THE STORY OF THE IRISH PUB

The Story of
The Irish Pub

An Intoxicating History of the
Licensed Trade in Ireland

Cian Molloy

The Liffey Press
in association with
The Vintners' Federation of Ireland

Published by
The Liffey Press
Ashbrook House, 10 Main Street
Raheny, Dublin 5, Ireland
www.theliffeypress.com

© 2002 Vintners' Federation of Ireland

A catalogue record of this book is
available from the British Library.

ISBN 1-904148-13-1

Printed in the Republic of Ireland by Colour Books Ltd.

Contents

About the Author

Cian Molloy is a freelance journalist who started his career in 1987 with a report for radio about the introduction of Guinness dual-flow pumps in Preston, Lancashire. Raised in an Irish-speaking family, he spent seven years in England working as a journalist before returning to his native Dublin in 1994. Today, he specialises in writing about business matters, technology, religion and social affairs. This is his first book.

The Story of the Irish Pub is published in association with The Vintners' Federation of Ireland (VFI), a Trade Association of publicans, for publicans and essentially run by publicans. It was founded in 1973 from a number of local Licensed Vintners Associations for the protection and betterment of the livelihood of the individual publican outside the Greater Dublin area. Today the VFI has approximately 6,000 members.

Acknowledgements

The author would like to thank the following people for their help: the individual vintners who shared their family histories; Tadg O'Sullivan, Elaine Comerford, Mairéad Howe and the staff of the Vintners' Federation of Ireland; Nicola Jamison of the Federation of Retail Licensed Trade of Northern Ireland; Frank Fell of the Licensed Vintners Association; Eibhlin Roche and the staff of the Guinness Archive; Professor Fergus Kelly of the Dublin Institute for Advanced Studies; Andrew O'Gorman of the Dublin Institute of Technology; archaeologist Rosanne Meenan; David Roe, Charlie Taylor and Willie Carr; Jimmy Jordan of the Breffni Lounge, Blackrock, Co. Dublin, and John and Della Costelloe of the Old Royal Oak, Kilmainham; Tony and Anna Farmar; Ronan Gallagher; the staff of the National Library and the staff of the National Museum; David Givens and Brian Langan at The Liffey Press; and, for her great patience, my wife Máire O'Reilly.

Dedication
This book is dedicated to my daughter Caoimhe and my goddaughters Emily Weber and Amy Sheraston-Baker. Respectively, they may not be served alcohol in an Irish pub until 2019, 2005 and 2010.

Photographs and Illustrations

The publishers are grateful to the following for photographs and illustrations used in the book: Guinness Archive, Ireland: cover photos and pages 41, 46, 53, 56, 59, 67, 70, 74, 76, 80, 87, 88; Guinness Irish Pub Concept: page 91; National Museum of Ireland: pages 21, 28; The Schøyen Collection, Oslo and London (MS 1717): page 6; University of Pennsylvania: page 7; British Museum: page 36; Murphy Brewery Ireland Ltd.: pages 13, 40, 45, 49; Bushmill's Distillery: pages 24, 84; *Punch* Magazine: page 43; Vintners' Federation of Ireland: pages 82, 85, 86. We are also grateful to the licensees who supplied us with the photographs which accompany the profiles of their pubs. Every effort has been made to trace the origins of all illustrations; if any omission has been made, we would be happy to correct this in any future printings of this book.

Foreword

"There is nothing which has yet been contrived by man, by which so much happiness is produced as by a good tavern or inn."

Those in the licensed trade would probably argue, and with some justification, that the claim in the quotation above is as true today as when it was made by Samuel Johnson in 1776. Whether referred to as an ale house, a tavern, an inn or the modern day pub, Irish men and in latter years Irish women have been frequent visitors to them. They come to slake a thirst, propose a toast, celebrate weddings, offer support in the sorrow of bereavement or mark the happy family or social occasion. Sometimes they come just to be there, to meet friends, to relax and unwind, to pass the time, to eat, to drink, to be merry, to be at peace.

This book is a celebration of these houses and perhaps more importantly the people who have lived and worked in them. In the pages that follow, you will read part of the history, perhaps even the sum of the history of the Irish pub as we know it. Some of the stories are funny, many are comic, few undoubtedly are tragic, but all are historic. They trace in excess of 100 years of direct family involvement in over 100 pubs throughout Ireland.

The book began as a simple idea by the Vintners' Federation of Ireland to mark the Millennium by investigating those pubs which had a direct family connection with the licence for in excess of 100 years. It quickly took on a life of its own. The more we delved the more we wanted to know. The more we learned, the more we sought to discover. Now the history of the pubs and the families that run them is gathered in one volume with what is essentially the history of the industry in Ireland.

Despite all the counter attractions the Irish pub today remains the single most appealing location for relaxation and social intercourse for the vast majority of the population of this island. The reputation of our pubs also makes them a magnetic attraction for millions of visitors whether on holiday or on business. Indeed, research shows that tourists to this country consistently report that a visit to an Irish pub is part of what makes a holiday in this country special.

The traditional Irish pub is an institution that is well-worth celebrating. It is the place where you will find a *Céad Míle Fáilte* (one hundred thousand welcomes) and the families that have served Ireland for generations. In that spirit, the Vintners' Federation of Ireland is delighted that *The Story of the Irish Pub* is now being told in all its glory.

Tadg O'Sullivan,
President,
Vintners' Federation of Ireland

THE STORY OF THE IRISH PUB
An Intoxicating History of the Licensed Trade in Ireland

Cian Molloy

Introduction

The pubs and licensees listed in this book belong to families that have liter-ally been serving Ireland for generations. The families that own these pubs are proud to be part of a living heritage that be traced back to the Iron Age. Surprisingly, very little has been written about the history of drinking in Ireland and much of that is inaccurate. Here we will try to separate facts from myths, while paying storytelling tribute to both.

One of the most honoured ranks in ancient Celtic society was that of *briugu*, or hospitaller, who was only worthy of the status if he had "a never-dry cauldron, a dwelling on a public road and a welcome to every face". According to the medieval historians, a brewer and a hospitaller were among the very first people to set foot on the soil of Ireland following the Great Flood of the Bible.

Today, there are just under 11,000 fully licensed premises in the Republic of Ireland, of which 88 per cent are family-owned. In Northern Ireland, there are 1,645 pubs, with family ownership estimated at just under 95 per cent. Of these 11,240 or so family-owned pubs, a tiny proportion, less than 200 in the year 2001, have been identified as being in one family for at least 100 years. Pubs qualifying for this "century club" status were identified with the help of the three main organisations representing publicans and licensees in the Republic and in Northern Ireland. The largest of these three organisations, the Vintners' Federation of Ireland, took the lead in this project and it was with their help that most of the pubs listed in the second part of this book were identified as being in the one family for over 100 years.

Only four family pubs in Northern Ireland identified themselves as being of over 100 years' vintage. It is reckoned that there are other pubs in Northern Ireland that qualify for listing in this book, but that many publicans in the north are still loath to draw attention to themselves or their premises. Such a sense of caution is within the traditions of the trade. In 1825, William Phipps, secretary of the Fair Trading Vintners Society and Asylum of the City of Dublin, counselled new licensees to "Be not too talkative, but speak as much as is necessary to recommend your goods and always observe to keep within the rules of decency".

It is no mean feat for a family business to be in operation for over a century, but publicans in Ireland faced particular obstacles if they were to survive and prosper. Being licensed by the law involves duties that can put a publican in direct conflict with his customers' desires — at its most banal, this involves refusing to serve someone outside of licensed hours — but in the 19th century it also involved not taking part in any boycott organised by the local community.

Several of the family pubs listed in this book narrowly escaped being burnt down because of their owners' suspected nationalist sympathies during the Black and Tan era. However, it was unusual for the British to take such drastic measures against suspect licensees — if a landlord showed signs of Fenianism, it was far easier to get a magistrate to refuse to renew the licence on the grounds of the publican's character. One can only guess at how many family businesses are no longer in existence because of violence and intimidation. One pub in our collection, O'Keeffe's in Co. Kildare (page 184), survived being targeted by rebels; it was looted in the Rising of 1798 when the town of Kilcock was identified as "a unionist town".

Among those pubs in the Republic of Ireland that have been in business for a century, there is a significant number which have close links with either

Fianna Fáil or Fine Gael, the Republic's two main political parties. Of those pubs with political links, the vast majority have a connection with Fianna Fáil, though there are pubs in our list that host meetings of both Fianna Fáil *and* Fine Gael. This is a remarkable achievement: how many buildings in the US host both Democrat and Republican meetings, or how many UK pubs host both Conservative associations and meetings of the Labour Party?

Whatever about political survival, financial survival was a much bigger issue 200 years ago. A licensee setting up in business for the first time at the start of the 19th century was more likely to go bankrupt than to prosper. Opening a public house was a very risky venture because of a liberal alcohol-licensing regime that produced over-competition. Indeed, William Phipps's advice to publicans about not being too talkative is contained within his book, *The Vintners' Guide*, which he specifically published to help new licensees to avoid bankruptcy.

Sadly, only one Dublin pub, John Kavanagh's of Glasnevin (page 170), could be included in this book, because it is the only pub in the city and the county to be in the one family for over a century. Over the last 30 years, the value of Dublin pubs has soared astronomically and the sons and daughters of Dublin's licensees have sold up. When the Licensed Vintners' Association researched Dublin pub ownership in the 1990s, only 140 pubs could be found in the city that had been in the same ownership for over 20 years. However, if you are looking for a social history of the licensed trade in Dublin, Kevin Kearns's *Dublin Pub Life and Lore* is recommended. For those interested in viewing Dublin pubs which retain some Victorian and Edwardian architectural details, a list of these is provided in an appendix to the rear of this book.

This book also does not cover any pub in Cork city, for the simple reason that in 1900 most of the pubs in Ireland's second biggest city were "tied houses" that belonged to the city's breweries. A hundred years ago, when a Cork publican died the licence was not passed on to the next generation; instead, the brewery appointed a new publican to run their premises.

Researching the history of the family pubs listed here was a daunting task, with much of it carried out by the licensees themselves. Tracing individual pub histories is hampered by the fact that most of Ireland's state archives were destroyed when the Customs House in Dublin was set on fire during the Civil War. Much valuable information about licensing in the 19th and early 20th century was also deliberately destroyed by the police. Acting on the orders of Dublin Castle, RIC officers destroyed all locally held police records before their barracks were handed over to the newly formed An Garda Síochána in 1922.

However, much valuable information was unearthed in parish records and in surviving deeds and titles. In some cases, the information retrieved was extensive, particularly in those pubs with sales ledgers from the 18th and 19th centuries. Some guesswork has been required to estimate both how long an individual pub has been in existence and how long it has been formally licensed to sell beers, wines and spirits.

Since we are dealing with the history of the sale of intoxicating liquor, this lack of accuracy may be excused. Certainly, for over two centuries the legal profession has complained about the bewildering nature of licensing law: one 18th century judge described them as "complex, uncertain and contradictory", while another said they were "complicated, puzzling and rather incomprehensible".

There are some 80 Acts directly concerning the pub trade on the statute book today. The oldest of these, the Drink on Credit to Servants Act, 1735, includes measures outlawing the practice of "tippling" or giving drink on credit. For more than 250 years, "a licensee who sells drink on credit has no right in law for recovery of the debt, nor has he the right to keep any pledge or pawn left as security for such a debt".

Pubs in Ireland were first formally licensed in 1635 and, in the intervening three and a half centuries, the licensed trade in Ireland has had to contend with, and deal within, some 200 different acts of Parliament. Happily, this is not a book for judges: we will keep the legal jargon to a minimum and only concern ourselves with laws that are historically interesting.

Nevertheless, such is the complex nature of licensing law that even today the Irish government admits to being muddled about it. As part of an investigation into ways of reforming licensing in Ireland in 1999, an Oireachtas Committee admitted that "little or no information is available to us concerning the number of licences issued prior to 1902 which are still in circulation in one form or another".

But before we start dealing with the complexities of modern licensing law in Ireland, let us first look back, and further afield, to the origins of brewing and the emergence of the first ever controls on alcohol consumption.

The First Drink

Man is now believed to have been brewing ale for at least 12,000 years, since wild barley was first domesticated and systematically harvested in the "Fertile Crescent" region of modern-day Turkey, Iran and Iraq.

Until the 1950s, accepted ethnological thinking was that man first domesticated wild grains to make bread. Now, it is increasingly believed that wild barley was first domesticated to provide ale. If the beer-first argument is true, the first ever property rules in agrarian society were probably alcohol-related licensing laws.

We can easily surmise how man learned to brew; indeed, we can also surmise how his efforts to improve his alcoholic beverages led to the discovery of baking. When raw wild barley is dormant, its grains are small, hard, bitter tasting, starchy and difficult to digest. Soaking the dormant grains in water causes them to send out shoots, a process known as "malting". As part of this process, the grains become larger, softer and more palatable as enzymes in the shoots remove the grains' bitter tannins and convert the grains' starch into sugar. Once grains are soaking in water, all that is needed to produce a weak beer is yeast, an invisible airborne microorganism whose contribution would have appeared magical to early man. Indeed, the basics of fermentation were not properly understood until 1857 when Louis Pasteur first identified the single-celled organism that converts sugar into alcohol. Before the 19th century, brewers knew that if they added old beer to a new batch of malted barley and water, more beer would be produced. But they did not truly understand the process involved and could only shrug their shoulders and say, "God is good".

When early man first tasted the frothy, cloudy liquid produced from leaving wild barley soaking in water for too long, he would have had his first taste of alcohol, an addictive and intoxicating drug; a drug that would provide enough physiological and psychological motivation to reproduce the process and to improve it by experimentation.

Brewing Techniques

Gradually, by trial and error, man would have learned that controlling the malting of barley could vary the taste and strength of the final product. Optimum sugar levels are reached when the shoots reach a certain length and drying the grain halts the malting process. If the dried malt is then boiled in water, further sugar is extracted from the raw material, giving the final fermented product even greater alcoholic strength. At first, the malt would have been

Sumerian tablet, c.3100 BC, showing stages in the brewing process

dried by exposure to the sun, but in climates such as Ireland's, fire would have been necessary to dry it. Indeed, in ancient Ireland we know that the malt was dried in cakes to be stored until needed for brewing. There is even a possibility that the baking of bread was learnt from brewing and the making of malt cakes.

In addition to its alcohol content, ale is more nutritious than a plain mix of water and barley. Yeast also produces amino acids and B vitamins, essential components of a balanced diet. Amino acids are the building blocks of protein, necessary for muscular speed and strength. B vitamins are necessary for both physical and mental health; B vitamin deficiency causes beriberi, skin rashes, anaemia and infertility, as well as mood swings, depression, rage, apprehension and an inability to handle stress.

Clearly, any tribe with ale in its diet had a marked advantage over tribes that did not.

It is now certain that from c.3500 BC onwards, the Sumerians were prolific ale drinkers with chemical proof of this found in pottery dating from 3500–3100 BC in the Zagros Mountains of western Iraq. Throughout Iraq, Iran and East Africa, pottery from the period 3000–2000 BC has also been found to contain calcium oxalate deposits, proving that the pots and jars once contained beer.

But our oldest depiction of alcohol being drunk is believed to be a Sumerian seal, dated at c 4000 BC, showing two figures drinking beer using traditional straws and container. Beer drinking using straws to avoid the foamy surface and grainy residues of early ales is depicted throughout Sumerian and Mesopotamian art from between c.2500 and 1500 BC. Another Sumerian clay tablet, dating from c.3100 BC, depicts what may well be the earliest example of an industrial brewing process. The tablet contains pictograms of barley, a brick building with a chimney, and containers with another barley symbol, possibly representing the finished beer.

The oldest known recipe for beer was found on a c.1800 BC clay tablet found at the city of Ur in modern-day Iraq. The brewing method described is roughly as follows: bake cakes out of malted barley, break up the cakes and mix with water and strain the resulting sweet-tasting liquid into large jars which should then be left aside to allow fermentation to take place. Interestingly, this use of malt cakes and the requirement to strain the liquor corresponds with what little we know about early Irish brewing techniques.

Oldest beer recipe, c.1800 BC

The world's oldest known licensing laws come from the Code of Hammurabi, a Jewish legal text from c.1700 BC, where it is written: "If a tavern-keeper does not accept corn according to gross weight in payment of drink, but takes money, and the price of the drink is less than that of the corn, she shall be convicted and thrown into the water"; and "If conspirators meet in a house of a tavern-keeper, and these conspirators are not captured and delivered to the court, the tavern-keeper shall be put to death".

Early Ireland

Unfortunately, no forensic evidence of prehistoric brewing has been found in Ireland and we have to rely on medieval history and law texts from the 12th century for clues about licensing law in Celtic and pre-Celtic Ireland.

However, pottery with traces of calcium oxalate (beer and ale residue) has been found at three sites in Scotland: Strathallen in Perthshire, Ashgrove in Fife and Machrie Moor in the Orkneys. The last two sites are Bronze Age, but the first is Neolithic with artefacts dating from c.2600 BC. We can be almost certain that if the Scots were drinking beer at this time, so were the Irish.

Ireland's first settlers were Mesolithic hunter-gatherers who arrived c.7000 BC. The first Neolithic farmers are reckoned to have arrived c.4000 BC and, as well as introducing domesticated crops, they probably brought brewing with them.

The beer traces found at Ashgrove and Machrie Moor in Scotland were found to contain immature lime pollen and traces of meadowsweet, suggesting that the ale had been flavoured to produce a primitive beer.

The general drinking public today uses the term "beer" to describe all manner of alcoholic brews. But within the brewing industry, "beer" specifically means ale that has been flavoured with hops, which give the ale a distinctive bitter palate. Since hops were not introduced into Britain until the 15th century, some would say it is incorrect to use the term "beer" for any ale brewed before the 1400s. Whatever about the technical niceties, the inclusion of meadowsweet was a good choice, as the herb prolongs the shelf-life of beer by inhibiting fermentation.[1]

In the absence of physical evidence of brewing in Ireland, our earliest clues about alcohol consumption in ancient Ireland are provided by Roman army reports from garrisons on the western coast of modern-day France. From the 1st century BC onwards, Roman commanders stationed in Gaul reported the arrival of strange warrior-like people who came from a mysterious island known as Hibernia to trade animal hides for wine. While the Romans considered all Celts to be fond of a drink, they noted that the Hiberni had a particularly strong taste for alcohol. The fact that they drank beer was remarkable enough for a physician named Dioscorides (c.40–c.90 AD) to write that the Irish "instead of wine, use a liquor called courmi or curmi made of barley".

For our next set of clues about the drinking patterns of the ancient Irish, we must move forward some 600 years to that great monastic period of learning that earned Ireland a reputation as a land of saints and scholars. At some stage shortly after the arrival of Christianity, Ireland's monks began recording what was known about the country's history in pagan times. These histories had been passed down orally through the generations, with bardic poets committing whole genealogies and epic tales to memory, and Ireland's 5th and 6th century monks were the first to write them down. While the earliest of these manuscripts have been lost, their contents were copied and survive in much more recent documents.

According to the 12th century *Annals of Leinster*, a brewer and an innkeeper were among the first people to settle on the island of Ireland in the aftermath of the Biblical Great Flood. This manuscript records the claim that Ireland was a wasteland for three centuries before it was settled by a tribe called

---

[1] Prolonging shelf-life was a major preoccupation of publicans and licensees until the middle of the 20th century when refrigeration and pasteurisation have taken the risk out of beer storage. Those who still remember the days when Irish pubs bottled their own Guinness remember the task as a major weekly chore. At best, they reckon a bottle of Guinness could be left on a shelf for up to three weeks before becoming unfit for sale — if a bottle was ever left on a shelf that long.

the Milesians, led by a chieftain named Parthalon. This tribe is said to have landed at Inver Scene in Bantry Bay, either 300 or 312 years after the Biblical Flood, one Tuesday in spring. It is noted that Parthalon's possessions included "a cauldron" and that "Of his company was Samailiath, by whom were ale-drinking and suretyship first made in Ireland. Of his company was Beoir, by whom a guesthouse was first made in Ireland."

Elsewhere, a tale of prodigious alcohol consumption is contained in the oldest surviving manuscript written completely in Irish, *Lebor na hUidire, The Book of the Dun Cow*, written at Clonmacnoise c.1100 AD. The tale, *Mesce Uladh* or the Intoxication of the Ulstermen, purports to be about events that occurred sometime before the arrival of Christianity in the 5th century. After a bout of heavy drinking at Samhain (Hallowe'en), the men of Ulster became enraged and decided to raid Tara, the ancient capital of Ireland, just across the River Boyne. But such is the drunkenness of the Ulster charioteers that they completely miss Tara and become hopelessly lost. They end up careering across the length of Ireland to Kerry where they are promptly imprisoned inside a house with iron walls. How much of the story is true and how long ago the original events supposedly happened, we cannot tell. Certainly the *Lebor na hUidire* account is greatly embellished, especially for humorous effect, but the kernel of the story may be based on an actual event. In any case, *Mesce Uladh* could well be the first story about drunken drivers coming to a bad end.

Saints

The first hagiographies of Ireland's early saints show that most of our holy men and women were fond of their beer. In 448 AD, St Patrick (then preaching in Ireland for 16 years) had built up a permanent retinue of some 35 people, according to the *Annals of the Four Masters*. Among Patrick's companions were "The priest Mescan, without evil, his friend and his brewer"[2] and "the youth Mochonnoc, his hospitaller".

---

[2] *Cruimther Meascan gan bine, a chara sa chirpsire.*

According to a 7th century writer, when St Patrick arrived at Tara on Easter Sunday, 433 AD, the kings, princes and druids were feasting and drinking wine in the palace of King Laoghaire.

Saint Brigid
— miracle brewer

The medieval histories also record that Ireland's most important female saint, St Brigid, was a brewer in her own right who, when pushed, could even short-cut the brewing process with the use of miracles. The saint's abbey included a leper colony which one day found itself without beer. The lepers went to St Brigid and explained their plight, but the abbess had no beer in stock. To remedy the situation, she called for the leper's bathwater to be brought to her and she blessed the murky liquid, promptly converting it into delicious ale!

When the missionary St Columbanus was travelling across Europe, it is said, he came upon a group of people in a forest clearing who were about to sacrifice a cask of ale to the pagan god Wodan. Using only his breath, St Columbanus caused the cask to shatter, before explaining to the pagans that they were about to waste good ale. According to the Irishman, the one true God loves ale, but only when drunk in his name. Indeed, St Columbanus seems to have loved ale too, as he is credited as saying: "It is my design to die in the brew-house; let ale be placed to my mouth when I am expiring, so that when the choir of angels come they may say: 'Be God propitious to this drinker.'"

Another Irish monk, Sedulius Scottus, the 9th century scholar, may have written the first Irish drinking song, as his poem "Request for Meat and Drink", includes the lines: *Ast nos tristificis perturbat potio sucies / cum medus atque Ceres, cum Bachi munera desint* (Of mirth-provoking sap I too have need / some beer, or Bacchus' gift, or perhaps some mead).

Ancient Law

There is no way of knowing how true the contents of the medieval histories are or how accurately they record life in pre-Christian and early Christian Ireland, but we know much about drinking in Ireland from the 6th century onwards. For a book about the history of licensing and trade controlled by law, it is a happy coincidence that this information comes from legal texts. Again, these texts date from the 12th century, but much of their contents were originally recorded in the 6th and 7th centuries.

Before the arrival of the Normans, Celtic Ireland had its own legal code, the Brehon Law, which is dotted with references to three alcoholic beverages: beer, mead and wine. Most scholars estimate that the great bulk of the Brehon Law we know about today was in operation in the 1st century BC, but that parts of it may date to 1000 BC or even earlier. Certainly, many elements of early Irish law echo concepts found in Indo-European legal codes, such as the Code of Hammurabi mentioned earlier.

We may speculate about just how old the Brehon Laws are, but it is a matter of fact that these laws were in operation in the 6th century and that they remained in use in those parts of Ireland not under Norman rule up until the late 17th century (at first the Viking and early Norman settlers were a law unto themselves, but their settlements gradually adopted Irish ways and Irish laws and it wasn't until the 1690s that English law was formally declared to apply to the whole of Ireland).

One of the foremost authorities on Brehon Law today is Professor Fergus Kelly of the Dublin Institute for Advanced Studies. As well as publishing *A Guide to Early Irish Law*, he has also written *Early Irish Farming*, a study based on references to agriculture in 7th and 8th century law texts. Professor Kelly says: "Beer (*cuirm*) is very commonly mentioned in early Irish sources and was clearly a drink of social importance. Many of our texts extol beer as an expression of hospitality which brings honour to the host who provides it."

Aside from beer, the texts clearly state that the ancient Irish drank plenty of mead, an alcoholic drink made from a fermented mixture of honey and water that is also known as *metheglin*. Mead had more prestige than beer and was associated with feasting — the main banqueting hall in Tara, home of the High King of Ireland, was known as *Tech Midchúarda*, "the house of the mead circuit". A seating plan for this banqueting hall survives in the Book of Leinster detailing where the different professions are to sit and which cut of meat is appropriate to their rank. The diagram is illustrated with a picture of a bard and a drawing of a cooking spit. Sometimes the Irish fermented a mixture of malt, honey and water to produce a drink known as *brocóit* or "bragget", which had a reputation for giving drinkers swollen red noses!

It is tentatively suggested by some scholars that the ancient Irish might have drunk cider. This claim is based on an obscure word, *nemadmim*, which is defined in a legal glossary as "the delicate juice of wild apples".

Medieval manuscript depicting a monk brewing beer

Wine was also drunk at major feasts (as well as being used by monks and priests for celebration of the Eucharist) and had even more prestige than mead. It is possible that vines were grown in Ireland and the Venerable Bede, author of the first comprehensive history of England in the 8th century, wrote that Ireland had "no lack of vines". However, given the Irish climate, is unlikely that vine growing was ever extensive and Giraldus Cambrenis, writing in the late 12th century, claimed that Ireland never had vineyards, but that there was plenty of wine sold here by foreign commerce. An indication of the amount of wine brought into Ireland is given in a story about Murchertach Mac Erca who was King of Ireland in 533 AD. While feasting with his nobles in the Palace of Cletty, "a revengeful woman" set the building alight; to escape the flames, Murchertach plunged into a butt of wine in which he drowned.

Most of the wine drunk in Ireland came from trade with Gaulish and Frankish traders, most usually with Irish merchants travelling to Bordeaux in Western France. In Roman times, Bordeaux was known as Burdigula and such was the town's reputation among the Irish that its name eventually became an Old Irish word, *bordgal*, meaning "a meeting place or a city".

However, beer was the drink of everyday life. A law text on status, *Críth Gabhlach*, states that even the lowest grade of freeman should have a cauldron for fermentation in his house with a mug of beer always available for callers.

Failure to provide food and drink to guests was an offence, particularly for someone belonging to the higher echelons of society. The *Críth Gabhlach* states that a king who cannot ensure a supply of beer for his household every Sunday is not a proper ruler and another text disparages a particular king because his guests did not leave his house "with the smell of beer on their breath".

The honour acquired by providing beer reaches its highest limit among those who earn the title *briugu* or "hospitaller". A chief briugu was of equivalent status to a minor king or a chief poet. By definition, all briugu were wealthy men because of the almost unlimited obligation on them to provide hospitality. One text tells us "he is not a briugu who is not the possessor of hundredfold wealth", i.e. 100 head of cattle.

Briugu status was totally dependent on keeping the supply of beer flowing, as once hospitality was refused the status was lost. The status had a number of advantages: unlike a king or a lord, a briugu had no military role; also, according to law, all duelling was banned on a briugu's lands. A woman had as much to be a briugu as a man, with one of the most famous briugu being the legendary Queen Maedhbh of Connaught.

Notably, there was one exception to the law of hospitality: under no circumstances were criminals to be harboured. (Today, licensees are still barred from "knowingly harbouring thieves or reputed thieves" under the 1871 Prevention of Crimes Act.)

The office of briugu continued in some parts of the country until the 16th century, with annals of this period using the term briugu to descibe men of a status higher than mere "guesthouse owners". Notably, these latter-day briugus are men who also belonged to high-paying professions, allowing them to fulfil a briugu's duties of hospitality: Matha Hua Mailruanaigh, who died in 1479, was a briugu and a goldsmith and Doctor Mac Eogain Í Duinnshléibhe, who died in 1527, was a briugu and an expert in medical arts. At this stage, commercial taverns and inns were in operation under the new order fostered by the Normans to increase trade. However, the hospitable traditions of the briugus continued into the 19th and 20th centuries. Many of the older publicans featured in the second part of this book described how their parents and grandparents regularly provided meals free-of-charge to almost every traveller who called looking for help at their door. Indeed, most Irish vintners today see hospitality as a duty of privilege, even though their customers must now pay for their beer.

In pre-Norman Ireland, beer was so ubiquitous that there appear to have been few licensing laws controlling its consumption. However, the raw material for beer-making, malt or malted barley, formed part of the taxation or the annual food-rent paid by base-clients to their lords. Furthermore, it appears that there were licensed and unlicensed malting houses. In a licensed (*dligtech*) malting house, the malt was subjected to three tests before being handed over as food rent. If the beer made from malt produced in an unlicensed malting house turned out bad, the base-client was obliged to make good the amount of malt originally donated and pay a heavy fine. However, if the beer turned out bad after it had passed the three tests in a licensed malting house, the client incurred no penalties.

Some rents involved beer rather than malt; for example, the sum involved in renting a knife included four mugs of beer, filled to the brim without froth.

Little is known about the brewing process except that it involved mashing pre-prepared maltcakes, straining the mixture and then sealing the liquid in vats. In large households, a professional brewer was employed and there was a place reserved for brewers at royal feasts. Professional brewers appear to have been all male, though it is recorded that while St Brigid's abbey included both men and women, it was the nuns who prepared beer for celebrations at Easter.

Brehon Law also makes some acknowledgement of the diminished responsibility caused by alcoholic intoxication. Most contracts agreed while either party is drunk are invalid. However, in law texts dealing with "ale house brawls", there is no reduction in the penalty for causing injury or death while drunk; this is in contrast with modern law which allows for a charge of manslaughter, instead of murder, for a killing committed while drunk.

Modern Beginnings

Alcohol licensing in Ireland today is rooted in Norman law from the 12th century onwards. At its simplest and most brutal, early Norman licensing was about who was and who wasn't permitted to trade within the towns and markets established by Ireland's new rulers.

The English detested the Irish habit of feasting out of doors, as this satirical drawing shows — note what appears to be a beer mug on table

To the Norman settlers, the native Irish were classed as "foreigners" who did not have the same rights as the town citizens. Only city freemen were allowed to set up permanent places of trade within town walls and all foreigners (i.e. the Irish) had to be outside the walls by nightfall. The effect of these sanctions can be seen on Irish town maps today, as frequently those areas outside the walls where the Irish were obliged to live are in townlands still referred to as "Irishtown".

European populations increased significantly in the Middle Ages as both trade and towns increased in size. In this new economic climate, the merchant guilds enjoyed monopolies of trade and wielded significant economic and political power. The first guild established in Ireland was the Dublin Merchant's Guild and its charter, granted by Prince John in 1192, states: "That no foreign merchant buy within the city from a foreigner, corn, hides or wool, except from a citizen. And that no foreigner have a wine tavern, except aboard ships."

It is here that we have our first legal reference to a tavern where alcohol is sold, as opposed to the briugu's house of ancient Ireland where the ale and hospitality were free of charge.

It was the Romans who gave Western Europe the "taberna", a place where food, wine and ale were sold and where trade was advertised with a display of vine leaves, both real and artificial, outside the doors. After the fall of the Roman Empire in the 5th century, these taverns disappeared from Northern Europe. However, brewing continued both in monasteries and, on a smaller scale, in private households. In England, it is known that in 7th century Anglo-Saxon society, commercial trade in beer had reached a level significant enough for Ethelred, King of Kent, to introduce controls on the number of brewers trading in his kingdom.

It wasn't really until after 1066 and the arrival of the Normans that taverns and inns began to become common throughout England. Similarly, it wasn't until after the Norman invasion of Ireland in the 12th century that taverns and inns began to be established in Ireland. Hence, Ireland's first taverns were in Norman strongholds in Leinster and the Pale. Evidence of this can be seen on modern maps: Winetavern Street in Dublin earned its name from the fact that, in the 12th century, it was the city's main centre for the alcohol trade.

The word "vintner" — originally meaning "wine merchant", but now a synonym for "licensee", dates from this period, as all taverners were wine merchants. Their customers were Norman gentry and nobles with continental wine-drinking tastes. The first taverns would originally have been set up as wine importation businesses where the primary business was in "off sales" — selling wine to stock the cellars of the local nobility. But gradually, these became places of social interaction and discourse, with food as well as drink available. Thus, in Norman Ireland the off-licence begat the pub, rather than the other

A medieval depiction of drinking to excess

way around. A host of professional business was conducted in the taverns, with lawyers, merchants and money-lenders meeting their clients and sealing deals over a glass of wine.

This distinction between alehouse and tavern has been extinct since the 17th century. For example, today, the chief Irish organisation representing licensees is the Vintners' Federation of Ireland, but the vast majority of its members can no longer be described as "wine merchants", as beer is the main drink that they sell.

Ale-making in Norman times remained very much a home-brew affair, with every large household having a brewer among their staff. Even in less well-off Irish households, brewing would be a standard domestic chore. In a list of household items commonly sold at medieval Irish markets, brewers' cauldrons feature prominently. It is not known how commercial alehouses emerged in Ireland, as there is little reference to them in Irish medieval texts. In contrast to the tavern, alehouses were frequented by the underclass. A notable distinction between the two in both Ireland and Britain is that alehouses were usually run by women, while vintners were exclusively male. In England, the first legislation concerning the licensing of alehouses notes this distinction. In a measure introduced to reduce the risk of fires caused by drying malted barley, the City Council ruled "that all alehouses be forbidden except those which shall be licensed by the Common Council of the City at Guildhall, excepting those belonging to persons who will build of stone, that the city may be secure. And that no baker bake, or ale-wife brew by night, either with reeds or straw or stubble, but with wood only". That order in

1189 predates the licensing of alehouses in Ireland by nearly 450 years, indicating how slowly commercial alehouses emerged in this country.

Blame the Pope

However, both wine and beer in Ireland would have been taxed from 1188, at the request of Pope Gregory VIII, who instituted the "Saladin Tithe", a tax payable by all those who could not take part in the crusade against the Arabs of the Holy Land. Henry II introduced the tithe in England and Ireland with all royal subjects paying "one tenth of his rents and movable goods" annually towards the fund. For taverners and alehouse keepers this would have involved a charge on one-tenth of wine and/or beer stocks. The Saladin Tithe was essentially an ecclesiastical tax, but notably it was a national tax collected by the civil authorities and, additionally, an early jury system was used to assess how much each individual should pay.

From 1203 onwards, vintners also paid a duty on wine imports, with one-fifteenth of all imported cargoes going to the Royal Treasury. Alehouses which used Irish malted barley did not pay duty.

In 1256, Henry III fixed the price of two basic foodstuffs: bread and beer. Any baker found guilty of overcharging was put in stocks and pilloried, but the penalty for brewers and alehouse keepers who overcharged was a potentially fatal punishment by ducking stool. Throughout the medieval period, the price of wine was also fixed both by local market officials and by statute.

The Church thrived during the Norman period and monasteries were large landowners, whose tenants had paid annual tithes long before the arrival of the new English rulers. As before, the monasteries all had their own breweries, with the beer being drunk as an important source of nutrition. At Jerpoint Abbey, for example, the monks had an allowance of a gallon of beer a day. This brew would have been known as "small beer" because it was weak enough to be consumed by children.

As well as benefiting from the patronage of the local Norman lords and increased food rents from improved Norman farming techniques, monasteries and episcopacies benefited from their involvement in trade. The Bishop of Waterford, for example, permitted no others to sell wine in his area and his cellars were filled with some of the best wines in Ireland. Monasteries also benefited from the growth in pilgrimages, which were the foundation of the tourist industry. Thousands travelled each year to Holy Cross Abbey in Tipperary, for instance, because it purportedly held a fragment of the True Cross. Monasteries set up guesthouses to cater for these travellers, laying the foundation for what were to become the first inns. An inn is distinguished from a tavern by the fact that an inn offers overnight accommodation.

General Licensed Trade

The success of the Norman settlement outside Dublin was helped to a great extent by the way trade in general was licensed. Under the new regime, Irish lands were given to Norman lords and Irish chieftains who swore allegiance to Henry II or his son John. As well as lands, Norman vassals were also given grants and charters to hold annual fairs and weekly markets that traded in the food surpluses created by improved agricultural methods.

In the 13th century, some 300 fair charters and some 200 market charters had been issued, with bishops and abbots being given 18 per cent of fair licences and 31 per cent of market licences. These charters for fairs and markets produced a handsome income for lords temporal and spiritual, as trading anywhere other than a licensed place was banned.

In the statutes, Edward specified that each barony had to pay him a royal fee of 40 pence, to be paid twice annually. For the local lords of the manor it was a goldmine: once a baron had paid his royal fee, he owned all the other revenue generated by market tolls and for the twice-yearly fee he could hold licences for several markets and fairs. If his town prospered with traders and vintners setting up shop permanently, so much the better; the local landlord or the town corporation still only paid a set fee to the crown.

Money

However, while the lords counted their wealth in pounds, early tavern and alehouse keepers had a small money problem. Ireland had a perennial shortage of coin until the second half of the 19th century, when the first copper halfpennies were issued. The first coins to be minted in Ireland were produced during the late 10th century in Viking Dublin during the reign of King Sitric. Before then, the Irish had been using foreign coins from, at the latest, 2 AD onwards. First they used Roman denarii, then Anglo-Saxon coins. The Normans were quick to introduce their own coinage following their arrival, striking their first coins in Dublin c.1185 AD; however, lower denomination coins remained perennially in short supply. In the 16th century, both Henry VIII and Elizabeth I issued debased coin to raise revenue, with the result that English coin was not trusted. In the 17th century, a myriad of coins were in use, with Spanish quarters and doubloons particularly valued but, even with these foreign imports, coin remained in short supply.

One way around the coin shortage was for vintners to mint their own "beer tokens" and "wine tokens". A hoard of 2,061 pewter tokens from the 13th century was found hidden in a cesspit during an excavation of Dublin's Winetavern Street and it is thought they were produced for selling ale. What monetary value the tokens had is not known, but it is believed they were hidden after Edward I issued his "round farthing" in 1279.

Sketches of 13th century "tavern tokens", found in Winetavern Street, Dublin

In 17th and 18th century Ireland, the mine and mill owners of the Leinster coalfield often paid their workers with tokens that could only be redeemed by certain retailers, usually shops and bars owned by the mine or mill company. This practice, known as "trucking", was outlawed in the 19th century, but is remembered still in the phrase "to have no truck with someone", indicating an unwillingness to do business with a person.

As well as coins, the Normans were quick to introduce their own standard weights and measures. The Magna Charta Hibernica of 12 November 1216 extended the provisions of the Magna Charta promulgated in England by King John the previous year. As well as recognising the rights and privileges of barons, freemen and the Church, the Magna Charta Hibernica includes the ruling: "There shall be one measure of wine throughout our entire kingdom and one measure of ale and one measure of corn".

Significantly, the charter does not include a measure for aqua vitae: this is because whiskey drinking did not become a popular drink until the 15th century.

Whiskey

It is falsely claimed by some writers that, when the soldiers of Henry II landed in Ireland in 1171, the invaders found the Irish drinking aqua vitae or whiskey. This claim is almost certainly based on a misreading of the word liquor,[3] but it may also be a product of "black propaganda" promoting the idea that the Irish were a feckless race, incapable of governance and economic development without the help of superior English/Norman know-how.

While the Chinese are known to have been distilling beer into whiskey in the 7th century, it wasn't until the 11th century that distillation of wines and beers began to be practised in Mediterranean countries. Originally, the spirit produced by heating and then condensing wines and beers was used for medical purposes only, and the distilled liquid became known in Latin as "aqua vitae" or "water of life". The Irish for aqua vitae is *uisce beatha* and its shortened anglicised form gives us the word "whiskey" or "whisky".

---

[3] A claim that the Welsh were distilling aqua vitae from mead in the 6th century is also most probably false as it is based on the line "May abundance of mead be given Maelgwn of Anglesey, who supplies us, from his foaming meadhorns, with the choicest pure liquor" in *Hanes Taliesin* (*Tale of Taliesin*), a 16th century manuscript.

There is no archaeological or textual evidence of aqua vitae being produced in Britain or Ireland before the 13th century. Indeed, of all the stills found in Ireland, none has been dated to before 1400, judging by the metals and solders used in their construction.

At the very earliest, most scholars agree, the knowledge for distilling spirits may have been brought to Ireland in the 12th century by monks returning from pilgrimage to Rome. For over 200 years after its introduction to Ireland, aqua vitae or whiskey remained a medicine rather than a drink for popular consumption. While whiskey is distilled from beer, the earliest reference to aqua vitae in Irish literature is contained in the *Red Book of Ossory*, written c.1300. While this distilling recipe uses wine rather than beer (and thus is not a recipe for whiskey), it is notable that Ireland's earliest record of distillation is about 200 years older than the first Scottish record, which dates from 1494, something which gives credence to the claim that whiskey distilling was introduced to Scotland from Ireland.

Whiskey began to become a popular recreational, as opposed to a medicinal, drink in the 15th century. According to annals, a minor Irish noble died in 1405 from the over-consumption of aqua vitae. The irony wasn't lost on the author of the *Annals of Connaught*, who recorded the death with a pun: "Risderd Mag Ragnaill, eligible for the chieftainship of the Muinter Eolais, entered into rest after drinking 'water of life' to excess: it was deathly water to him."[4]

There is no reference to whiskey or aqua vitae in a statute of the Irish parliament meeting in Drogheda in 1450 which ruled that "Irish wine, ale or other liquor" is to be properly sold by the king's measure, that is, by "the gallon, pottle, quart pint and half pint", indicating that even though whiskey and spirits were becoming more popular, they had not reached a situation where they deserved a description separate from "other liquor". But over a century later, in 1556, the Irish parliament, again meeting in Drogheda, noted that "Aqua vita is

---

[4] *Risderd Mag Ragnaill adbur taisig na nEolusach quieuit iar n-ol usci bethad co himarcach, & dob usci marbtha do Risderd.*

now universally taken throughout the realm of Ireland" and enacted a statute licensing distilling in Ireland for the first time.

The penalty for those distilling without a licence was £4 and imprisonment, but "peers and gentlemen owning property worth £10 and borough freemen" were permitted to make aqua vitae without a licence.

Bushmill's Distillery. Co. Antrim

In the event, the requirement for a licence was ignored. One notable exception was the Bushmills distillery in Co. Antrim, which obtained a seven-day distilling licence in April 1608. As a result of its adherence to the law, Bushmills can today claim to be the world's oldest whiskey distillery.

There were subsequent efforts to license distilling in Ireland in 1661, 1731 and 1770, but these efforts were largely unsuccessful in rural areas, with only large-scale whiskey manufacturers in towns and cities obtaining licences.

Measures to tax and regulate the wine trade were regularly introduced from the 14th century onwards, but beer wasn't subjected to a specific tax until the 17th century.

The Normans can also be credited with making cider a popular drink. While the Celtic Irish had fewer than half a dozen varieties of apple, the Normans introduced dozens of new varieties, many of them specifically grown for cider making.

Norman Decline

At the end of the 13th century, the Normans controlled four-fifths of Ireland, but this was eroded during the 14th century: a third of the population was killed by the Black Death, which arrived in Ireland in 1348; a series of risings saw the Irish regain their estates; and, finally, there was the phenomenon of Norman lords "going native" and becoming more Irish than the Irish themselves. Among the ordinary people, there was a high-level of emigration to England, something that depleted the country's population further.

By 1485 and the end of the War of the Roses, England controlled only part of counties Dublin, Meath, Kildare and Louth. The rest of the country was ruled by a patchwork of lordships, many of them more Gaelic than Norman.

The first Tudor king, Henry VII, was anxious to enforce his rule in Ireland, particularly as there were Yorkist supporters among the Irish lords. For the next two centuries, Ireland would be embroiled in a cycle of resistance and suppression that greatly hindered the development of trade. Even Dublin went into decline between the 15th and 17th centuries. However, commerce did continue in those cities and towns established or developed during the Norman period; the largest of these were Kilkenny, Galway, Tuam, Limerick, Kilmallock, Tralee, Cork, Youghal, Clonmel, New Ross, Wexford, Carlow, Athy, Kildare, Trim, Drogheda, Carrickfergus and Coleraine.

During the Tudor period, the single biggest upset to the trade in alcohol and the manufacture of beer in Ireland was Henry VIII's dissolution of the monasteries in 1539. Closing the monasteries did away with a whole system of inns and guesthouses. Travel was also hindered by the fact that the national road system fell into disuse. The ancient Irish had maintained national roadways for millennia, but during the Tudor era, these roads became overgrown with scrub or sank into boglands. Overland travel became increasingly dangerous and rare. Although the number of pubs and alehouses increased within cities and towns, according to Edward MacLysaght's *Irish Life in the 17th Century*, there were hardly any inns providing overnight accommodation to travellers. MacLysaght writes:

> "At the beginning of the century inns providing beds were so scarce that in the cities lodgings were appointed by the urban officials for travellers and even in Dublin nearly a hundred years later, visitors stayed in lodgings, not

in public inns. Bourchier in 1623 remarks on the scarcity of inns, especially in the Pale, adding that travellers had to find accommodation in gentlemen's houses. Travellers enjoyed the prescriptive right of demanding accommodation at inns where such existed. William Edmundson describes in his journal how he arrived one evening at Mullingar and, being refused shelter and refreshment by the innkeepers on the ground that he was a Quaker (and so a potential cause of disturbance on the premises), he repaired to the constable and insisted on that official finding him lodging."

As late as 1672, the Mayor of Limerick complained that he was hardly capable of finding two beds available in the city's 80 or so alehouses.

Much of the turmoil which led to this shortage of traveller resting places was due to Elizabeth I, a woman who drank beer for breakfast. When Henry VIII's daughter took to the throne in 1558 she was determined to bring Ireland under English control once and for all. In the resulting military campaigns, Elizabethan adventurers plundered Ireland and there was little of the economic stability necessary for the development of normal commercial trade.

Elizabeth also introduced a new tactic for eliminating Irish unrest: plantation, where the Irish were ejected from their lands and replaced with loyal English settlers. The most successful Elizabethan plantations were in Laois and Offaly, which were renamed Queen's County and King's County. In these counties, the traders and vintners in plantation towns would have been exclusively English. These traders would have left a country where a national licensing system had been in operation since Edward VI's reign when an Act of parliament requiring "Keepers of alehouses and tippling houses to be bound by recognisance" was passed in 1552 and where licences from local justices of the peace were required to sell alcoholic drink. But the licensed trade in Ireland was still a bit of a free for all. Indeed, long after the Act of Union in 1800, Irish and British licensing laws varied greatly. Some subsections of English and Welsh laws never applied to this country while other measures were not introduced here until decades after they were introduced in Britain.

One of the most quoted sources for information about drinking patterns in Ireland at the start of the 17th century is the English pamphleteer Barnaby Rich, who wrote in 1610:

> "There is no merchandise so vendable, it is the very marrow of the common wealth in Dublin: the whole profit of the towne stands upon ale houses and selling of ale. There are whole streets of taverns and it is a rare thing to finde a house in Dubline with out a taverne, as to find a tavern without a strumpet."

Rich compared most of the ale he drank in Ireland to "hogges-washe" and "un-fit for any man's drinking but for common drunkards", but he noted that while malted barley was half the price in Dublin as it was in London, beer sold in Dublin was double the price of beer sold in England's capital. Another English traveller, William Dyott, who visited Cork in 1785, is widely cited as having described Irish ale as "the very worst". However, according to MacLysaght, visitors to Ireland were as likely to praise Irish beers and ales as to disparage them. One of the difficulties of researching daily life in Ireland is that the Irish wrote very little about themselves and we have to rely on English or continental sources for our information. However, it is tempting to believe that Rich's and Dyott's remarks are given such prominence in Irish histories because their views support the idea that Ireland had no decent beer until the arrival in the 18th century of certain porter breweries that are still manufacturing in Ireland today.

It is notable that Rich uses the words "taverne" and "alehouse" inter-changeably — by the 1600s, the distinction between a place selling wine and a place selling beer was disappearing, with both being described in legislation and in normal conversation as "public houses", which was abbreviated during the Victorian period to give us the word pub that we use today. His complaint about the price of beer in Dublin may have been due to the fact that hops, the ingredient needed to turn ale into beer, did not grow well in Ireland's climate. Hops were usually imported and their use did not become common in Irish brewing until the mid-18th century.

Another difference between drinking habits in the 17th century and the present day is that 400 years ago most ale and beer was drunk from wooden utensils. In 1602, an Englishman, Dr Alexander Nowell, discovered that ale could be stored for longer if kept in cork-sealed glass bottles, but it wouldn't be until the second half of the 18th century that beer in bottles, and glassware in general, would become common. Indeed, it wasn't until the end of the 17th century that pewter mugs and tankards became common as an alternative to drinking from wooden utensils.

Four bottles found in Ireland, dating from (L–R): c.1680; c.1750; 1729; and 17th century (the third bottle pictured here belonged to Dean Swift, author of Gulliver's Travels; *his seal can be seen on the front)*

The Start of Pub Controls

The first statute to control the number of pubs in Ireland was enacted in 1635, by which time Dublin is reckoned to have been home to 4,000 families and 1,180 public houses, most selling their own homebrew. Most commentators argue that the act was introduced because of growing public concern about high levels of public drunkenness. Certainly, the first laws to curb public drunkenness in England were introduced during the reign of James I with four Acts of Parliament aimed at reducing public intoxication introduced between 1603 and 1619,[5] but none of these Jacobite laws was enacted in Ireland. As the preamble to the 1635 Act makes clear, the introduction of licensing in Ireland

---

[5] The title of the 1606 legislation, "An Act for repressing the odious and loathsome Sin of Drunkenness", gives an insight into how closely Church and State law were intertwined at the time.

was as much about political control as it was about controlling alcohol consumption:

> "Forsomuch as it is found by daily experience, that many mischiefes and inconveniences doe arise from the excessive number of alehouses, from the erection of them in woods, bogges, and other unfit places, and many of them not in towne-ships, but dispersedly, and in dangerous places, and kept by unknown persons not under-taken for, whereby many times they become resceptacles for rebels and other malefactors and harbours for gamesters and other idle, disordered, and unprofitable livers, and that those that keep those alehouses for the most part are not fitted or furnished to lodge or entertaine travellers in any decent manner: For the redresse of these inconveniencies, and many other mischiefes dayly observed to grow by the course now held, and to reduce those needless multitudes of alehouses to a fewer number, to more fit persons, and to more convenient places."

The Act failed in its effort to restrict or reduce the number of alehouses, particularly in Dublin where, by 1667, there were over 1,500 premises selling alcohol, according to minutes of the city corporation. However, the way the Act and subsequent licensing laws gave Ireland's rulers control over who could own alehouses and sell intoxicating liquor helped increase England's domination of Ireland. One reason why the number of licences continued to increase is that the monies from licence fees were an important source of income to the exchequer.

Better Brews

Most of Ireland's licensed premises were alehouses, but many of them were no longer selling ale that had been brewed on the premises. From the mid-17th century onwards, taverns and alehouses increasingly sold beer from "common brewers" or "public brewers". One reason for this was that drinkers were becoming more discerning and the craft of brewing was being developed. In Dublin alone, there were 91 commercial breweries in 1672 and by 1696 the brewers had sufficient economic power to demand representation on the common council of Dublin Guilds.[6] The Brewers' Guild had St James as its patron and James's Street, which is still the home to Guinness's Brewery, was the main centre of brewing in Dublin with at least half a dozen breweries in the district. With the formation of the guild, brewing became a respectable trade, but it was not an activity for gentlemen until the end of the 18th century — in 1750, the Leeson family abandoned brewing when they had amassed sufficient wealth and social standing to be made the Earls of Milltown.

The Curse of Cromwell

Cromwell — Son of a brewer and a drinker of small beer

Because of a lack of records, it is difficult to gain a picture of how the licensed trade developed outside Dublin during the 17th century. It is likely that the growing number of alehouses in Dublin did not follow the national pattern as the period between 1649 and 1658 was one of the bloodiest periods in Irish history. The suppression of the Catholic Church and its followers was ruthless, estates were seized and the dispossessed were either executed, transplanted to Connaught or transported to the Americas. Notably for our story, Cromwell's rise to power is indirectly linked to the licensed trade in two ways: he was the son of a brewmaster and the English Civil War was partly funded by the first direct tax on beer. In 1643, the Parliament established an excise service to impose duties on home-produced goods, with the first goods to be taxed being ale and beer. The Royalists followed suit almost immediately with their own excise service and beer duty. Both sides promised that after the Civil War the tax would be removed, but there has been a beer

---

[6] Vintners had been represented on the council since 1565 when their society was amalgamated with the Guild of Cooks.

duty in Britain ever since. A year after the restoration of the English monarchy, Charles II introduced a customs and excise service in Ireland in 1661 and we have had beer duty ever since.

Time Please

The first formal restriction on licensed trading hours — other than local requirements related to town and city curfews — was the Lord's Day Act of 1685, which prohibited Sunday trading "during the hours of divine service". The measure had been introduced in England in 1618 during the reign of James I, but it wasn't until 77 years later, during the reign of William III, that the measure was extended to Ireland.

Indeed, even following the Act of Union, licensing laws in Britain and Ireland differed greatly. Even in Victorian times, subsections of new licensing legislation didn't necessarily apply to Ireland, something that continuously added to the confusion surrounding Irish licensing law. In many cases, there was a delay of several years before trading laws in England were applied to this country.

As well as being the first restriction on opening hours, the Lord's Day Act is significant for two other reasons: it placed a duty on constables to enter pubs during restricted hours to apprehend anyone found drinking "after hours", and it also introduced the requirement that alcohol licences be renewed annually.

Fair Dues and Dirty Gaugers

That early Irish 17th and 18th century licensing was about political control, rather than controlling sales of drink, is underlined by the fact that it was possible to set up a beer stall at a public fair, race meeting or market without having a licence. Providing one had a certificate to show that one had bought the beer, and paid the necessary duty, at a public brewery, no offence occurred. Indeed, under an Act of Parliament introduced in 1760, the last year of George II's reign, it was possible for an unlicensed person to sell beer at a public event, but an alehouse keeper who brewed his own beer was barred from doing so. Guidance on this exception to the law is contained in *The duty and authority of*

Justices of the Peace and Parish Officers for Ireland, by E.D. Bullingbrooke, which was published in 1788. Describing himself as a "doctor of laws and an advocate in the ecclesiastical courts", Bullingbrooke counsels:

> "It ſhall be lawful for any perſon, except such perſons under licence, who brew their own beer or ale for retail, who shall buy beer of ale at any publick brewery, and obtain a certificate from ſuch brewer, as alſo from the gauger of the diſtrict, that such beer or ale was brewed in ſuch publick brewery and hath paid the exciſe, to ſell the ſame without licence at any fair, aſſiſes, ſeſſions, race, or other publick meeting, without being liable to any of the penalties herein before contained."

The gauger referred to was an official of the customs service, who was responsible for ensuring that barrels of ale, beer, wine and whiskey contained no less than 40 gallons and that half-barrels held no less than 20 gallons. If the barrel contained less than the legal amount, the gauger had the power to seize and destroy barrels, as well as to impose heavy fines on the barrel's manufacturer and owner. As a person with the ability to bring financial hardship to anyone with faulty measures, gaugers would not have been popular with market traders, which may be why "you dirty gauger" remains an insult in Ireland today.

The ban on alehouse keepers trading at fairs and public races appears to have lasted until 1825, when they were allowed to set up stalls next to their unlicensed competitors. An attempt was made in 1862 to make unlicensed fair-day and race-day beer-stalls illegal, but such was the public outcry that the ban was overturned the following year and it wasn't until 1874 that all trade in alcoholic drinks in Ireland required a licence. Today, occasional licences are issued to cover the sale of alcohol at "special events" like annual dinner-dances or special festivities in venues that would otherwise be unlicensed, but these occasional licences can only be obtained by existing licensees. In 1971, the Supreme Court held that "bi-weekly cattle and pig markets in a county town were not special events".

Certainly, the fact that unlicensed beer sales were allowed during court assizes indicates that these quarterly visits by justices of the peace were important social events that were accompanied by a carnival atmosphere that included balls and fairs. Following independence, the Free State replaced the royal assizes with the circuit courts, which are in operation today and where the atmosphere is sober.

Bullingbrooke's legal handbook provides many insights into 18th century law and it is clear that licensing wasn't uppermost in the minds of the legislature at the time — the handbook contains 10 pages giving guidance on licensing law, but it has 30 pages about laws suppressing "popery". This was a time when the Church of Ireland was very much the Church of the establishment and where Church sanctions were part of the punishment involved in criminal law.[7] As such, Bullingbrooke notes:

> "If any offend their brethren by drunkenefs, the churchwardens and fidemen fhall prefent the fame to the ordinary, that he may be punifhed by the feverity of the laws, according to their deferts; and fuch notorious offenders fhall not be admitted to the holy communion, till they be reformed."

One of the more unusual laws found in Bullingbrooke concerns the crime of "enhancing the price of ale" where:

> "No perfon fhall fell or caufe to be fold by retail any ftrong beer at a lower price than 2½ penny by the quart; nor any fmall beer at an higher price than one penny for each quart, upon pain of forfeiting for each offence 5L [£5]."

Since Irish independence, as we shall see later, the main concern of politicians and the powers that be has been keeping the price of the pint down and there has been little concern in the last century about possible below-cost selling of alcohol.

---

[7] Transportation to America is described by Bullingbrooke as a punishment for those whose crimes demand that they be "excluded from benefits of clergy". Ironically, many of those who were transported were Catholic priests, with the only clergy recognised as legitimate being those belonging to the established Church.

Other Measures

As the 17th century progressed, the licensed trade became increasingly regulated with additional restrictions and duties placed on publicans. For instance, in New Ross in October 1680, keepers of alehouses, taverns and brandy shops were ordered to hang out their lights on dark nights from 6 p.m. to 9 p.m. under penalty of a fine of 6d "for every neglect".

From 1689 onwards, under the terms of the Mutiny Act, public houses were obliged to provide billeting for soldiers and army officers' horses during times of unrest. This was a measure that forced Irish licensees to go beyond obeying English law to actually become indirectly involved in the enforcement of law and order in their locality. It may be argued that this provision in the Mutiny Act later led to the tradition of policing among a number of licensing families, as many the son of a publican pursued a career in the Royal Irish Constabulary or the Gardaí.

As fresh clean water became an increasingly scarce resource in urban areas, brewers' use of alcohol came under increasing scrutiny and regulation. In Kinsale, in 1714, a local bylaw was passed prohibiting the collection of gutter water for brewing except between November 1 and February 28 of each year.

It should be remembered that for a large proportion of Irish society, the development of taverns and alehouses meant nothing. Agricultural labourers were mainly cottiers who received no wages at all; instead, their payment was access to land on which to live and grow crops. Those who lived in this cashless economic existence literally didn't have the money to buy beer and wine in alehouses or taverns.

London coffee house, c. 1690
— competition for taverns

In the large towns, where there were customers with money, alehouse keepers and taverners had a new rival in the second half of the 17th century: coffee houses. Among Dublin's merchant classes, the tavern was forsaken for the coffee house as a place to do business. Coffee houses were also found in Limerick, Cork, Galway, Kilkenny, Clonmel and Wexford. Chocolate and tea also arrived in Ireland in the late 17th century; tea has become the most consumed beverage in Ireland today. Notably, sellers of these non-alcoholic beverages were also licensed, with a grocer being defined in law as "a retailer licensed to trade in, vend, and sell, coffee, tea, cocoa, nuts, chocolate or pepper".

Signs of the Times

The second half of the 17th century was also a time when English-style pub signs became common. During the 17th and 18th century, pub names like The Bear & Ragged Staff, The Nag's Head and The Mitre became common in Ireland, with pubs having decorative signs illustrating their names as an aid to those who could not read. These signs had been in use in England by law since 1393, but the Irish were slow to adopt them. In the late 19th century and 20th century, the Irish abandoned this form of pub name, choosing instead to name the pub after the current licensee or the family name of the pub's founder.

In rural districts, homemade whiskey or poteen was starting to become a more common drink than home-brewed beer, though for much of the 17th century whiskey was a drink mainly of the upper classes. Following the introduction of the potato as an alternative source of carbohydrates and vitamin B, beer became a less important element in the diet of the rural poor. The move from beer to whiskey drinking is reflected in the word "shebeen" used in Ireland, Scotland, the Caribbean and South Africa to describe illegal drinking dens. The original Irish word *séibín* meant "ale, especially bad ale", but since the 18th century, when the word entered the English language, shebeen has meant "a place where alcoholic drink, especially whiskey, is on sale illegally".

As home-brewed beer declined, distilling whiskey became more common. Efforts had been made to gain licensing revenue from all distillers, but this had been mostly unsuccessful. Whiskey was distilled in houses big and small. Among the nobility, whiskey was frequently drunk at mealtimes in the same way that wine is drunk today.

Orange Gin

The repercussions of the Battle of the Boyne in 1690 are still being felt today in the politics of Northern Ireland, but one of the most immediate effects of the battle was the widespread availability of cheap alcohol at the start of the 18th century. The victorious King William of Orange was fiercely anti-French and banned all imports of brandy, promoting his favourite tipple, Geneve or gin, instead. There were hardly any restrictions on distillation and, in London and Dublin, gin shops proliferated with devastating effects on the urban poor. In the mid-18th century the political caricaturist William Hogarth produced engravings depicting "Beer Street" and "Gin Lane" side by side.

"Beer Street" by William Hogarth   *"Gin Lane" by William Hogarth*

The beer drinkers are depicted as plump, healthy and enjoying life, but the scene in Gin Lane is one of chaos and squalor, with one of the figures being a mother so drunk on gin that she drops her infant in the street. Such were the effects of gin in London that although the city's sanitation improved in this period, its population fell as people literally drank themselves to death. As middle-class concern grew, the British government was forced to introduce the Gin Acts of 1744 and 1751, which increased the duty on spirits and changed the law so that only licensed "keepers of public houses" could sell spirits. The Act is credited with closing up to 1,700 gin shops in London alone, but at the height of the gin epidemic there were more than 8,600 gin shops in the city. Many gin shops acquired public house licences and then traded in both spirits and ale.

William of Orange also deserves commemoration by Irish drinkers for giving us fair measure, for it is he who introduced the legal requirement that all pint vessels in pubs bear an assay mark, certifying that they hold a full pint measure. The 1700 Act gives an indication of the wide variety of drinking vessels in use at the time, requiring that the "essay" be stamped or marked on all vessels, be they made of "wood, earth, glass, horn, leather, pewter or of some other good and wholesome metal".

The oldest statute still in effect that applies to the licensed trade in Ireland is the Drink on Credit to Servants Act of 1735, which states that a licensee who sells drink on credit to "Servants, Day Labourers and other Persons, who usually work or ply for Hire or Wages" has no right in law for recovery of the debt. This reversed a previous law, enacted in 1603, which allowed innkeepers to detain guests until bills were paid in full. Under the 1603 Act, an innkeeper could also seize a guest's horse as surety against unpaid bills and once the horse had eaten its value in fodder, the animal became the innkeeper's property.[8]

The administration of licences was further tightened up and subjected to greater monitoring by a law in 1753 that required all clerks of the peace to

---

[8] Another peculiarity of the 1603 Act was that an innkeeper was responsible for any property stolen from a guest, only if the guest was in credit; if the guest was in debt, the innkeeper bore him and his property no duty of care.

keep a record of licence holders in their localities. Theoretically, the days of the shebeen were over, but many unlicensed premises continued to operate openly, particularly in Dublin, until the 1930s. The crowded slums of Dublin made it difficult for police to raid illegal shebeens without their arrival being spotted well in advance by lookouts. As a result, shebeens were still active, though less publicly so, in Dublin until the 1950s.

Marriage Licences

Before the mid-18th century, many people were married in pubs. All that was needed was a public declaration of consent, a vow before witnesses and consummation, and the marriage was legally binding and permanent. When agreed on the spur of the moment, under the influence of drink, and consummated in the upstairs room of a tavern, many marriages were doomed to failure and unhappiness.

Many a poor girl who thought herself wed to the man of her dreams quickly found herself deserted. In 1753, under the Marriage Act introduced by Lord Hardwicke, it became illegal to be married in a pub. From that year on, it has been necessary in Britain and Ireland to have a marriage licence and for the marriage vows to be given in a place registered for that purpose.

Coach Houses

The start of the 18th century saw the development of the first major stage-coach services in Ireland, something that provided a valuable source of income to many Irish pubs of the time. As well as the business generated by accommodating overnight travellers, inns also benefited from contracts to stable coaching horses. Coaching inns were substantial buildings for their time. Stables were usually found in an enclosed cobbled yard to the rear of the pub with a high arch providing access to the main road. Byrne's Irish House in Kilcoole (see page 146), Co. Wicklow, had a purpose-built platform attached to the front of the pub so that coach passengers could alight without dirtying their feet in the muddy road; there was then an external stairway which gave the passengers access to a dining room on the first floor.

By 1737, there were regular services from Dublin to Drogheda, Kilkenny, Kinnegad and Athlone. A permanent service between Dublin and Belfast, running three days a week, was established in 1788, by which time there were a total of 12 provincial centres linked by stagecoach service to the capital. The expansion of the national postal service in 1789 saw the coaching inns gain further income and by 1834 there were 28 mail coach lines in the country. As well as catering for travellers, until the 1820s coaches were also accompanied by a military guard, with the soldiers providing further income for the pubs.

The Wet War

One of the biggest developments in the licensed trade in Ireland during the 18th century was the arrival of British beers in Irish pubs. In the twelve years before 1727, no beer or ale had been imported into Ireland, but as English brewers' capacity increased, they began expanding into their nearest colonial market.

What became known as "The Wet War" started in 1732 when a law was passed banning the Irish from importing hops from anywhere other than England. Previously, although most hop imports came from England, Irish brewers could also buy hops from Holland, France and Spain and the price was competitive. Once the law was changed, hop prices soared because of the English monopoly. The excise laws also worked against the Irish brewers because they were charged a higher beer duty than their English rivals and English brewers were also given grant aid for their exports. In Dublin alone, the number of breweries fell from 70 to 30 in the face of unfair competition.

In 1773, the Dublin Brewers Guild petitioned the Irish parliament to set up a committee to "enquire into the reasons of their distress and to gain them fair play". In the enquiry, a young Arthur Guinness said that such was his plight that he had decided to shut up shop in Dublin and was planning to brew in Caernarvon or Holyhead in Wales instead.

18ᵗʰ century London porters

Unfair competition aside, the English also had the advantage of "porter", a tasty new brew that was developed in London in the 17ᵗʰ century because of market conditions involving taxation, economies of scale and a growing sophistication of taste among beer consumers. Porter's name is believed to be derived from the fact that porters working in London's markets particularly favoured it. At first, it was known as "three thread", because it was originally made from a blend of three different ales — pale ale, mature dark ale and immature dark ale — that were kept in kegs behind a pub's bar counter. In 1722, a London brewer named Ralph Harwood produced a beer that could be supplied in a single barrel, yet which still had the complex aroma and taste of "three thread" porter beer. The fact that the new brew was now supplied in a single keg also made it ideal for export.

Genesis of Genius

In 1787, Arthur Guinness became the first Irish brewer to produce porter, with other Irish brewers following suit; as a result, British beer imports started to decline. This decline accelerated in 1800 when the Act of Union ended trade inequalities.

The story of large-scale/industrial brewers like Guinness is central to the history of licensing in Ireland from the mid-18ᵗʰ century onwards.

The Guinness brewing dynasty was founded by Richard Guinness, who was born in 1690, the year of the Battle of the Boyne. He became a land agent (rent collector) for the Rector of Celbridge in Co. Kildare, where his duties included brewing ale for the rector's household. When the rector died, he left £100 to Richard's son, Arthur Guinness, who bought a small brewery in Leixlip in 1756. Arthur had bigger plans and three years later he moved to Dublin, taking out a

9,000-year lease on a disused brewery in James's Gate, Dublin, for an annual rent of £45. By 1787, Arthur was brewing porter and 12 years later, in 1799, he took the decision to brew only porter. One of the factors that was to lead to Guinness's dominance of the Irish market was its successful use of innovations in transportation, firstly using the canals from 1820 onwards and then using railways from the second half of the 19th century. One pub that benefited from being on the banks of a canal was Thomas O'Keeffe's in Kilcock (page 184), where the family also supplied Guinness to other pubs in the district.

Arthur Guinness, 1725–1803

Poteen

The increased duties on spirits imposed by the Gin Acts of 1744 and 1751 led to increased beer consumption within the licensed trade, but it also led to a boom in an unlicensed trade in whiskey, described as "poteen", from the 18th century onwards. While gin was popular in Ireland, the spirit of choice was usually whiskey. In the 1740s and 1750s, nearly every town in Ireland had its own distillery, usually producing only between 200 to 300 gallons per year. Gradually, these distilleries were forced out of business by British taxation policy. Not only did the duty increase almost fourfold in the space of 30 years, from 10d in 1775 to 6s 1.5d in 1815, but the law also favoured those who distilled large amounts of spirits. A minimum duty charge meant that legal distilleries had to produce more than a certain amount of whiskey every month to remain profitable. Irish distillers were obliged to fire their stills twice a week, then once every day. The regulations forced the makers of legitimate "parliament whiskey" to cut corners and produce their finished product at an ever faster rate. As a result, illegally made poteen, made at a time-honoured pace,

*Poteen still seized near Killyleagh,
Co. Down, c 1930*

was usually the better drink. In fact, it is reckoned that more than half of the whiskey sold in Ireland between 1780 and 1820 was illegally distilled poteen. Not only did it taste better, but those who bore political resentments against England felt more patriotic when drinking poteen.

It was not until the end of the 18th century that duties were reduced and regulations were changed to allow legitimate distillers to produce a better quality drink. By this time, however, most of Ireland's legal distilleries had vanished, but it appears that many pub licensees discreetly sold locally made, but illegal, poteen at this time. *The Vintners Guide*, published in 1825, gives full instruction on how poteen is made. The instructions are introduced with the words, "It may not be uninteresting to insert in this place extracts on distilling", indicating that the recipe has not been included for reasons of idle curiosity: until the mid-19th century, the words "interesting" and "uninteresting" were only used in connection with matters of commercial profit. Certainly, several of the pubs listed in the second part of this book were founded by former poteen makers, notably O'Sullivans in Co. Kerry (page 248) and Harkin's in Co. Donegal (page 276).

Spirit Grocers

In 1791, the gin shops returned in a new form following the passing of a new Spirit Licences Act that was very much in keeping with the new political dogma of free trade and *laissez-faire* economics. Less than 50 years after gin shops had been more or less abolished in 1744, the new British government orthodoxy held that there should be few limits on the trade in hard alcohol. As a result, the gin shops returned in a new form: the spirit grocery.[9]

Getting a spirit grocer's licence was relatively easy. Prospective publicans needed to present character references from "three or four respectable and substantial householders" attesting that they were "of good fame and sober life and conversation", but no such references were needed when applying for a retail spirits off-licence. One reason for this is that grocers were, by definition, already licensed to sell goods like tobacco, coffee and tea.

When spirit grocers' licences were first introduced, it was argued that they would act as an aid to temperance, because they would allow women to purchase spirits without risking the moral dangers and temptations of a public house. However, the lax laws meant a return to the worst days of the gin epidemic — customers would order gin by the naggin bottle[10] and sip the contents while standing at the bar.

Improvements in glass, mirrors and gas lighting meant that the spirit grocers were very well illuminated for their time, earning them the nickname "gin palaces" among the urban poor. In 1877, there were 641 spirit grocers in Ireland, 321 of them outside Dublin.

---

[9] When the Orange Order, a Protestant fraternity dedicated to sustaining the "glorious and immortal memory" of King William of Orange, was established in 1795, one of its founders, Dan Winters, was a spirit grocer. His home in Armagh is now a museum, with the 18th century cottage complex featuring a dwelling, a spirit grocer's and a weaving shed.

[10] In the UK, the word "noggin" describes a measure of quarter of a pint and the Hiberno-English word "naggin" is rarely listed in dictionaries, despite the fact that a "naggin bottle" appears in James Joyce's *Ulysses*. Interestingly, in Ireland in 1825 a naggin was considered equivalent to two glasses of spirit measures, indicating that even then spirit measures in Ireland were twice the size of those in the rest of the UK. Whiskey is still sold by the "naggin bottle" in Ireland today, but now the bottles contain 200ml, which is closer to three-eights of a pint than quarter of a pint. For more on the various measures used in the 19th century, see Appendix C, page 294.

Further Liberalisation

As public concern about drunkenness caused by consumption of cheap gin grew once more, the Duke of Wellington sought to cure the problem by liberalising the pub trade. The Beer Act of 1830, which applied to England and Wales, transferred the responsibility for issuing licences from magistrates to the excise service. While prospective publicans in Ireland still had to make court appearances, and provide sureties and statements of good character, in England two guineas paid to HM Excise was all you needed for a pub licence.

Those who would argue for liberalising Ireland's licensed trade today would do well to look at the English experience: the market was flooded with new pubs, hundreds went bankrupt and Britain ended up with a system of "tied houses" as the breweries bought up most of the country's alehouses for knock-down prices. Paradoxically, when the 1869 Wine and Beer House Act de-liberalised the English and Welsh licensed trade the tied-house system there was reinforced, because the value of the breweries' licences and tied-houses suddenly increased in value. And when it came to discouraging drunkenness, the 1830 Beer Act was a total failure as instead of getting intoxicated by spirits, the public chose to do so with cheap beer. The British author Sydney Smith wrote:

> "The new Beer Act has begun its operations. Everyone is drunk. Those who are not singing are sprawling. The sovereign people is in a beastly state."

The Licensing (Ireland) Act of 1833 included many of the measures contained in the Duke of Wellington's Beer Act for England and Wales three years earlier. The Irish Act removed any limit on the number of licences that could be issued annually. While it was still necessary in Ireland to apply for a licence in a magistrate's court, magistrates could only refuse licence applications on one of three grounds: the unsuitability of the applicant, the unsuitability of the premises or because there were already too many licensed houses in the neighbourhood. The last provision was almost totally ignored and a vast number of licences were issued between 1833 and 1902. When it came to licence renewals, the law was even slacker: the Excise Service granted renewals on payment of an annual fee and production of a certificate signed by six local householders as to the "good and peaceful conduct" of the house during the previous year.

Competition

Those setting up as publicans in the 19th century had a wide range of beer suppliers to choose from, as Ireland had over 100 different commercial breweries dotted around the country in some 80 different towns. Most of the breweries were in Leinster, though there were seven towns with breweries in Co. Galway and six in Co. Mayo. In 1830, there were 13 breweries in Foxford alone, indicating the Mayo mill town's economic importance at that time.

The oldest of these breweries still in operation is the St Francis Abbey Brewery in Kilkenny, which was founded by John Smithwick in 1710.[11] Smithwick's was the second commercial brewery to be established in Kilkenny in the 18th century: the St James's Street Brewery founded in 1702 traded until the end of the 19th century, but its local market suffered

18th century engraving of a small scale brewery

because of post-famine emigration and its English export market was destroyed by the arrival of the "tied house" system of pub ownership.

---

[11] Guinness took an interest in Smithwick's in the 1950s, had overall control of the brewery in the 1960s and sole control in the 1980s. Guinness and Smithwick's are now part of Diagio plc.

In the City of Dublin in 1816, there were 35 breweries, with others close by in Cloughran, Clontarf, Leixlip, Celbridge and Kingstown (Dún Laoghaire). There was a commercial brewery in nearly every county in Ireland, with the exceptions of Donegal, Tyrone, Sligo, Cavan, Monaghan and Clare. In counties Derry and Fermanagh, there were no breweries outside Derry city and Enniskillen. Generally, because of a poor supply of barley, there were fewer breweries in Ulster than in the other provinces; in total, Ulster had 21 breweries, nine of which were in Belfast.

Guinness's St. James's Gate Brewery
in the early 19th Century

While Guinness had the largest brewery in Dublin at the start of the 19th century, its brewery was not the largest in the country. That title was held by the Cork Porter Brewery which was founded in 1792 by the partnership of Richard Henrick Beamish and Arthur Frederick Sharman Crawford. By 1805, Beamish & Crawford owned the third largest brewery in the British Isles and the biggest in Ireland, producing 100,000 barrels of beer a year.

The intense competition between breweries in Ireland led to attempts to operate a tied-house system, where pubs were brewery-owned and licensees were tenants, contractually obliged to sell only the brewery's beer.

Starting a pub also became increasingly easy, thanks to the relative ease of obtaining a licence and the fact that breweries were more than willing to provide credit to new licensees. As a result, there was a huge growth in the number of licensed premises and there were many vintners who started in business who ended up bankrupt shortly afterwards.

The Vintners' Guide

Such was the number of vintners and vintners' families in distress that the Fair Trading Vintners Society and Asylum was founded in Dublin in 1818. As a further measure, the society's secretary, William Phipps, published the first ever handbook for the Irish licensed trade in 1825, with the hope that "by means of this little work, I shall be the instrument of saving industrious and well-disposed persons from ruin".

In his introduction to *The Vintners Guide*, Phipps wrote:

> "Those who live by the occupation of vintner are generally speaking persons who have not been brought up to any business. Such as have little capital saved prefer it to any other, calculating on the quick return of money from the desire which is so prevalent for the use of strong liquor.

> They in many instances never consider it a business of much labour and circumspection and some will go so far as to think scarcely any knowledge of the business necessary but what can be easily obtained. They think to draw a naggin or a measure of whiskey or strong liquor cordials etc. or a pint of porter an easy matter.

> But how very much mistaken in this point, never did any business require more circumspection and few comparatively from the many in the trade are adapted for carrying it on respectably and giving satisfaction to the frequenters of their houses. Failures in trade, which I'm sorry to say are very numerous, are the consequence."

Under "Remarks on House Taking", Phipps writes:

> "Generally speaking houses are taken at random, and as if it were a matter of indifference with the proprietors whether they succeeded in them or not. Brewers are very friendly on these occasions to offer their services and often are induced to venture their property with persons of no capital on speculation, in houses thrown on their hands by insolvent vintners.

> I have often witnessed houses puffed off and saw inexperienced vintners occupy them no doubt with golden dreams of making certain fortunes with

them; they were completely ruined in a short time and incredibly almost as it may seem I have seen another and another in quick succession following on the ruin of his predecessor and sharing the same fate without ever considering the causes why none succeeded until at length the house was completely destroyed."

As well as giving counsel on indispensable cleanliness, an obliging deportment, holding one's tongue and the importance of choosing a good location, Phipps is almost evangelical in some of his advice:

"Endeavour to be perfect in the calling you are engaged in and be assiduous in every part thyself. Be strict in discharging all legal duties. Endeavour to be as much in your shop or warehouse or whatever place your business properly lies as possible you can — leave it not to servants to transact, for customers will not regard them as yourself. Be complaisant to the meanest as well as to the greatest, you are as much obliged to use good manners for a farthing as a pound. Take care as much as you can whom you trust; neither take nor give long credit, but at the furthest annually settle your accounts; deal at the fountainhead for as many articles as you can and if it is in your power for ready money; this method you will find is the most profitable in the end. Aim not at making a great figure in your shop or warehouse in unnecessary ornaments, but let them be neat and useful. Strive to maintain a fair character in the world — that will be the best means for advancing your credit, giving you the most flourishing trade and enlarging your fortune. Condescend to no mean action, but think it a lustre to trade by keeping up to the dignity of your name."

Repeatedly, Phipps tells vintners not to become indebted to brewers. His reasoning is simple: if you are in debt to your brewer you will probably find yourself forced to sell poor quality beer and your trade will further suffer.

Beer aside, the range of drinks sold in up-market public houses in the early 19th century appears to have been extensive. *The Vintners Guide* lists a variety of imported spirits, plus advice on preparing a wide range of flavoured wines and cordials. Among the recipes given by Phipps are instructions for making the following homemade wines: blackcurrant, ginger, berry, cowslip, alder and raisin. As already mentioned, Phipps gives a recipe for poteen, but he also gives instructions for making a very strange drink which he calls "usquebaugh" and whose ingredients include brandy, Spanish liquorish, raisins, currants, dates, tops of broom, mint, savoury, thyme, rosemary, cinnamon, mace, nutmeg, aniseed, coriander seed and orange peel.

Anti-popery Porter

Such was the level of competition between brewers in the 19th century that appeals to sectarian sympathies and fears were made to licensees and drinkers. In pamphlets produced in 1815 to promote Pims Ale, drinkers were warned that their favourite beverages might be brainwashing them. The pamphlet claimed that "brewers of anti-popery porter" had mashed up Protestant bibles and Methodist hymnbooks in the brewing mix "thus impregnating the volatile parts of the porter with the pure ethereal essence of heresy". The Guinness brewery was specifically targeted by the pamphlet, with the claim that in recent years that brewery alone had consumed 136,000 tons of bibles and 501,000 cartloads of hymnbooks and Protestant catechisms.

Murphy's — a "Catholic porter"?

In the 1920s, Guinness's own sales representatives in Cork would complain that sales in Cork were suffering because priests were advising people to drink Murphy's because it was a "Catholic porter".

One brewery that benefited from being identified with Catholicism was the O'Connell brewery, which was founded in 1832 by Daniel O'Connell, son of the Liberator, who had £2,000 invested in the enterprise. The O'Connell brewery was still in operation in the first decade of the 20th century and today the Dublin Brewing Company, founded in 1996, produces a brew called "O'Connell's Ale".

Ireland Sober, Ireland Free

The reaction against the increased public drunkenness perceived to have been caused by a liberal licensing regime, excessive competition and, in particular, spirit grocers can be linked to a resurgence of nationalist feeling in early 19th century Ireland. The first temperance societies founded in Ireland were anti-spirits societies formed in New Ross, Belfast and Dublin. Although later temperance movements advocated total abstinence from all forms of alcohol, spirit grocers and "gin shops" remained the main target of temperance crusaders.

The most successful pre-Famine temperance movement was that led by a Cork Capuchin friar named Fr Theobold Matthew, who claimed to have administered the teetotal pledge to five million people. Perhaps his crusading zeal led him to exaggerate his own achievements, but if this claim were true he would have given the pledge to over half of Ireland's then total population of eight million people. Nevertheless, Fr Matthew found huge support and he drew thousands to his rallies.

Daniel O'Connell — brewing pioneer?

Among those to take the pledge was Daniel O'Connell, the political leader known as "The Liberator" for his role in achieving Catholic Emancipation in 1829. Despite having a financial interest in his son's brewery, O'Connell took the pledge in 1840, the same year he established the Repeal Association to work for an end to the Act of Union. As well as giving O'Connell the idea for "monster meetings" that drew tens of thousands of people, Fr Matthew allowed the Repeal Association to use temperance halls for planning meetings and temperance bands also provided the music at emancipation rallies. O'Connell even went so far as to administer a "repeal pledge" to election candidates seeking his support. With sobriety keeping O'Connell's monster meetings peaceful, it's no wonder the phrase "Ireland sober, Ireland free" was coined at this time.

The temperance crusaders finally succeeded in having the spirit grocer's licence abolished in 1910, but by this time there was little difference between a public house and a spirit grocery. At the start of the 20th century, most pubs in rural Ireland had a grocery counter and selling groceries was usually a bigger source of income to publicans than selling drink.

Laissez Faire

The liberalisation of the licensed trade at the start of the 19th century sprang from the ideology of *laissez faire*, which held that there should be no restriction on private commerce. It was an ideology that compounded the suffering caused by the Great Famine, as the British government were slow to begin a relief programme when the potato harvest failed: it was held that market forces would eventually lead to famine relief being provided, but thousands starved because the market responded too slowly. When grain was available, the poor did not have the money to buy it.

Some local restrictions were placed on brewing and distilling to make grain available, but beer production appears to have been only slightly affected, with output falling by 12 per cent. The economists Patrick Lynch and John Vaizey estimate that Irish beer output in 1846 was 732,000 barrels and in 1847 it was 617,000 barrels.

Folklore tells us that many general merchants did go out of business during the Famine; some bankrupted themselves feeding the hungry and over-extending their credit lines, while others were forced out of business after they attempted to profit from the misery of the starving. Certainly, *The Freeman's Journal* reported that many tradesmen, such as cobblers and stonemasons, were idle through lack of work, but there are no reports of merchants going bankrupt as a direct result of the Famine. Indeed, modern historians have found little evidence of vintners and other merchants suffering hardship or bankruptcy because of events surrounding the Great Hunger.

One reason for this lack of evidence of Famine-related business failures may be that, before the disaster struck, business failures among public houses were already commonplace because of excessive competition. Another reason may be that, as already noted, those most affected by the failure of the potato crop lived in a virtually cashless economy and were never in a position to be regular customers of taverns and alehouses. In 1845, more than half of Ireland's population of 8.5 million people lived in dire poverty: some 3 million people belonged to shareholding or cottier families while another 1.5 million were classed as "landless labourers".

Indeed, if anything, the flight from the land brought a new line of business to general merchants who became ticket agents for the emigrant boats taking the desperate and the hopeful to England and the United States.

After the Famine

It is an uncomfortable fact that life after the Famine in Ireland was a great deal better for most people than life before the Famine. Although poverty was still rife at the end of the 19th century, overall economic conditions improved. With fewer labourers available, wages were higher. The building of the railways saw thousands employed. Even where there was no commercial work available, public works schemes provided the poor with an income. The end of the penal laws meant that it was easier for Catholics to enter the professional middle classes and many did so by becoming publicans.

Among those who emigrated to America, there were some who prospered sufficiently to return to Ireland to set up business in the old country: three such pubs still in business today are Tigh Bheaglaoich in Baile na nGall, Co. Kerry (page 210), The Criterion Bar in Bundoran, Co. Donegal (page 271) and Rabbitt's Bar in Galway city (page 133).

In the long term, beer got better too. A method for prolonging beer's shelf-life was detailed in *Études sur la Bière*, published by Louis Pasteur in 1876.

Another 22 years would pass before the pasteurisation process was applied to milk.

Railways and Canals

The second half of the 19th century saw the establishment of the greater part of Ireland's railway network, a development that would greatly benefit the licensed trade. One of the reasons the Guinness brewery achieved such dominance in Ireland is that it successfully harnessed the power of first the canals and then the railways to dispatch its beers all over Ireland. But all manner of goods were transported on the railways and those pubs that also traded as general merchants

A Guinness barge makes its deliveries

were now able to offer their customers an almost unlimited choice of goods. The vast numbers of people employed in building the railways were also, in the first instance, responsible for the founding of two of the 100-year-old pubs listed in this book: Harkins Bar in Brockagh, Co. Donegal (page 276) and The Sycamore House near Enniscorthy, Co. Wexford (page 195).

Once the railways were built, they created a new industry — tourism — which benefited many publicans. The Criterion Bar in Bundoran (page 271) and The Roadside Tavern in Lisdoonvarna, Co. Clare (page 257) are both situated in towns that became tourist resorts as a direct consequence of the arrival of the railways. Some pubs, notably The Rustic Vaults in Tuam (page 135), also benefited from the fact that a large part of their clientele were railway company employees.

Nevertheless, some pubs lost out as a result of the arrival of the railways: Thomas O'Keeffe's in Kilcock, Co. Kildare (page 184), lost out because its location beside a harbour on the Royal Canal declined in importance, and the arrival of the railways saw Patrick C. Kelly's in Monivea, Co. Galway (page 113), lose its coaching business.

One of the indirect consequences of the railways' arrival is that all pubs in Ireland became obliged to keep the same opening hours as one another. Before the 1880 Time Act, every town in Britain and Ireland kept its own hours based on when the sun reached the highest point in the sky in their locality. As a result, for instance, the time of day in Cork was 11 minutes later than it was in Dublin. This situation was impractical for railways, which require uniform timetables, with no local variations. The 1880 legislation, officially entitled "An Act to remove doubts as to the meaning of Expressions relative to Time", introduced Greenwich Mean Time (GMT) for all of Great Britain and Dublin Mean Time (DMT) for all of Ireland.

As a result, for the next 36 years, the time of day in Ireland was officially 25 minutes and 21 seconds later than anywhere in England, Scotland or Wales. Following the Easter Rising of 1916 new legislation was rushed through Parliament to bring the time difference to an end, with the Time (Ireland) Act, "An Act to assimilate the Time adopted for use in Ireland to that adopted for use in Great Britain". At precisely 02:00:00 a.m. Dublin Mean Time on Sunday 1 October 1916, it became 02:25:21 GMT on both sides of the Irish Sea.

Pubs and Politics

As publicans prospered, they became pillars of their communities and many went into local or national politics. Among the pubs listed in our collection, there are several where the licensees were involved in political activity, including Thomas Kenny's in Ballygar, Co. Galway (page 115); O'Donnell's Bar in Carrick, Co. Donegal (page 282); Mellett's of Swinford in Co. Mayo (page 121); McClafferty's in Church Hill, Co. Donegal (page 278); Forde's (The Country Club) in Claremorris, Co. Mayo (page 101); Thomas Connolly's in

Sligo Town (page 99); O'Donovan's Hotel in Clonakilty (page 251) and Herbert's in Castleconnell, Co. Limerick (page 226).

In those pubs where licensees were elected as county councillors or town commissioners, they had to temporarily transfer the licence to a spouse or relative because the law prohibited councillors and commissioners from being licensees.

Also disqualified from becoming a licensee under the Licensing (Ireland) Act of 1833 are "Any distiller, rectifier, compounder of spirits, bailiff, gaoler, turnkey, constable, sheriff's officer, peace officer, keeper of a turnpike or any person not being a householder". Moneylenders and pawnbrokers are also prohibited from being licensees under laws passed in 1933 and 1964.

Pubs and Policemen

Despite the prohibition on constables holding licences, there is a strong tradition among licensed families of having sons who served in either the Royal Irish Constabulary (pre-Independence) or An Garda Síochána. In several cases, when serving police officers inherited their parents' pubs, they gave up their policing careers to become licensees.

Ireland can claim to have the world's first organised police force, founded as the "Peace Preservation Force" in 1814 by Sir Robert Peel. After the experimental force proved a success, a permanent national constabulary was founded in 1822 (seven years before the metropolitan police were established in England). In Britain, the new police force had severe problems with discipline with up to a quarter of officers being dismissed for drunkenness while on duty — in 1834 in Oldham, Lancashire, the town's entire police force was sacked after they were all found in a severe state of drunkenness in an unlicensed premises! In 1872, it became an offence for licensees to "knowingly harbour" a constable on duty or to supply an officer on duty with "any liquor or refreshment".

Under the Garda Síochána Discipline Regulations drawn up in 1926, a garda may be dismissed for "corrupt practice" if he "places himself directly or indirectly under pecuniary obligations to any publican, beer retailer, spirit grocer, or any person who holds a licence". A Garda may also be dismissed "if he enters while on duty any licensed premises, or any other premises where liquors are stored or distributed, when his presence there is not required in the execution of his duty".

When the force was founded in 1922, more than half the officers belonged to the Pioneers of the Sacred Heart, a total temperance organisation. Outside the force, many perceived the new Civic Guards as over-zealous in the enforcement of licensing laws. In 1923, a man convicted in Kilkenny District Court for after-hours drinking protested that he had done so for 40 years and was "never interfered with by the old RIC". This view was echoed during a Dáil debate in 1924 when Sean Lyons, TD, declared,

> "Years ago, during the British régime, the RIC used very often allow a man to go in to get a drink in his town on a Sunday. The publicans now, however, at the sight of a member of the Civic Guard, start to shiver like blancmange on a plate."

Drinking on duty? Two uniformed men in a posed photo, c. 1900

Such was the emphasis placed on sobriety among Ireland's new police force after Independence that from 1926 onwards, disciplinary action could be taken against any officer who "while on or off duty, shows as the result of consuming intoxicating liquor, the slightest departure from strict sobriety". The Garda regulations caused particular difficulty for one licensee in Feakle, Co. Clare (page 212). Bridget Fitzgerald's husband, Michael Bohan, was a Garda when the couple married in 1932. Immediately after their wedding, Michael was transferred from Feakle to Ennis where he lived for the next 22 years, cycling the 18 miles home once a month to see his wife and family.

Further Restrictions

The 19th century saw a great deal of new controls being placed on licensees in both Britain and Ireland. In Britain, many of the measures were aimed at preventing "unrule", while others were aimed at preventing the spread of venereal diseases by prostitution; in Ireland, the licensing laws were also aimed at suppressing nationalist political activity. In 1833, the law was changed so that a publican's licence could be annulled if they were found guilty of a misdemeanour or any offence of a greater nature.

The Licensing Act of 1836 made it an offence for a publican to display "any sign, flag, symbol, colour decoration emblem except the sign of the house" and the penalty for a second offence was forfeiture of a licence. This measure was repealed in the Republic in 1960.[12]

Under the Coroners Act of 1846, a coroner could direct that a dead body be brought to the nearest "tavern, public house or house licensed for the sale of spirits" and the owner or occupier of such a place was required to allow the body to be kept there until an inquest had taken place. The Templeogue Inn in south Dublin was situated beside a dangerous bend in the road and road accident victims were laid out on the pub's marble tables so frequently that it became known as "The Morgue". This legal provision obliging publicans to store the bodies of the dead wasn't removed until 1962. Before the age of the motorised ambulance and hearse, the provision made good sense for several reasons: publicans usually had cool store rooms where bodies could be kept from decomposing, and many publicans also ran undertaking businesses.

The Licensing Act of 1872 was part of a Victorian crusade against the crimes of prostitution and drunkenness. The Act made it an offence for a publican to "knowingly permit his premises to be the habitual resort of, or place of

---

[12] In Northern Ireland, nationalist publicans were effectively banned from displaying the Tricolour under the Flag and Emblems Act of 1954, which defended the right of unionists to display the Union Flag but which allowed the RUC to remove any emblem that a police constable believed might occasion a breach of the peace. Flying of tricolours in Northern Ireland only became permissible following the Good Friday Agreement in 1998.

meeting of, reputed prostitutes", with the penalty being immediate permanent disqualification from holding a licence. Under the Act, it is not a crime for a publican to serve drink to a prostitute and allow her "reasonable time" to consume it, but the licensee must not encourage the prostitute to "resort habitually" in his pub.

The 1872 Act also made it illegal for a person to be drunk in public. It also distinguished between simple drunkenness — i.e. being drunk on any highway or other public place, or on any licensed premises or when entering a designated sports event — and drunkenness with aggravation — i.e. being drunk and disorderly, refusing to leave licensed premises when requested, being drunk whilst in possession of any loaded firearms or while having charge of a child aged under seven.

In 1880, a new word was added to the English language when the Land League organised their first concerted campaign against a Mayo land agent, Captain Hugh Cunningham Boycott. The tactic of getting a whole community to refuse to deal with a landlord was extremely effective and was of major concern to the landlord class, many of whom also served as Justices of the Peace. Not surprisingly, very soon after 1880, judges started to refuse to renew the licences of publicans who had taken part in boycotts on the grounds that such publicans had placed a question mark over their good character. This view was backed by the Criminal Law and Procedure (Ireland) Act of 1887, which outlawed boycotting as a "criminal conspiracy" and specified that any licensees prosecuted under the Act should have their conviction recorded against them.

Bona Fides

In addition to trading restrictions, the Licensing Act of 1872 introduced a great new freedom: the right of "bona fide travellers" to be served outside of normal opening hours.

According to the rules, to qualify for late-night drinking or all-day drinking on a Sunday in Ireland and Britain you had to have "travelled in good faith" for a distance of at least three miles, by public thoroughfare, from the place where you spent the last night. In Australia and New Zealand, the rules were similar, except that the distance travelled to qualify was greater; in Australia, the qualifying distance was 25 miles or more.

The distance involved could be less than three miles as the crow flies; the measurement was three miles by road or public footpath — if you had a short-cut, via a back gate or private land, then lucky you.

Travelling in good faith meant that you could not be "travelling for the purposes of taking refreshment", but you could be "one who goes into an inn for refreshment in the course of a journey, whether of business or pleasure". This is a narrow distinction, but it proved enough for one 19th century traveller to escape prosecution after he told the court that he had walked into his local town, cross-country, for "a glass of water for his health"; once that task was accomplished, he then refreshed himself after his journey with beer.

In Southampton, a defendant claimed to be a bona fide traveller because he was more than three miles away from his home by land when arrested. However, the court found him guilty after ruling that he had travelled a shorter distance by public thoroughfare having made his way to the pub by boat across Southampton Water on a regular ferry route.

In Cavan, there was a case of a man who walked more than three miles into Mullagh and drank his fill in one of the town's pubs. After a while, the farmer moved on to another pub, where he was charged with drinking illegally. The court found him guilty, ruling that he "had been supplied with necessary refreshment in the first instance".

A worker taking a quick "refreshment break" and a mug of beer

While those "posing as travellers" were regularly charged and prosecuted, it was difficult to prosecute licensees, who had a handy escape clause in the law. To find a publican guilty, the prosecution had to prove that the licensee did not "honestly believe" that his customer was a bona fide traveller when serving outside normal opening hours. In one case, concerning a publican who owned a bar within a railway station, the licensee had a doorman checking that all drinkers had a train ticket on them when entering the bar — any ticket would do, even a third class 1d ticket to the next station down the line. The police observed that there were several customers who frequented the bar outside normal opening hours but never got on a train and that the station's ticket inspector was "very lax" in his duties. The case against the publican failed when the police couldn't prove any "connivance" between the pub's doorman and the railway company employee.

In an age when people travelled by foot, horse or rail, the bona fide laws were quite acceptable. But with the growth in the use of the motorcar, the provision fell increasingly out of favour. The provision was never intended to encourage drink driving, but it was increasingly being linked with deaths on the road. The car was also making a mockery of the licensing laws. In some places, bars would be crowded with customers at a time when all locals were barred. In Dublin, come 10 p.m. closing time those drinking in the city centre would drive to the suburbs to continue their sessions, while those in the suburbs would drive into town. Myles na Gopaleen boasted that, as a bona fide traveller, he had driven himself to drink.

All night drinking was getting out of hand. The law was changed in 1943 so that bona fide travellers could not be served between midnight and 6 a.m. and in 1953 the concept of bona fide travellers in pub licensing law was abolished.

The concept of bona fide travellers remained in licensing law as far as rail travellers were concerned, however. Under the 19th century laws, rail travellers may still be served alcohol in "railway refreshment rooms" on Good Friday, when normal public houses are barred from opening their doors, providing they are in possession of a valid ticket for a journey of more than three miles distance. Where there is a buffet carriage on a train, rail travellers may also be served alcohol on Good Fridays.[13] Theoretically, the bona fide rail traveller exception also applies on Christmas Day, the other day of the year when pubs are obliged to remain close, but there are no rail services in Ireland on 25 December.

Muddled M'lud

As more and more licensing laws were passed by parliament in the 19th century, judges grew increasingly concerned about their complexity. Much of the licensing law peculiar to Ireland was found in sub-sections of Acts that otherwise had been completely repealed. As a result, one judge writing in 1874 complained that he was dealing with a completely new Licensing Act, plus surviving fragments from 12 other Acts that had otherwise been repealed.

Another difficulty is that new kinds of licences, such as the spirit grocer's licence, were added to the existing range of licences in a piecemeal fashion. By 1890, there were 15 different intoxicating liquor licences in operation. There were four different types of public house licence: seven-day, six-day, early-closing and a six-day early-closing licence. Those with public house licences could sell alcohol of any kind — beer, wine, sweets[14] and spirits — on specific premises during specific opening hours, though they could also apply for "occasional licences" allowing them to set up counters for trade at race meetings, fairs and other, officially approved, public events.

Other valid licences in 1890 were a beer off-licence, a beer dealer's licence, a spirit grocer's off-licence, a spirit dealer's licence, a methylated spirits licence, a shopkeeper's wine off-licence, a wine dealer's licence, a refreshment house wine and sweets on-licence, a sweet dealer's off-licence, a theatre licence and a packet-boat licence. The difference between a "dealer's licence" and a pub, grocer or shopkeeper's licence is that dealers were restricted to minimum levels (e.g. spirits in quantities no smaller than 4.5 gallons), while retailers had maxi-

---

[13] The concept of bona fide traveller still exists under the common law right to remove obstacles on a public right of way.

[14] Any liquor made from fruit and sugar.

mum limits imposed (e.g. no more than 4.5 gallons of beer and/or half a gallon of spirits to any one person in any one day).

Since 1890, the following licences have been created: an aerodrome licence, an aircraft licence, a bus station licence, a greyhound race track licence, a hotel licence, a passenger vessel licence, a railway refreshment room licence, a railway restaurant car licence and a turf camp licence.

Not surprisingly, numerous parliamentary commissions examining the sale of intoxicating liquor have called for the law to be simplified, to little avail. Such calls were made in 1925, 1957 and, most recently, in 2000, but the area has remained extremely complex.

Sanity Returns

The start of the 20th century saw the end of the chaotic situation caused by the excessive liberalisation of the licensed trade in 1833. An immediate brake was put on new pub licences on 31 July 1902, when "the Clancy Act"[15] came into effect. The Act's restrictions were made permanent in 1943, until such time as they are changed by the Oireachtas, and as a result the 1902 Licensing Act is still regularly debated in any discussions about current Irish licensing law.

In urban areas, for a new pub licensing application to be successful, the applicant had to show that there had been a 25 per cent increase in the local population since the 1901 census; in rural areas, an applicant had to extinguish two licences elsewhere in the country before a new licence could be granted to him.

A new licence could also be issued when another licence in the "immediate vicinity" is extinguished. Using only case law to guide us, the most precise reckoning of what counts as immediate vicinity in urban areas ranges from "of no account" to "in easy walking distance"; so far, in precedents set by court

---

[15] Named after the MP and barrister John J. Clancy, who steered the Sale of Intoxicating Liquors (Licences) (Ireland) Bill 1902 through parliament for four years before it was passed with a massive majority in both Houses of Parliament.

cases, an application involving a distance of 510 yards has been allowed, but a distance of 645 yards has been rejected.

In rural areas, the distance allowed for "immediate vicinity" was greater, with an application involving a distance of 2.25 miles between premises being allowed in 1943. Indeed, in rural areas, a case in 1944 established that walking doesn't come into it, as the judge ruled that the two premises in question had served the one community, even though the new premises was in Burtonport and the old premises was on Rutland Island, half a mile off-shore.

Drunkenness

The Clancy Act was seen as a small step in a public reform campaign against alcohol abuse that had begun in the 19th century, notably with the 1872 Act's prohibitions on drunkenness. Alcohol abuse was increasingly being portrayed in the British press as a particularly Irish problem with the Irish frequently being caricatured as drunken louts.

There was some truth in the caricature: in 1875, arrests for drunkenness in Dublin exceeded those in London, despite the fact that London had a population 10 times greater. In 1876, the House of Lords established a Select Committee on Intemperance to investigate insobriety in Ireland and the role of public houses.

The committee accepted that the public house was "a legitimate and beneficial social institution when well conducted". It also considered reducing the number of pubs by order, but decided against it on the basis that it would be socially inequitable to take action against pubs without taking action against gentlemen's

A typical 19th century anti-Irish cartoon from Punch *magazine*

drinking clubs. Nevertheless, 20 years before the Clancy Act, this committee recommended that a limit be put on public house licences. Their report of 1878 also recommended a campaign against drunkenness on licensed premises, a measure that was also included in the 1902 Act.

After the Clancy Act was passed, publicans and licensed grocers were obliged to display notices reminding customers that "any person found drunk and incapable in any public place or licensed premises is liable to be apprehended and punished"; that licensees were obliged to take all reasonable steps for "preventing drunkenness" and "procuring drink for drunks". In particular, the notices drew attention to one measure and the fine involved: "The licence holder must not sell, or allow any one to sell, intoxicating liquor to any convicted habitual drunkard for three years after such a conviction; maximum penalty for first offence £10."

Trouble Brewing

At the time the 1902 Act was passed, there were 31 independent breweries operating in Ireland; by the end of the 1960s, there would only be three. In 1902, Guinness was available almost everywhere, but there were other breweries supplying local markets throughout Ireland. In Dublin alone Guinness had five competitors: Phoenix, D'Arcy, Jameson Pim, Watkins and The Mountjoy. Elsewhere, several towns had more than one brewery: Belfast had McConnell's and Caffrey's; Drogheda had Cairns and Casey's; Dundalk had McArdle Moore and the Great Northern Brewery, with the Castlebellingham Brewery also supplying pubs in Co. Louth; Kilkenny had Sullivan's and Smithwick's; Waterford had Kiely's and Davis Strangman's; and Cork City had Beamish & Crawford and Murphy's. The other breweries were: Perry's of Rathdowney, Down's in Enniskillen, Foley's in Sligo, Livingstone's in Castlebar and Westport, Cassidy's in Monasterevan, Egan's in Tullamore, the Marquis of Waterford Brewery in Dungarvan, Murphy's in Clonmel, Feehan's in Carrick-on-Suir, Deacy's in Clonakilty and Allman, Dowden and Co. in Bandon.

Guinness achieved dominance for four reasons: its brew proved better than many of its rivals and the company paid close attention to quality control; it successfully harnessed developments in transportation to expand into the Irish countryside; it had a large export market and therefore enjoyed greater economies of scale; and, lastly and most importantly, it undercut its rivals ruthlessly.

In 1859, the Dublin brewers signed an agreement stating that discounts would only be allowed to customers who sold more than 100 barrels of beer each year, but the agreement did not apply to Guinness's "agents", regional middlemen who earned up to 15 per cent commission on the beer they sold. To gain new customers, these agents frequently sold Guinness without charging their full commission rate.

In 1862, Guinness unilaterally broke the agreement against discounting and introduced a price reduction for all its customers. For the next 20 years, the brewery waged a price war which saw its profit margins decrease by 30 per cent while its market share continued to increase. Gradually, Guinness's rivals merged, went out of business or were bought up by the now giant Dublin brewery.[16]

Travellers' Tales

From the mid-19th century onwards, as well as independent agents who sold their porter, Guinness also employed "travellers" to report on market conditions across the country. These reports show us how Guinness was establishing a stronghold on the Irish beer market at the turn of the century. In 1906, the travellers report: "Clifden — we have a monopoly of the trade" and "Thurles — we have all the trade. [This is] Considered the best business town between Dublin and Cork". Again, in 1910, entries read: "Cavan — we have all the trade"; "Bundoran — a typhoid epidemic spoiled the tourist season. We have gained against other breweries and our prospects are good".

In Dublin, Guinness's main trade was in porter, rather than its premium product, double stout. In 1904, the brewery's income in the capital city was £144,271 for extra and £435,790 for porter. The company did not consider

---

[16] According to Guinness marketing figures for the period, in the first quarter of 1898, rival Irish brewers produced 184,721 barrels of beer; by the first quarter of 1902 the combined rivals' total had more than halved to 85,919 barrels.

trading conditions in Dublin to be good, with a report noting that the city had "40,000 people suffering from want".

During the first decade of the 20th century, the Guinness travellers' reports give an insight to local booms and depressions in trade. Sales of extra porter in Tullamore increased by 29.7 percent due to "return of military" after the Boer War in 1902. In Wexford town, sales went up 21.77 per cent "consequent of the new railway works" in 1906, a year which saw porter sales in Letterkenny go up 209.09 per cent "due to the construction of the new railway line to Strabane".

It wasn't all going Guinness's way, though; in 1906, the travellers' reports make frequent mention of sales being hit by local temperance crusades. This appears to have affected porter sales in particular; perhaps the drinkers of extra stout, a more expensive product, were immune to religious-led exhortations to stop enjoying their pints. In Navan, for instance, while sales of extra stout were up 12.55 per cent due to "a good hunting season", porter sales were down. In Dingle in 1906, sales of extra stout were down 31.39 per cent and porter was down 87.69 due to "energetic working of the temperance movement", with the traveller glumly reporting, "It's improbable that any recovery will be shown here for some time".

Not that religion and drinking didn't go hand in hand: noting a fall in trade in Armagh, the report says this is due both to the temperance movement and "a falling off in numbers of visitors to the new cathedral".

The same report notes a greater sophistication among Guinness drinkers, recording:

> "Complaints of our article were principally in the nature of caskiness and it suggests that, as we hold and have held for some time almost the entire trade of the city, the public are becoming more educated to differences in soundness and condition and, where drink would have passed some years ago, it is now objected to if at all faulty."

By the start of the 20th century, Guinness had a sophisticated quality control department. Licensees who sold Guinness by the bottle were obliged to use

Guinness labels, which bore the promise that the bottler bottled "Only Guinness Genuine Extra Stout and Porter, and no other".

To ensure that the promise was being kept, the brewery regularly tested the beer being sold by licensees, sometimes taking samples away with them for testing by the brewery's laboratories in Dublin. Licensees were sued if they weren't selling the genuine article. This didn't just mean licensees who were selling non-Guinness beer in Guinness bottles; those who diluted extra stout with plain porter were also taken to court. Tests for adulteration or dilution were carried out in Guinness's laboratories: a drop in alcohol strength was an immediate giveaway, but samples were also colour-tested for "redness" and "yellowness".

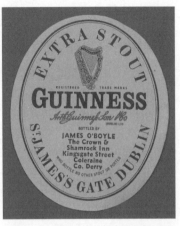

A trademarked Guinness label from the 1960s

Court cases against licensees who adulterated Guinness occurred regularly in the first half of the 20th century. In 1925, the brewery's legal counsel, Mr Overend KC, admitted that the practice "was becoming common". In all court actions, Guinness sought damages that included the publication of prominent newspaper advertisements headed "Mssrs Guinness and Co" and bearing the words "I [name of licensee] do hereby tender an 'unqualified apology' to you for having sold as your porter an article that was not your genuine porter".

Black and Tans

While the Rising of 1916 was mainly a "Dublin-only" event, the Irish War of Independence was not. As the country became more and more ungovernable for the British, a new auxiliary police force, known in infamy as "the Black and Tans" was introduced. From the evidence collected for this book, the Black and Tans' reputation for bloody and pointless violence is justified with licensees in Carlow, Donegal, Galway, Limerick, Longford, Offaly, Sligo and

Tipperary still remembering how their families were intimidated. However, it also should be mentioned that two licensees interviewed for this book also said they received compensation for damages caused by rioting Black and Tans, and that several licensees stated that civility and fairness were more usually the mark of a British army officer.

Many pubs had a close relationship with the forces of law and order. At one time, for instance, Burke's of Colemanstown in Galway (page 96) secretly supplied a gallon of beer a day to the local RIC barracks, with the Guinness being marked as "milk" in mess room invoices. Many pubs had more official arrangements, supplying goods to the local barracks under a British Army victualling contract. For these army suppliers, the disappearance of a British army barracks from their towns sometimes meant more financially than losing the off-duty soldiers' drinking trade.

One of the few commercial organisations still trading in Ireland today with records from the War of Independence and the Civil War is the Guinness Ireland Group. Its records from the period make for interesting reading. For example, shortly after the outbreak of the Civil War, in June 1922, every Irish licensee who sold Guinness received the following letter from the brewery:

> "Dear Sir (or Madam),
>
> Owing to the present unrest in Ireland, postal arrangements are seriously disorganised and we should be glad if you would address all communications (including your orders) on receipt of this advice to Messrs A Guinness & Co Ltd, London and North Western Railway Hotel, Holyhead, until further notice. We do not anticipate difficulty in sending forward any stout you may require subject to receiving your orders."

As lawlessness increased, armed men would regularly seize barrels from publicans or while they were in transit. A Guinness memo dated 15 February 1921 notes the case of Mrs J. O'Regan, Sunday's Well Road, Cork, who had a kilderkin (an 18-gallon barrel) stolen by armed men. The memo notes:

"We are prepared to share the loss with Mrs O'Regan and propose therefore only charging her one-half of the invoiced price, namely £3.7.6, in connection with the loss of the cask and we trust she will consider we are treating her fairly by so doing."

In a case where a quantity of Guinness was stolen while in transit by rail in May 1922, the brewery wrote to its customer, T.M. Boland Wine and Spirit Merchant, Ballinagh, Co. Cavan, stating:

"We shall be glad to hear what steps you have taken in this matter and whether you have submitted a claim for compensation to the government. If so, please give us a copy of the claim, in order that we may record the information in our books. As the empty cask has reached the brewery a claim for it is not necessary."

Cask Shortage

Beer became a publican's property once it left the brewery gates, but kegs remained the property of the brewery. Wooden casks were expensive pieces of hardware and breweries were particularly concerned about their loss.

In September 1922, Guinness issued an "Important Notice to Customers", stating:

"The frequent cessation of both Rail and Road transport since June last has created a serious situation and unless every trader makes a special effort to Return Our Casks directly they are empty we may shortly find ourselves without sufficient casks to supply their requirements.

Under our trade terms each trader is responsible for the prompt return of Empty Casks at his own expense to the station or berth from which they are ordinarily dispatched to Dublin, to bear a portion of the extra cost of cartage to secure a quick return we therefore ask all traders:

1) to ensure that his casks are returned to Dublin immediately they are empty;

2) to advise us, our agents, our stores or our travellers of any difficulties or extra expense. In the latter case a carrier's receipt should be issued."

Cooperage Yard at Guinness, c 1900

Two of the biggest irregular beer-raids involved Guinness being transported by boat. In April 1922, six kilderkins were taken by armed men from a canal boat at Quaker Island, Lough Ree, Carrick-on-Shannon, and in September of that year ten kilderkins were stolen by armed men at the quay at Kenmare.

While beer was stolen, it seems that the old IRA sometimes promised to pay for its whiskey. At Kate O'Grady's pub in Stoneyford, Co. Kilkenny (page 181), there is a 1922 credit note headed "North Tipperary Batt. Flying Column" with the words: "Please give the bearer two bottles of best Irish whisky and charge same to above account". The bill has never been paid.

Insurance

Compensation payments for Civil War damages ended on 12 May 1923, even though irregular beer seizures continued. In December that year, Guinness sent "the representatives of Mrs Margaret Daly" the following note:

"Dear Sirs,

Kilderkin No 590007.

We regret to enclose herewith a debit for 19/6d respecting this cask. We note from your post card dated October 8 that you have consulted your solicitor on the subject; we do not know what steps he may advise as regards attempting to recover from the railway company the value of the cask and contents and you will no doubt be guided by his advice.

We would however remind you that public notice was given by all railway companies that they would only accept for traffic or conveyance if it was agreed 'to relieve the company and all other companies or persons over whose lands the goods set forth in this consignment note may pass from all liability for loss, theft, damage, expense, injury or delay, directly or indirectly caused by or resulting from or in pursuance of any civil commotion, rebellion, boycott, unlawful assembly, raid, riot or any illegal acts in connection there with'.

It's therefore improbable that you will be able to recover the loss you have sustained and unless you are prepared to take the risk of such losses in the future, it will be necessary for you to effect an insurance against losses arising out of raids etc."

An internal Guinness memo kept with the archived letter, notes: "We cannot run the risk of allowing a trader for a 'raids' loss; it would create a precedent and might create systematic raids! Traders can insure for 3.5d per kilderkin."

Insurance has continued to be a major issue for the licensed trade. In 1943, a Hibernian Insurance advertising campaign made much of a £375 damages award to a customer who "slipped on a cork lying on the floor of a licensed premises". Since the 1970s, there has been a growth in "compo culture" with the general public becoming much more litigious. In the 1980s and 1990s, publicans were sued after customers fell while drunk or were convicted of drunk driving. The high cost of insurance is a major issue today for all Irish businesses, not just the licensed trade.

Unionisation

The late 19th and early 20th centuries saw labour being increasingly unionised, but it wasn't until four years after the Great Dublin Lockout of 1913 that bar workers were specifically targeted for trade union organisation. In September 1917, a special meeting of the Grocers' Assistants' Association (GAA) passed the following resolution:

"In view of the future outlook of our Trade, the time has arrived when it is absolutely necessary that a strong national union of Assistants engaged in the

Grocery and Liquor Trade throughout Ireland should be formed and become linked up with other labour bodies through affiliation with organised labour in Ireland."

The GAA had originally been formed in the 19th century as a Dublin-based provident benefit society specifically for employees in the licensed grocery trade, probably for the same reasons as the Fair Trading Vintners Society and Asylum was founded in 1818.

In 1873, the Association's president was able to report that "all our members are employed in the most respectable houses in the city and suburbs and there is not at present one member unemployed. The health of our members is, on average, very good".

However, the Association became increasingly radicalised by Labour movement leaders like James Larkin and James Connolly. The grocery and bar employees found Larkin particularly inspiring, as they had witnessed themselves how "Big Jim" had almost single-handedly ended the corrupt practice of sub-contractors and "jobbies" paying casual labourers their wages in pubs. On being paid, the worker was under an unspoken obligation to buy his employer a pint to ensure that he would be employed again. The practice had been illegal since 1883 when the Payment of Wages in Public Houses (Prohibition) Act was passed,[17] but it was rife in Ireland's docklands until Larkin suppressed it in the first decade of the 20th century.

At the inaugural meeting of the Irish National Union of Vintners Grocers & Allied Trade Assistants, there were delegates from 30 branches representing 1,500 trade union members. In 1920, over 700 members of the union in Co. Dublin were involved in one of the fiercest strikes in Irish history, over union recognition and a substantial wage increase. The union was always strongest in Dublin and its industrial actions have not adversely affected most small rural pubs, which are still almost completely staffed by individual licensees and their families. As well as having one of the longest abbreviated names in Irish trade

---

[17] In 1807 and 1843, Acts of Parliament were passed prohibiting the payment of "coal-heavers" in pubs, a move significantly at odds with the general *laissez faire* economic philosophy of the time.

union history, the INUVG&ATA holds the dubious record of the longest-running strike in Irish history. The strike at Downey's Pub in Dun Laoghaire[18] ran for 14 years and did not end until May 1953 when the licensee died.

The main union representing bar workers in Ireland today is Mandate, which was founded in 1994 when the INUVG&ATA amalgamated with the Irish Distributive and Administrative Trade Union.

The Price of a Pint

Very quickly after national independence, Irish politicians started to complain about the price of a pint. The first was Sir James Craig, who raised the thorny matter in a debate about the cost of living in October 1922. Sir James told the Dáil:

> "I have been told quite seriously by seriously-minded people that if the working man can get his pint of porter at a decent price he will not object to his wages being reduced. But so long as he is compelled, or asked to pay, one shilling a pint for porter, and if he consumes three or four pints in the day, the amount of money spent at the end of the week will be so great that it will be utterly impossible for the wages to be brought down."

Following Labour Party objections about this slur on the working classes, Sir James apologised for suggesting that "the working man takes any more stout or porter than his neighbours".

After the Christmas recess of 1923, the very first question to be asked in the Dáil in 1924 also concerned the price of the pint, with Deputy Ailfrid O'Broinn asking the president of the executive, William T. Cosgrave, to take steps to "reduce the tax paid on beer, porter, and stout in the Free State to the same level as that paid on the same goods in Northern Ireland and Great Britain".

---

[18] The Dun Laoghaire Shopping Centre now stands where Downey's (and the strikers) once stood on Upper George's Street.

Pub interior, possibly in the 1940s

In his reply, Cosgrave replied that the government was "working with brewers and publicans to reduce the retail cost of a pint of porter to sixpence". He added: "It appears, however, that in most parts of the country porter is already retailed at this price, and that it is chiefly in Dublin that the price is higher." While beer in Ireland is still cheaper outside Dublin, throughout the country the cost of a pint is now 100 times what it was in 1922.[19]

Early Irish efforts to reduce the price of the pint were thwarted by the outbreak of the Second World War, which led to a massive increase in the price of barley. The war also led to rationing of beer and a wide range of goods sold by pubs with grocery counters — tea, sugar, flour, bread and sweets. In 1947, the price of a pint of stout broke the shilling mark when an extra 3d of tax was introduced in the budget of that year: stout now cost 1/1, with a pint of porter costing 11d. During the 1960s, and particularly the 1970s when Ireland was hit by high inflation, the price of the pint rose steadily. Nevertheless, the price of a pint of Guinness was well below the £1 mark as late as 1980, when the price went from 58p to 62p.

New Licensing Laws

By 1924, the Dáil had progressed sufficiently with national reconstruction to try to reform the licensing system inherited from the British administration and "a Committee of Inquiry on Intoxicating Liquor" was established by the

---

[19] Half a shilling (6d) is equivalent to 2.5p or €0.03. See Appendix B, page 293.

government. Ireland's new political leaders wanted to rid the country of its overseas image as a country that was ridden with alcohol.

Those who rallied to the call "Ireland sober, Ireland free" were delighted when the first major piece of licensing legislation passed by the Free State in 1927 included a measure to have all pubs closed on St Patrick's Day. Like Christmas Day and Good Friday today, for over three decades the 17th of March was a "dry day". When the law was changed in 1960 to allow pubs to open their doors on St Patrick's Day, they were required to keep Sunday hours and close their doors in the afternoon. All-day opening on St Patrick's Day became legal again in 1988.

The 1927 legislation followed a nationwide investigation by the Committee of Inquiry, which reported in 1925 that "the drink problem has lessened, thanks to improved social conditions, cheap entertainment, tax on drink and a reduction in its strength".[20] Certainly, the committee's figures supported its conclusion: in 1870, there were 85,470 arrests for drunkenness; in 1914 that had fallen to 15,339 arrests; and in 1925 that was down to 6,862.[21]

Pub Numbers

Nevertheless, the committee was firmly of the opinion that Ireland had too many pubs, with 13,427 pubs and hotels in Ireland. When it came to alcohol abuse the committee argued that "the major factor in the problem is the supervision of the sale of drink", but that "excessive competition leads to illegal trading". The final report reckoned there were too many pubs in the country

---

[20] With bread supplies rationed during the First World War, alcohol strengths on spirits were reduced to conserve barley. Notably, during the First World War, while the alcohol strength of British beers was also reduced, no such reduction was imposed on beers brewed in Ireland. After the war, Guinness was able to make inroads into the English markets because of its higher alcohol content.

[21] In 1999, there were 933 convictions for simple drunkenness and 523 convictions for drunkenness with aggravation in the Republic of Ireland. However, there were also 478 convictions for attempting to drive while drunk, 167 convictions for being in charge of a vehicle while drunk. In addition, 4,633 motorists were convicted for being "over the limit".

and recommended that the number of intoxicating liquor licences be reduced from a ratio of one licence for every 230 people to one licence for every 400. In Scotland, the ratio at the time was one pub for every 695 people.

The problem of too many pubs was primarily a problem outside Dublin; the pub-to-people ratio in the capital was one pub for every 700 people.

In the 1960s, customers could be trusted to drink on both sides of the bar

The committee identified particular towns across Ireland where it was believed the number of licences was excessive. In Ballymote, Co. Sligo, there were 200 houses, 27 of which were pubs; down the road in Gurteen, six of the village's 15 private houses were licensed premises; Blacklion in Co. Cavan had 20 houses and eight licences; Donegal town had "approximately 100 houses", 26 of which were licensed; Killybegs had 62 houses, 10 of which were licensed; in Castletownbere, Co. Cork, there were 24 pubs serving a town of 40 families.[22]

Not surprisingly, with many pubs being only marginal businesses, most licensees also ran other businesses apart from the licensed trade. In 1925, it was reckoned that "in 90 per cent of premises outside the cities, the licensed trade is carried on side by side with other businesses".

---

[22] The reason for the high number of pubs in Castletownbere was that it had formerly been used as a port by the Royal Navy.

Throughout Ireland there were general stores, drapers, hardware stores, grocers, butchers and shoe shops with bars selling alcohol for consumption on the premises. The committee saw an opportunity to reduce licences and it recommended: "The police should be given authority to oppose a licence if the publican does not make an adequate attempt to set up partitions and separate counters to separate licensed and unlicensed trade."

In the event, the Intoxicating Liquor Act of 1927 included the measure in its sections dealing with "Reduction of Licences". Both the District Court and a new compensation authority were given the power to abolish licences based on considerations of "the character of the licensing area, the number of licensed premises in the area in proportion to the population of the area, the volume of business done by licensed premises in the area, the amount of drunkenness in the area, and any other matter which appears to be relevant".

In choosing which licences to abolish, the court and the compensation authority were to base their reasons as follows:

> "that the volume of business transacted in the premises to which the licence is attached is small, that the structural condition and state of repair of the said premises is bad, that the accommodation in the said premises for customers is unsatisfactory in character or extent, that the business carried on in the said premises is not properly conducted, that the situation of the said premises is such as to render supervision thereof by the police difficult."

The compensation scheme ran for one year only and led to 299 licences being abolished by the end of 1928. By 1956, there were 11,953 licensed premises in the Republic, down 1,474 on the figure in 1926. The reduction wasn't great enough, according to a Liquor Commission report presented to the Dáil in 1957, and in 1960 further measures were introduced to prevent lapsed licences from being renewed after they had remained idle for more than five years.

In 1969, the Republic of Ireland had 11,800 public house licences, for a national population of 2,850,000, i.e. one pub licence for every 242 people. The pub-to-people ratio has increased since then. In 1999, there were 10,898 fully licensed premises in the country (not including off-licences); of these licensed premises, 8,751 were pubs, 491 were hotels and 403 were restaurants. With the 2002 census finding that the Republic had a population of 3,917,336 people, this means that there is currently one licence for every 359 people and one pub for every 448.

However, there is a huge difference between the distribution of pubs per population in County Dublin and other parts of the country. In Dublin, there is one pub for every 1,187 people; but in Leitrim, there is a pub for every 152 men, women and children.

The pub-to-people ratio in Connaught currently is one pub for every 232 people, while in Munster it is one pub for every 283 people.

Goodbye to Grocery

Government initiatives to end mixed trading in Irish pubs were mostly un-successful, with pubs-cum-shops being the norm in rural Ireland through-out the 1960s. As late as 1969, an Irish tourist guide book, *Irish Pubs of Character*, could claim: "The impression that many English visitors have got of Irish villages is that you can get a drink in every shop." In the end it was market forces, not government initiatives, that would see mixed trading come to an end in the 1960s and 1970s.

Today, it is difficult to appreciate how important the grocery trade was to licensees 50 and 100 years ago. In 1935, *The Licensed Vintner and Grocer* magazine could boast that "The Trade sells 95 per cent of all Foodstuffs and consumable Household Requisites used in the country".[23] Before the arrival of "packet tea", Ireland's favourite hot drink was often a licensee's biggest-selling stock item. Licensees prided themselves on their blends of tea as much as their blends of whiskey; during Second World War rationing, often a licensee earned

---

[23] Other claims made in 1935 by *The Licensed Vintner and Grocer* magazine were: "The trade has more accounts in the banks than any other single organisation. The trade owns more commercial motor vans, lorries and private cars than any business circle in the country; it is the largest user of paper and twine, and ordinary account books, in Ireland."

more kudos from his customers for being able to supply a good cup of tea than for his ability to produce whiskey on demand.

In an age where whiskey or brandy were usually the only spirits sold, there was no big collection of bottles behind the bar counter. Instead, it was more usual to find rows of drawers containing blends of tea, tobacco, spices and flavourings. If flour and meal were also sold, these would be kept in purpose-built bins. Potatoes, if sold, would be in sacks on the floor.

As well as selling groceries, many licensees bought farm produce — chiefly milk, butter and eggs — which they then sold wholesale in Dublin, Cork or England. Such a trading relationship, particularly when credit was involved, was fraught with potential difficulties. At the end of the 19th century, the derogatory word "gombeen" was used to describe anyone who exploited the poor through unfair trade or money lending. Most licensees had quit butter and egg dealing by the 1920s, but for some licensees it remained an important business until the mid-1950s. There were high levels of rural poverty in Ireland during the 1940s and the 1950s and many licensing families remember those two decades as "the hungry years". The market for Irish agricultural produce in Britain was greatly reduced because of a continuing trade war, the post-war depression and the arrival in England of butter from New Zealand. By the 1960s, there were hardly any publicans left still involved in wholesale butter and egg dealing.

As the farming co-operatives expanded further to supply animal feedstuffs and farm supplies to their members, mixed-trading licensees saw that part of their business decline too. The groceries run by publicans also faced new competition following the arrival of supermarkets, something that was exacerbated by greater car ownership and mobility among the general public.[24]

---

[24] In the first half of the 20th century, many licensees also operated mobile-shops that sold groceries on the doorstep of their customers. By the 1960s, these travelling shops were made even less profitable by the arrival of greater car ownership.

Lounges, Ladies and Lager

The disappearance of the grocery counter coincided with the arrival of the lounge bar, a separate room in a pub where both the levels of comfort and the drink prices were higher than in the public bar. Lounges were brightly lit, airy places, with an atmosphere more refined than the ambience of the "public bar". Not everyone was admitted to the lounge; men in their working clothes were often barred for fear their clothes would soil the furnishings or the up-market atmosphere. A lounge bar was a place where gentlemen could entertain ladies and where "respectable women" could be seen to drink alcohol publicly.

No men, no pints: women drinking in the 1970s

Before the 1960s, Irish bars were almost exclusively male-only. Some pubs had snugs — small, screened-off rooms — for female customers, but the majority of premises did not allow women to consume alcohol on the premises.

In the 1970s, it was still common enough to see women and children sitting waiting outside a pub while husbands and fathers were drinking inside and it did not become illegal for a licensee to refuse to serve a woman because of her sex until the Equal Status Act was passed in 2000.

The arrival of women made a huge difference to Irish pubs: they became cleaner, better-lit and more comfortable, with soft furnishings often being introduced for the first time. Largely thanks to women, toilet facilities in pubs for both males and females improved. Indeed, one joke about the state of the Irish health service has it that the two big differences between Ireland in the 1950s and Ireland now is that the pubs have got cleaner, but the hospitals are dirtier.

In 1969, the difference between the traditional male-only pub and the modern lounge bar is noted in these two paragraphs by Maurice Gorham in the guidebook *Irish Pubs of Character*:

> "The windows on the street need show no more than a liquor licence or framed showcards for brands of whiskey, not necessarily those still available inside. Women are not seen in the bar, not many women frequent the pub and those that do are tucked discretely inside a little compartment known as the snug. That is our vision of the traditional Irish pub, the pub of 10, 20 or 50 years ago and pubs of this kind are still with us.

> But a new trend has set in, the pubs of today are more often light and spacious with wide leather settees, carpets under foot, taped music playing or a television set interrupting the conversation; places where women are expected and catered for and where there is no snug. Probably, the pub itself is all lounge and has no simple straightforward bar, where waiters circulate carrying trays laden with a bewildering variety of drinks."

One thing Gorham didn't note is that drink prices are usually more expensive in a lounge bar.

As well as lighter, brighter premises, the arrival of lounges signalled the arrival of new lighter drinks targeted mainly at the emerging market of women drinkers. There was a move from dark stouts to lager ales and from whiskey to vodka.

The first ever lager brewed in Ireland was produced 1891 by the Dartry Brewery in Dublin, but neither the lager nor the brewery proved a long-term commercial success. The first Irish-brewed lager to become widely available was Regal, which was brewed in Kells until 1952. In the 1930s, Patzenhofer was widely available in Ireland and sold under the brandname "Patz". Brewed in Germany, but pasteurised and bottled in Dublin for the Irish market, Patzenhofer was once the world's biggest selling lager, but the outbreak of the Second World War stopped its supply in Ireland. By the 1950s, German lagers were on sale again in Ireland, with Patz, Spatenbrau and Lowenbrau being the three

main brands. Overall, during the 1950s, there was a five-fold increase in Irish lager sales.

In response to the growing market for lighter beers, Guinness established the Harp Lager Brewery on the site of the old Great Northern Brewery in Dundalk in 1959 and by June 1960 the first bottles of Harp were on sale in Irish bars. By 1969, Harp was on sale in 10,099 of the Republic's 11,800 pubs.

In 1962, the Canadian brewer Carling O'Keeffe bought Beamish & Crawford in Cork and began brewing Carling Black Label lager there from 1964. The Cork brewery also started producing Bass Ale in 1968 and it started brewing Carlsberg Lager in 1973. Heineken has been brewed for many years at Murphy's brewery in Cork, which was bought in 1983 by Heineken International. Budweiser lager has been brewed in Kilkenny by the Guinness Ireland Group since 1986.

At the start of 2002, both Budweiser and Heineken claimed to be Ireland's biggest selling lager, with both claiming over 30 per cent of lager market share. What neither of the two breweries dispute is that lager now outsells the "traditional" black pint of stout.

Dark Spirits

In spirit drinking, there has also been a move towards lighter-coloured drinks. In the 1950s, vodka sales in Ireland were negligible, but by 1971 a vodka drink accounted for one out of ever ten glasses of spirits sold; by 1980 vodka accounted for a fifth of spirits drunk in Irish pubs.

This change in Irish drinking habits was partly responsible for licensees giving up the business of bonding and racking their own whiskey. Until the late 1960s, most of the whiskey sold in Irish pubs had been bottled by a vintner and not by the distillery. On pub shop fronts dating from before the 1950s, and on the shop fronts of overseas "traditional Irish pubs" founded in the last 10 years, the words "whiskey bonder" are often proudly displayed in gold lettering.

Whiskey bonding was a trade filled with craft, mystery and — until the 1950s — profit. When first produced, even after undergoing three separate distillations, Irish whiskey is raw tasting and not very pleasant to drink; like most illegally sold poteen, immature whiskey contains higher alcohols that can cause severe hangovers and permanent brain damage. Raw whiskey is also light-coloured, but it takes on a darker hue after it has been matured in wooden casks. Usually, fresh Spanish oloroso sherry casks are used, but casks that previously held American bourbon whiskey, rum, port or fino sherry are also used, as are casks that previously held Irish whiskey and casks that never held any alcohol at all.

While it is maturing, whiskey undergoes subtle and complex transformations. Each year, the alcoholic strength weakens at a rate of about two per cent of alcohol volume — a phenomenon that has long been known as "the angel's share" and is the result partly of higher alcohols forming complex chemical compounds with material contained in the wood of the cask, and partly of evaporation. When first produced, whiskey is about 60 per cent alcohol by volume; when it is being prepared for bottling, its strength is reduced further by being diluted with water. After bottling, all chemical changes in whiskey cease and the alcoholic proof remains the same.[25]

---

[25] The Irish Whiskey Act 1980 stipulated the minimum strength for whiskey as 40 per cent per volume; premium whiskeys have a higher proof, but their higher strength makes them more expensive because tax is paid on the alcohol content.

Spirits safe in Bushmill's Distillery

While it is maturing, the whiskey is kept under government lock and key, sometimes in a "spirits safe" on a licensee's premises, but more usually in a purpose-built bonded warehouse. Matured whiskey would not be released by Customs and Excise until tax was paid on it and, as a result, whiskey bonders had to use their skill and experience to decide when to release stocks from bond. Once released from bond, whiskeys from different casks were blended together to produce as pleasing a taste as possible. The mixture was (and still is) diluted with water to reduce its alcohol strength, as required by law. If the colour of the whiskey wasn't yellow enough, the colour was improved with the addition of some caramel.

Because duty wasn't paid on bonded whiskey until it was ready for bottling after several years of maturation, it was a good investment — providing demand for whiskey didn't fall and providing taxes on alcohol didn't increase severely in the intervening period. In good years, after five years a whiskey bonder could expect a return of over 25 per cent on his initial investment.

Unfortunately for whiskey bonders in the 1950s, taxes on alcohol increased while demand fell. In the 1952 budget, the price of a glass of whiskey rose by a sixth, from 3s to 3/6d, and the effect on whiskey consumption was dramatic; the additional taxation had been predicted to earn an extra £1 million for the government, but revenue from tax on whiskey fell by £591,713.

One reason for the fall in demand was that the quality of whiskey on sale to the general public was still suffering the effects of wartime rationing. In England, whiskey rationing was introduced because it was believed that wartime industrial production was being affected by munitions workers spending too much of their overtime money on strong drink. In Ireland, the government ordered farmers to grow wheat for bread, instead of barley for beer and whiskey, and rationing was used to conserve beer and whiskey stocks. One tactic used by Irish licensees to sell their limited supplies as fairly as possible was to sell whiskey only between specific hours on specific days. When stocks became particularly scarce in some pubs, whiskey was sold for only a few minutes once a week. After the war, wheat commanded a much higher price than barley and fewer Irish farmers than before were prepared to supply the country's breweries and distilleries with their main ingredient.

The distillers themselves were also partly responsible for their difficulties. With the exception of John Powers, Irish whiskey manufacturers appear to have been hopeless at marketing. When prohibition was repealed in America in 1934, the Irish government secured an import quota for Irish whiskey into the US, but the reaction of the Irish distilleries was to declare that they wanted to keep all their whiskey stocks for the home market. Even though the Scottish made inferior whisky to Irish distillers, they dominated the American market and their

Power's Gold Label —
a favourite since 1886

whisky was making inroads into the Irish market during the 1950s and 1960s. During the 1960s, Scottish distilleries spent more on advertising their product in the US than all of Ireland's distilleries combined earned from exports to America.

Gradually, whiskey distilleries in Ireland were going out of business and in 1966 three of the survivors, Jameson, Powers and Cork Distilleries, united to form the Irish Distillers Group.[26] All three distilleries were steeped in whiskey-making tradition — Jameson was founded in 1780, Powers in 1791 and Cork Distilleries in 1825 — but Powers could claim to be the only one of the three

---

[26] The Bushmills distillery in Armagh joined the Irish Distillers Group in 1972 and since 1988 Irish Distillers has been part of the multinational Groupe Pernod Ricard.

with a tradition of innovation. In 1886 John Powers became one of the first whiskey manufacturers in the world to supply its product bottled and ready to drink. Another innovation was the "Baby Powers" bottle, small enough to be carried in a breast pocket. Thanks to the Baby Powers bottle, the distillery was one of the first in the world to have its own corporate logo — the little bottles held three large mouthfuls of whiskey and, in a visual pun, the Powers' logo features three swallows in flight.

Even though Powers bottled its own "gold label" whiskey in bottles, the bulk of its product was bottled by licensees who sold the finished article in "white label" bottles bearing the Powers' name and logo and the licensee's name.

Jameson Red, a label first used in 1968

Before the Irish Distillers Group was founded, all Jameson whiskey was sold wholesale to be matured and bottled by licensees. Jameson did not supply pre-bottled whiskey until 1963 when it launched the "Jameson 10" label, a brand that was superseded in 1968 by the Jameson Red Label bottle that is familiar to whiskey drinkers today. As Irish Distillers concentrated their marketing efforts on selling its own bottled whiskey, it became increasingly unprofitable for licensees to bottle their own whiskey. The final straw for many licensees who blended their own whiskey was the increasingly high cost of insuring against fires in bonded warehouses.

While it was impossible not to notice the disappearance of grocery counters in pubs, few people noticed that whiskey bonding in pubs disappeared during the 1970s. A centuries-old trade disappeared, like the alcohol that disappears from whiskey barrels left in bond.

Losing Your Bottle

In addition to this move to lighter beers, the dark stuff changed too. The Draught Guinness we drink today is a very different drink to that which was consumed in the days of Double Stout and Plain Porter. In fact, one of the biggest changes to Irish drinking habits was the introduction of Draught Guinness in 1961. Supplied by the brewery in ready-to-use pressurised metal kegs, Draught Guinness was smoother and creamier than its predecessors; drunk at a lower temperature it was also a lot less prone to fizzi-neess. The introduction of the sealed aluminium keg meant an end to the weekly task of bottling, which was a messy chore that sometimes went on for days as bottles were washed, sterilised, filled, capped and labelled by hand. It was an arduous task, involv-

Metal kegs being delivered to Kehoe's in Dublin, c.1960

ing work with boiling hot water in unheated sheds, and most publicans hated the chore.

As well as selling bottled Guinness, throughout the 19th century and the first half of the 20th century many pubs also sold draught beer direct from the barrel, but the procedure for dispensing the fizzy beer was much more complicated than the method used to pour draught Guinness today.

The art of pulling a pint, 1957

Before the arrival of metal kegs, beer for sale on draught was kept in wooden casks held in racks above the bar counter. Unlike the handpump method used to pour cask ales in Britain today, barrels of beer in Irish pubs were emptied by gravity. When a customer ordered a pint of draught, the beer was first emptied from the barrel into a jug and then poured from the jug into the customer's glass. While the glass was being filled, it was held over a basin where any spillages would be collected and poured back into the serving jug. Pouring the draught beer twice, and re-using spillages, helped make the pint less fizzy when it was consumed.

Such was the fizziness of beer that great care was required when tapping a barrel — should the publican make a mistake while tapping the barrel, he and his walls and floors could end up being drenched by a fountain of beer.

Unification and Division

Ireland's entry into the EEC in 1973 helped to introduce an even wider range of alcoholic drinks on the Irish market and European unification also helped boost wine drinking in Ireland during the 1980s and 1990s.

In the same year that Ireland joined the Common Market, the Vintners Federation of Ireland was officially founded following the amalgamation of the Irish National Vintners Federation (INVF) and the Licensed Vintners Association (LVA). The uniting of the two organisations marked the first time that nearly every publican and licensee in the Republic of Ireland belonged to the same trade organisation — for nearly a century, publicans in Ireland had been represented by over a dozen different organisations.

The INVF was solely Dublin-based, but by 1973 the LVA was a national organisation. Through the LVA and Licensed Vintners and Grocers Association, the Vintners' Federation of Ireland could trace its roots back to the Fair Trading Vintners Association founded in 1818.

However, tensions caused by different trading circumstances in Dublin and the rest of the country proved too great for the new unified organisation. While the capital city had a mushrooming young population, bigger pubs and unionised staff, rural pubs had shrinking clientele, smaller pubs and labour that was "in-house". Matters came to a head in 1980 and "Dublin LVA" withdrew from the VFI: the publicans had split. It was an amicable break-up, but pundits couldn't help but make comparisons with the "republican split" in Sinn Féin a decade earlier. Today the two organisations collaborate closely on matters of mutual concern.

By the time the VFI marked its 25th anniversary in 1998, Tom Flynn, a founder member of the organisation, said both Ireland and its pubs had gone through "tremendous changes in all respects — to the benefit of both the trade and its customers". He pointed to a new era of diversification in Irish pubs as licensees introduced bar food, restaurants, entertainment and leisure facilities.

The VFI had also made the life of licensees easier by introducing pension and insurance schemes, a hospital cash plan and a benevolent trust. On a wide range of issues, the organisation helped its members and became one of the strongest lobbying organisations in the country. At present, the VFI is the organisation that is most calling for a mandatory national ID scheme to counter the problem of under-age drinking; already it operates a voluntary ID card scheme which covers one-fifth of the 150,000 young people aged between 18 and 20 in the Republic. The VFI has also been behind campaigns to increase drug awareness among licensees, helped licensees take a lead when organising community events and festivals and assisted in making premises less smoky, literally improving the Irish pub atmosphere.

In terms of leisure facilities, by the 1980s the colour television made the pub the next best place to watch a match after seeing the game live at the stadium itself. The era of big screen television was heralded by the Republic of Ireland's

European soccer campaign in 1988. That same year, VFI chief executive Tadg O'Sullivan could point to the growing choice of drinks and beverages in Irish pubs and say: "Older drinkers will remember the times not long ago when the choice of draught drinks in even the best bars was restricted to one stout, one ale and, sometimes, one lager."

Today, many young women would be shocked to learn that less than 30 years ago there were many pubs where they wouldn't get served if they approached the counter. It wasn't until the 1960s that it became socially acceptable for women to drink in pubs. Indeed, it wasn't until the passing of the Equal Status Act in October 2000 that it became illegal for a licensee to refuse to serve a person "on grounds of gender, marital status, family status, sexual orientation, religious belief, age, disability, race or membership of the Traveller community". The scope of the Act is broad, but it doesn't remove a licensee's right to refuse to serve particular customers with good reason.

The Last Decade

The 1990s heralded the era of the "superpubs", licensed premises where over 1,000 people can be comfortably accommodated at the one time. But ordinary family pubs also got larger, with more than a third of pubs nationwide increasing their retailing space in the five years before 1999. For decades, despite their reputation for being fond of alcohol, the Irish drank less per capita than their European neighbours, partly because of the high number of people here who don't drink any alcohol at all. However, Irish per capita consumption of alcohol increased by 41 per cent between 1989 and 1999.

While some pubs have benefited from increasing levels of alcohol consumption and greater custom from Ireland's booming population of young adults, in many rural areas licensed trading is a marginal business.

The precarious nature of licensed trading is highlighted by the fact that so few licensees have been in one family for over 100 years — less than 1.8 per cent of the total number of pubs in Ireland. If such a lack of stability of ownership was to be found in farming, it would be declared a national scandal.

Today, we celebrate the Irish pub as part of our cultural heritage and we have exported "the Irish pub concept" to almost every major city in the world. You can now order a traditional Irish pub from firms such as the Guinness-owned Irish Pub Company and the Irish Pub Design and Development Company, who will assemble your pub for you wherever you require. The second company offers six "stylistic" choices: the cottage pub, the old brewing house, the shop pub, the Gaelic pub, the Victorian pub and the "contemporary pub".

A traditional Irish pub? No — The Fadó pub in Atlanta, Georgia, as designed by the Irish Pub Company

History has become a commodity: in a recently published guidebook, *Historic Pubs of Dublin*, several pubs were listed that had been almost completely rebuilt and renovated in the last 10 years — the pubs were only listed because their premises featured interiors made from salvaged architectural material collected elsewhere.

Who knows what the next 100 years will hold? Perhaps by 2070 it may be possible to compile a book featuring over 100 overseas Irish pubs that are over 100 years old. Who knows how many of the pubs featured in the second part of this book will still be in existence? There may be more, but it is probable that there will be fewer. Increasingly, licences are held by companies rather than named individuals, as the courts have ruled that corporate bodies can enjoy a good reputation, in the same way as an individual licensee can enjoy renown.

Nevertheless, politicians, particularly those calling for radical changes to Ireland's licensing laws, would do well to listen to the counsel of those families that have served Ireland for more than a century. These licensees have a vocational approach to their trade, their heritage stretches back to before the dawn of Christianity and what is good for these families is good for the licensed trade.

The Irish pub is part of a living tradition; it is part of our unique culture and it deserves to be cherished and celebrated. Let me finish with a traditional drinking toast — *Sláinte agus go marfaidh sibh an céad* — Good health and may you outlive a hundred!

Family-Owned Pubs of Connaught

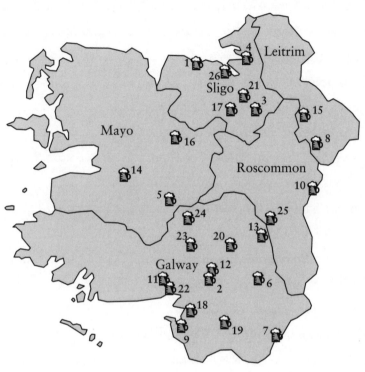

BATTLE'S

Seamus Battle, Dromore West, Co. Sligo

The licence for Battle's Bar in Dromore West, Co. Sligo, has been in the one family for over a century, but it has only been known as Battle's Bar since 1985, when the current licensee, Seamus Battle, took over.

The bar was first established as Mulligans in 1895 when a woman known today only as Mrs Mulligan bought an old coaching house. The building had once been a famous halfway house for coaches on the main Sligo to Ballina route and once had a large dormitory where paying guests slept. It is likely that alcohol was sold on the premises during its coaching days.

Once she had bought the coach house, Mrs Mulligan had the building demolished and replaced with a purpose-built bar and general store.

When Mrs Mulligan died in 1916, the bar passed to her only surviving relative, her nephew, John Howley. He renamed the bar Howley's and ran the business with his wife Anne until his death in 1931.

Their son, Paddy Howley, became the next licensee and something of a local legend when he became the first car owner in the region. In fact, he later became the subject of a song, after he was ambushed in the Sligo mountains and his car was stolen. Paddy's grandson, Seamus Battle, remembers locals singing the song, "Stealing the Howley's Motor Car", in the bar when he was a child, but sadly he never wrote the lyrics down.

In 1956, Paddy became ill and died the following year. The licence then passed to Paddy's daughter Bridget and her husband, John Battle.

There were many changes to the business during John and Bridget's tenure. Draught Guinness was introduced in 1961 and Seamus says: "It took a while for draught to catch on with the locals. I can remember bottling beer during the mid-sixties. When the kegs would arrive at the bar, we'd have to leave it a few days to settle, then it was all hands on deck for the bottling and the whole family would join in until the kegs were empty."

Seamus also remembers the time when women were barred from drinking in the bar. "It wasn't until the 1970s that women were allowed to drink freely in the bar. Before that, they would only be allowed into the parlour after a funeral."

The general store remained in operation until 1983 when Seamus started to take charge of the business. He turned the old bar into a lounge and built a new bar where the general store had been. The shopkeeper tradition lived on, however, as Seamus's brother opened up a new supermarket nearby. Battle's is one of five bars trading in the Dromore West area. Seamus says that it's much harder running a bar these days because people's drinking habits have changed, but he still enjoys being a publican and he aims to continue serving his locals for some time yet.

BURKE'S

Frank Burke, Colemanstown, Ballinasloe, Co. Galway

A pub like Burke's of Colemanstown can't help but be a community pub. And it's not a pub you are likely to miss — Burke's is the only commercial premises in the Co. Galway village.

Today, Burke's comprises a pub, grocery, sub-post office and petrol pumps, but when it was purchased by Ulick Burke in 1889 it was officially only a grocery, becoming a licensed premises shortly afterwards.

The business previously had two owners and the façade is from the early 19th century, pre-dating the Famine.

If you were to believe the records that survive from Ulick's time as publican and grocer, you would swear that the local police had a great taste for milk. According to the books from 1905, the local RIC barracks was ordering a gallon of milk nearly every day. In fact, it wasn't the white stuff, but the black stuff that Her Majesty's constabulary were drinking. By avoiding the excise on alcohol, the RIC men were supping pints of porter at a rate of 6d a gallon!

After Ulick's death in 1907, his wife Margaret was licensee until she handed over the business to her son Thomas, known as "Sonny", in the 1930s. Today, the licensee is Frank Burke, grandson of Ulick, who has been running the business for nearly 40 years now.

Both the bar and lounge were extensively refurbished in 1997, but the informal ambience has been preserved. You can't help feel that all of Colemanstown meets and relaxes here. As well as being home to Colemanstown Soccer Club and the Colemanstown Golfing Society, Burke's also plays host to the local branches of Fianna Fáil and Fine Gael, though admittedly the two political parties usually hold their meetings on different nights!

THE CASTLE VIEW BAR
Gary McDermott, Castlebaldwin, Co. Sligo

In 1900, Michael and Elizabeth Flannery bought what had been a "thatched shebeen" which had been owned by the Osborne family.

The couple lived in the small cottage for barely a year, while a new two-storey building was built next door by the Tansey family. Once they moved into the new building, the old thatched cottage was demolished.

In 1958, Elizabeth died and the pub passed to her daughter Clare Flannery, who married Matthew McDermott.

Today the pub is run by the couple's son, Gary McDermott, grandson of Michael and Elizabeth. Gary's customers include Osbornes descended from the pre-1900 licensees, and Tanseys, descended from the builders of the current bar.

The pub is named the Castle View Bar because it stands opposite the ruins of Castle Baldwin, which was burnt down while Lord Baldwin was away on holiday.

CONNOLLY'S

Gerard Nicholson, Markievicz Road and Holborn Road, Sligo Town

Tthe oldest family business still trading in Sligo is reckoned to be Connolly's Pub, which has been in the same family since 1890 when it was bought by Thomas and Denis Connolly, two brothers who had returned home from the United States a few years before buying the pub.

The business they bought was a going concern that had been in existence for at least 150 years previously. Early maps of Sligo show a tavern on Holborn Road and by 1800 the tavern's owners were prosperous enough to install a Kilkenny marble floor, which can still be seen today.

The Connollys bought the pub from a James Hannigan, who is believed to have been a distant relation, though the exact family connection has not yet been established.

Today, the pub is a much larger premises with two adjoining bars with entrances from Holborn Road and Markievicz Road. Regularly, drinkers leave via one door, turn round the corner and enter via the second door, thinking they are entering a totally different pub.

The Markievicz Road side of the pub dates back to the mid-18th century, when the street was built as part of a famine relief scheme. The Holborn Street side is much older and once comprised three separate premises — as is apparent from the fact that this side of the bar is on three levels and only one of these has antique marble flooring.

By the time Thomas Connolly became licensee, he was a prominent political figure, being elected later in 1890 as Mayor of Sligo, standing on a Nationalist Party ticket. This was at a time when the Nationalist Party was disintegrating, because of the scandal surrounding the party's leader, Charles Stewart Parnell. In December 1889, Parnell had been named as a co-respondent in a divorce case because of his affair with Kitty O'Shea and public opinion had turned against the man once called "The Uncrowned King of Ireland". Nevertheless, Parnell came to Sligo to support Thomas's election campaign and a civic reception was organised. However, a mob blocked the entrance to the banqueting hall with a barricade, which Thomas promptly pulled down, to clear the way for his party leader.

After Thomas's death from TB in 1896, his brother Denis became licensee. Thomas had two sons who went on to study at Trinity College Dublin, but both of them died of TB when they were in their twenties.

In 1902, Denis retired, passing the business on to two nephews, Tom and Roger Fox, the second of whom became licensee in 1904. Following Roger's death in 1951, the pub passed to another nephew, Gerard Nicholson, son of Katie Fox. At this time, the grocery was still an important part of the business. Gerard Nicholson produced his own blend of tea, which was highly sought after with customers travelling from as far as north Donegal to purchase it.

Following Gerard's death in 1986, the licence was transferred to his wife Maureen, whom he had married in 1956. Their son, Gerard Jnr, was prohibited from becoming licensee because he was a serving Garda. Policing has been as much a family tradition as licensing for over a century — Gerard Jnr's great-uncle Jim Fox had been a member of the Royal Irish Constabulary. Six years after his father's death and with a total of 10 years' service in the force, Gerard Jnr quit the Gardaí on 6 May 1992, becoming licensee four days later.

While the pub no longer has a grocery, the family business now includes a chemist shop next door, run by Gerard Snr's wife Maureen.

Gerard says that, as well as being a traditional pub, Connolly's today is very much a sporting pub. Gerard Nicholson Snr was a chairman and a treasurer of Sligo Rovers Football Club and a founder of Sligo Horse Racing. Connolly's has enjoyed a close relationship with cycling: Sean Kelly is a regular visitor and one of the bar's walls is adorned with a jersey belonging to Mark Scallon, winner of the Junior World Cycling Championships in 1998.

Such is the sporting atmosphere that the bar's interior was rebuilt in a film studio for a Heineken advertisement during the 1990 Irish World Cup campaign. Not that this is a Heineken pub; Guinness is the biggest seller and Gerard reports a 42 per cent increase in sales of the black stuff in the year 2000.

The pub also specialises in vintage whiskeys — entirely appropriate for a licensed establishment that is probably over 250 years old.

THE COUNTRY CLUB
Malachy Forde, Hollybrook, Claremorris, Co. Mayo

In America, a country club is where people play golf or tennis and sip cocktails, but in Mayo, "The Country Club" is where Carramore GAA and their followers play football and socialise.

Situated on a crossroads between Claremorris, Carramore, Hollymount and Ballindyne, this pub was originally known as "Andrew Forde's" after its founder,

who purchased the main pub building and 100 acres of surrounding farmland sometime in the mid-19th century.

A year after his purchase, Andrew opened a hardware shop that was licensed to sell alcohol six days a week. Apparently, Andrew was of the view that "six days is enough for anyone to work". Once the business was established and Andrew in a position to enjoy his Sabbath, he took a wife, Sarah Stevens of Mayo Abbey, with whom he had six children.

As Andrew's family grew, so did his business. As well as hardware, the business became a general merchants and family grocery. Forde's started trading in eggs, wool and farm produce. A 19th century handbill advertising the store describes Andrew Forde as a "Family Grocer; Tea, Wine, Spirit and Provision Merchant" and draws the reader's attention to the fact that he was also an "Agent for Gouldings and Richardsons manures". On fair days and during the run up to Christmas, over 100 horse-drawn coaches, carts and carriages would surround the store. As well as making purchases, people travelled from as far as Kilmaine, Shrule and Ballindine to sell their wool, eggs and other farm produce at Forde's.

Andrew's prosperity allowed him to buy another 30 acres adjoining his farmland, so that when he died in 1920, he handed on to his son Malachy a thriving business and a farm that is still bordered on three sides by the River Robe.

Malachy proved to be every bit as enterprising as his father. Shortly after taking over the business, he expanded into ice cream, founding the Hollybrook ice cream factory in Claremorris which for decades manufactured the only ice cream available in Connaught. During the Second World War, which the Irish government officially described as "The National Emergency", Forde's was given a special exemption from sugar rationing so that ice cream production could continue.

Rationing, and the scarcity of meat in England during and after the war, led Malachy to expand even further into the rabbit export trade. Malachy's vans collected caught rabbits from collection points he set up all over Galway and Mayo, with the rabbit carcasses being processed at premises adjacent to the Church Street ice-cream factory.

In the 1937 general election, Malachy decided to stand as an Independent Farmers Candidate. His travels across the province had helped him develop a large personal organisation, which threatened to take a seat from Fianna Fáil in particular. He also had a grasp of advertising techniques: as well as putting up posters, his supporters also used tarred road surfaces for electioneering. On the main roads leading into Ballyhaunis, Knock, Ballinrobe and, of course, Hollymount, the roads were decorated with the three-line slogan: FARMERS, VOTE NO. 1, FORDE. Unfortunately for Malachy, his name proved an easy one to sabotage to the benefit of Fianna Fáil and a week before the election the graffiti was amended to read: FARMERS, VOTE NO. 1, FOR DEV".

In the event, although he polled more than 1,900 votes, Malachy was not elected a TD and he never stood as a political candidate again. Instead he concentrated on his business and family. He married May Higgins from Carramarla, Claremorris, and had eight children, the eldest being Malachy, who inherited the business and farm in 1964.

The ice cream factory stopped trading in 1959 and young Malachy also wound up the hardware business, concentrating on improving the pub and developing the farm.

In 1966, he extended the pub and added dressing rooms, so that in 1967 it could become the home of Carramore GAA club. For some years previously it had been an unofficial home of Carramore, who played in a field to the back of the pub on Forde family lands. It was at this time that the pub's name changed to "The Country Club".

It's very much a multi-purpose pitch today. For the last 18 years, The Country Club has hosted an annual gymkhana on the last Sunday in May and it is also host to a Vintage Tractor and Engine Show, which is usually held on the first Sunday of July. One of the annual exhibits is a 1948 Ferguson 20 Diesel, which is Malachy's main source of transport when travelling around the farm.

In 1981, Malachy married Helen Connolly, from Cloonfad in Co. Roscommon, and the couple have two children, Andrew and Karen.

CUNNINGHAM'S

Patrick Cunningham, Newbridge, Ballinasloe, Co. Galway

You can tell Cunningham's of Newbridge wasn't originally meant to be a place of relaxation and enjoyment: the walls on the original building are three feet thick with narrow windows.

This was originally a police barracks, built by Mrs Gerard of Netherville Lodge, a landlord who was despised locally for evicting tenants. However, the barracks on the main Galway to Roscommon road were never used by the RIC, as Dublin Castle would not sanction the manpower to staff it.

In 1870, Patrick Turley acquired the building and made it his home. Two years later, the home was also a licensed premises, containing a small grocery and bar counter in one room.

At the turn of the century, it passed to Patrick's son, John Turley, who, during the War of Independence had to deal with police on the premises: Black and Tans who regularly ransacked the premises.

The business then passed to Annie, one of John's three daughters, and she ran the bar and grocery with her husband Michael Cunningham. In 1954, the business was transferred to the couple's son Patrick Cunningham, the current licensee.

In the 1960s, Patrick added a lounge to the premises by moving the grocery to an adjoining building. The grocery business continues today, but deals mainly in foodstuffs; in the 1960s, its wares also included farming provisions, drapery goods and watches.

Despite the addition of the lounge, this is still a small rural pub. Its main clientele are farmers and local sports enthusiasts, particularly followers of St Brendan's GAA club and Shiven Rovers soccer club.

CURLEY'S

Ronald Curley, Brendan Street, Portumna, Co. Galway

This pub has been in the one family since the late 1800s, though its exact origins are uncertain. It is known that an Ellen Salmon inherited the pub from an aunt sometime about 1890; details are unsure.

Following Ellen's death, the pub passed to her daughter Ellen, who ran the business with her husband Michael Curley. It then passed to their son Leo, who ran the business for only a few years, before it was taken over by his brother J.P., with his wife Lily.

Before J.P. and Lily took over the business, it was just a one-room grocery and bar that accommodated no more than 40 people. J.P. and Lily added a licensed restaurant to the business, but the bulk of their income came from providing accommodation to coal and zinc miners employed locally.

Following a decline in mining locally, both the lodgings business and the restaurant came to an end in the 1970s.

The pub is now run by Ronald Curley, son of J.P. and Lily, and his wife Phyllis. The couple have been running the pub since they married in 1984, with Phyllis now being the licensee. Ron and Phyllis have extended the premises to the rear of the building with the pub now accommodating up to 200 people.

According to Ronald, the pub enjoys a good local trade, boosted by tourism between April and October each year. The pub is very much involved in local community life, being sponsors of Portumna GAA.

THOMAS DUIGNAN

Gabriel Duignan, Main Street, Drumsna, Co. Leitrim

The Duignan family's involvement in the licensed trade can be traced back to 1890, when the grandmother of the current licensee, Mary Elizabeth Garvey, bought three separate neighbouring premises in the centre of Drumsna in 1890. At the time she bought the house, pub, grocery and wholesale egg warehouse, the town was entering a period of recession.

Drumsna's history dates back to the Stone Age when it was an important ford over the River Shannon. Because of the ford, Drumsna was also the most northerly navigable point on the Shannon until 1850. All waterborne goods — including beer barrels — were ported here for transportation by land to the Northwest.

Drumsna's main source of income was its quays and accompanying warehouses, but that all changed with the opening of the Jamestown Canal that allows vessels to travel north to Carrick-on-Shannon and beyond.

Three years after making her purchase, Mary married Thomas Duignan and the Duignan name has been on the pub licence ever since. The couple had seven children with the pub being passed on to Patrick Joseph Duignan, the youngest son, more usually referred to as "Joe". Thomas Duignan died in 1918 with Mary surviving him by another 10 years.

As well as a pub and grocery, Joe also inherited a hardware store, with all three shop counters in the one room! He also ran a travelling shop, which was a substantial part of the business, having regular runs throughout the district six days a week. Both the hardware and the travelling shop are now gone and the grocery has moved into a supermarket next door.

In the bar today, some fittings from the old grocery remain; there is an open fire and decorations including old whiskey casks and relics of the days when Guinness was bottled on the premises.

After Joe's death in 1979, the pub was run by his wife Mary B. Duignan who is still very much involved in the business, though day-to-day management is carried out by her sons, Noel and Gabriel, with Gabriel being the current licensee.

The two sons remember the days Guinness was bottled out the back, with Gabriel saying: "I don't remember those days very fondly. It was me who had to wash out the bottles and it was a pain of a job!"

Duignan's is one of four pubs in Drumsna, which today has a population of 200 people. Leitrim has more pubs per head of population than any other in Ireland. "Go three miles down any road out of Drumsna and you will come across another pub," complains Noel. "No one is making any money. You couldn't survive today without the grocery business."

GREEN'S

Mary Green, Main Street, Kinvara, Co. Galway

Kinvara is another west of Ireland town that prospered in the 17th, 18th and 19th centuries because of its importance as a port at a time when there were few good roads in Connaught.

A permit to hold regular fairs in the town was granted by King James I of England in 1616 to Oliver Martyn, a Mayor of Galway who occupied Dun Guaire Castle just outside Kinvara, but the town's heyday was between the 1850s and 1950s when it was an important sea port in South Galway.

A new harbour was built as part of a public works scheme following the Famine and from here timber from Derrybrien Woods near Loughrea was exported to England and grain was exported to the breweries and distilleries of Dublin. The port was also used to import turf from Connemara, as there was little of the fuel available in south Galway.

There are no records of any Greens in Kinvara until the mid-19th century. The family name is not recorded in tithe books for the Parish of Kinvara and Dooros in 1826, but several branches of the family are listed in *Griffith's Valuations* of 1850.

Sometime in the 1860s, Michael Green is believed to have taken possession of the three-storey building that holds the pub that still bears his name, M. Green, above the door. Certainly, situated facing the harbour and overlooking Galway Bay, the port would have been a major source of income for his new business. The building was originally a private dwelling, probably occupied by the family of a port official or merchant, and built sometime between 1820 and 1839, according to the town's earliest maps, *Griffith's Valuations* and the records of the St George family who live next door to the pub.

Certainly, Michael's business was up and running by 1863, when his son Martin was born. Michael may have had family assistance in setting up the new business, as he was a relative of Tom Fahy, who in 1850 owned a hotel in New Quay. Tom's son Francis A. Fahy was a well-known songwriter who composed *Galway Bay* and several other popular ballads, one of which, *The Old Plaid Shawl*, is the name of the hotel formerly owned by the Fahys in New Quay.

In Michael Green's time, his pub would be filled to capacity on fair days, as farmers, cattle jobbers and buyers made their bargains at the bar. Up until the 1940s, when the local roads were improved, boat loads of turf were also sold inside the pub with deals being sealed with "a pint and a half-one", as whiskey drinking was far more common then than it is today.

The date of Michael's death is not known, but he was succeeded by his son Martin Green who was licensee until he died in 1928. Martin's wife Belinda (née Connolly) then ran the business until 1945, before passing it on to her son Michael Green three years before her death.

Following Michael's death in 1971, the pub was run by his widow Helena, who was licensee until 1994. In 1980, Helena closed the grocery, as competition from supermarkets and the decline of the harbour as a commercial centre no longer made the shop counter a viable concern.

Since Helena's death, her daughter Mary has been licensee. She is proud of her licensing heritage. The pub's shopfront façade is original with the letters "M. Green" above the door referring both to Mary and her great-grandfather Michael Green.

She has some regrets about the loss of the pub's snug during the refurbishment that followed the closure of the grocery counter. Mary claims: "The snug was a unique aspect of the traditional Irish bar, which arose from the belief that it was not nice to see a woman — 'a lady' — drinking with men, even if the men included her own husband.

"The snug also played another social role: it was the place where the match-maker was found. The match-maker was usually a trusted old man who would discreetly arrange marriages between the sons and daughters of local farmers and shop keepers."

However, while the snug is gone, the grocery shelves and drawers remain in place. Instead of holding groceries, the shelves now positively sag under the weight of "Green's Bottles", a vast collection of whiskeys, brandies and unusual liquors. Indeed, Mary claims: "You would be hard pressed to name an alcoholic beverage that cannot be found on our shelves."

Selection of beverages at Green's

The pub's two busiest periods are during Kinvara's *Fleadh na gCuach* (Cuckoo Festival) in May and the *Cruinniú na mBád* in August, when the town celebrates its maritime heritage with one of Ireland's biggest gatherings of Galway Hookers and traditional sailing craft. However, throughout the year you will find impromptu traditional music taking place in the pub. Much of the pub's décor relates to the two annual festivals, but there are also posters advertising races held in Kinvara in the late 19th and early 20th centuries.

"Green's Bar remains a traditional pub of character and distinction," says Mary with pride. "There are no gimmicks — just great Guinness and as fine a selection of drink as you will find in any bar in Ireland."

KEENAN'S BAR
Barry Keenan, Termonbarry, Co. Roscommon

This small pub on the Shannon is a great favourite with boating enthusiasts, who can moor beside the pub and enjoy their refreshment in a spacious beer garden.

In the 19th century, the pub was in the Reynolds family, but in 1912 the then licensee, Ellie Reynolds, sold the business to Michael McDonald, a returned emigrant who had made his fortune in the United States. This pub would not be included in this book were it not for the fact that Ellie's daughter, Norah, married Michael two years after he bought the pub. In 1954, the pub passed to the couple's daughter Eileen, who ran it with her husband Joe Keenan and, ever since, the name Keenan has been above the door.

Barry Keenan, Joe and Eileen's son, has been licensee since 1996 and he runs the pub with his wife Annette. They recently added a restaurant to the pub, which is open all year round, but which is busiest during the summer months when tourist traffic on the Shannon is at its height.

The original shop frontage is more or less original and the interior is still small by modern standards, holding fewer than 40 people.

KELEHAN'S
John and Mary Kelehan, Bushy Park, Galway

Three miles from Galway city centre is Kelehan's of Bushy Park, a large pub and restaurant that has become a favourite of Galwegians and tourists alike. Overlooking the Corrib, to the rear of the pub is a large covered beer garden where barbecued meals have been served for over a decade.

It takes some imagination to picture it when it was founded as a small country grocery in a townland of five houses, which in the mid-19th century was well outside Galway city limits.

Today, as well as being a much bigger establishment, the level of the original bar has been raised to compensate for the fact that the level of the road outside has risen by over a foot following years of resurfacing. Forty years ago, you took a step down into Kelehan's bar.

Records relating to the family are confused, partly because the authorities (and the family) were slow to decide on a standard English-language spelling for their surname Ó Cheileacháin. The earliest records relating to the business date back to 1863, when "Thomas Kellehan" is listed as a small grocer, but after 1875 he is listed as "Thomas Kelihan". Neither of the two English-language surnames matches the spellings used by Thomas's father, a local farmer listed as "Peter Keallahan" and "Peter Keleher".

This relaxed attitude to the spelling of English-language surnames continued into the next generation; among Thomas's eight children, five different spellings are used: Kelaghan, Kellaghan, Keaghlaghan, Kelechan and Kelehan.

After Thomas's death in 1896, the pub passed to his wife Mary, who was licensee until 1901 when the pub passed to her son Peter Kelehan. Since Peter, the family has stuck to that spelling of the surname — in three generations, members of the family were known by at least 10 different spellings of their surname!

According to family folklore, the family was targeted during the Tan years because of their republican sympathies and police raids were a common occurrence, with minor damage caused on each occasion. One raid in particular stands out: an auxiliary who had smashed bottles suddenly grabbed the large jug behind the counter where the takings were kept, but he was ordered to put the money back by an RIC officer who balked at the idea of any policeman committing theft.

On another occasion, Peter's brother Tom and another local man Joe Carr were arrested, driven down the road and released on the far side of town immediately before curfew. They had to make a desperate dash home, because after a few minutes passed, if the Black and Tans caught them they would be executed for breaking the curfew order. Luckily, they were able to reach the Corrib and crawl back to the safety of the pub.

Before major roads were built locally, the Corrib was the chief thoroughfare in this part of Galway and during the 1950s it was common for drinkers in Menlo to use boats to cross the river to Kelehan's to enjoy a pint.

In 1956, the pub passed to Peter's son Augustine, who ran the business with his sister Mary-Anne. Augustine was a flamboyant character remembered for having a great singing voice and for his love of fast driving. He was a young man when he died of cancer in 1972.

Though the pub and licence passed to Augustine's brother John, it was their sister, Mary-Anne, who was to be found most often behind the bar during the

50 years she worked there. Though she never held the licence, many referred to the pub as "Mary-Anne's bar" and she is remembered as being strict but fair, with the same welcome for all her customers, be they the highest or the lowest in the land. She used to tell her co-workers to treat all equally, "for you never know, they might be in heaven with you".

Following John's death, the pub passed to his son Peter, who decided to concentrate on farming and to sell the pub and grocery. The businesses were bought jointly by Peter's brother, sister and brother-in-law — John Kelehan, Mary Kelehan and her husband John O'Connell — who run the business together today.

The three have significantly expanded the business since taking joint ownership, extending the pub and adding the large covered roof garden at the start of the 1990s. In 1998, the family grocery next door to the pub was replaced with "Mary-Anne's Restaurant".

Now catering for a large local, corporate and tourist trade, Kelehan's employs five chefs and earns more of its revenue from food than from drink. Nevertheless, the pub still has a "local" flavour — there are two rooms set aside for regulars to play pool and the pub sponsors St Michael's GAA Club.

PATRICK C. KELLY
Kevin Kelly, Monivea,
Athenry, Co. Galway

There has been a public house on the site of Patrick C. Kelly's in Monivea for at least 250 years, but the Kelly family's involvement with it began in 1885 when Patrick Christopher Kelly, from nearby Skehane, married the licensee, Ann Davin. She had obtained the pub and grocery from her uncle, a man with the surname Madden, who had owned it since 1815.

It was a thriving business as P.C. Kelly's was an official Bianconi coach stop and much trade was carried out on the premises — an old weighbridge house, where goods including hay, potatoes, corn and turf were weighed, still stands here.

However, both Monivea and the Kelly business suffered a major blow with the opening of the Midland and Great Western Railway between Galway and Dublin in 1851, with the nearest railway station 50 miles away in Athenry.

Ann Davin died childless, but P.C. Kelly married again and had two sons with his new wife, Mary Costello.

P.C.'s grandson, Kevin Kelly, is the current licensee. While the premises is now a pub and a bed-and-breakfast, he remembers a time when it was an important place of wholesale, as well as grocery, trade. He says: "A lot of trading was carried out by barter with people bringing in eggs to swap for tea and other groceries — this all stopped at about the time we joined the EU [in 1973]."

Another story told by Kevin dates back to the War of Independence: "The RIC Barracks is across the road and the story is told that one night the Black and Tans came in here and held a gun to a woman's head until she would play a tune they wanted to hear on the pub piano!"

On entering Kelly's today, it is still possible to see original shop shelving and counters the early 1900s. The pub also features an original open fireplace with hobs and crane.

The stables, once used to house coaching horses, have been converted into bed-and-breakfast accommodation. Kevin's great-uncle, Cardinal Cook of New York, is probably the most famous person to have stayed there overnight.

KENNY'S

Thomas Kenny, Ballygar, Co. Galway

The Kennys became involved in running this 200-year-old Co. Galway pub in 1859 when Patrick Kenny, from Ahascragh, married Winifred Feeney.

Her family, tenants of the landlord, Denis Henry Kelly, had been running a public house in Ballygar since the 1790s, but the Feeney connection with the pub — which also sold groceries, farm provisions and delph — ended when Winifred, and her first child, died while she was in labour.

Patrick re-married, only for his second wife to be the victim of an early death. It wasn't until he married a third time that his son and heir, Thomas Kenny, was born in the 1860s.

Thomas was as much a republican as a publican. During the general elections of 1918 and 1927, de Valera enjoyed the Kenny's hospitality when he came to Ballygar.

Kenny's was also an IRA safe house during the War of Independence — according to Thomas's daughter, Winnie Kenny, who died aged 92 in 1996. One night, a meeting was taking place in an upstairs room when three Crossley tenders full of Black and Tans arrived at the door. Sure that they had been betrayed, the revolutionaries upstairs prepared to shoot their way out. But the Tommies were only hunting late-night drink. While the Black and Tans drank the bar dry, little did they know that their enemies were hiding only a few feet away above.

Winnie also used to say that while some Black and Tans were no more than dangerous brutes, there were gentlemen among them. Sometimes the Tans would take over the bar and demand free drink, but on other occasions they would be on their best behaviour, with a senior officer paying all bills in full, plus a generous tip.

After national independence, Thomas served as a Fianna Fáil county councillor and Kenny's can still be described as "a Fianna Fáil pub".

Another tradition that survives from this era is the Kennys' custom of naming their firstborn sons after the child born to Patrick Kenny more than 140 years ago. The last two licensees have been named Thomas. The first took over the pub in 1945, but lived only to 1966, dying at the age of 45 from lung cancer.

The current licensee, Thomas Kenny, was a 16-year-old Inter Cert. student when his father died and had to leave his boarding school and his education to help his mother Nora run the pub. Of course, he had been involved in the business long before he was sent off to Dublin to be a scholar. During his national school days, when the pub was going through about a firkin of beer a week, it was his job to wash 128 half-pint bottles a week.

Guinness was available on draught before the arrival of "the iron lung" in 1968. But in the first half of the century, draught beer in Kenny's meant beer drawn from wooden kegs into an enamel jug and then poured into pint glasses. An enamel bowl was used with the jug, so that drips and spills could be captured for use when pouring the next pint of draught Guinness.

For a time, Watney's Red Barrel draught ale was available and the pub sold Bulmers Woodpecker Cider in flagon bottles. But Thomas says: "If you drank cider at any time between the 1950s and 1970s you would be regarded as a loose cannon. We also sold Barley Wine, which was called 'poor man's whiskey' and by law we were not allowed to sell anyone more than three bottles of it."

The delph side of the business ended in the 1940s and the pub stopped being a general store in the 1950s. In 1958, the pub shared its premises with the family's butchering business and you could enjoy your pint beneath the carcasses of dead pigs and sheep. Health regulations only led to the butcher's being moved to new premises in 1982!

Thomas is extremely proud of his family's heritage — though he has broken with tradition by using Irish in naming his first son Tomás, who it is hoped will become the next licensee when five generations of Kennys will have held the licence. The pub has received numerous tourism awards, for, as Thomas says, "the public bar is a museum in itself". Inside, there are all kinds of paraphernalia including whiskey barrels from his grandfather's time, plus public notices and advertising. There are Guinness labels bearing the name "Nora Kenny" and a large reproduction of a label belonging to the first Thomas Kenny with the number 898181, the date of the first of August 1898 written backwards according to Guinness's numbering system.

Among a host of photos, there is, of course, one of de Valera. There are dozens of photos of County Galway all-Ireland teams, with pride of place given to the hurling champions of 1956. Naturally, both "Sam" and the McCarthy Cup have been visitors to Kenny's more than once. On one wall, Ballygar's most famous son, Patrick Sarsfield Gilmore, writer of the anthem "When Johnny Comes Marching Home", is commemorated. There is also a photo of the heavyweight boxing champion Floyd Patterson enjoying one of Kenny's black pints.

Today, during the summer months there is even an antique jaunting car outside, with a horse that never moves — and that is because it is made of fibreglass!

McEVILLY'S
Walter McEvilly, Ballyheane, Co. Mayo

A disused police barracks originally housed McEvilly's Bar in Ballyheane, says its current licensee Walter McEvilly, who reckons the pub to be at least 120 years old.

The earliest surviving historical record is a coroner's report recording the death of "John McEvely, publican, aged 56" in 1883. It is not known how long John had been trading on the premises, but given that the pub was a former police barracks, the bar cannot predate the 1820s, as Ireland only began to have a national constabulary from 1814 onwards.

Following John's death, the business passed to his son James, who changed the spelling of his surname to McEvilly for reasons unknown. The 1901 census records James's profession as both "farmer and publican".

From James, the pub passed to his son Michael who ran it until his death in 1973 when it passed to the current licensee Walter, who runs the pub with his wife Pauline.

This part of Mayo has been hit hard by rural depopulation for decades, something that has affected the pub's business. "In the seventies, it looked as though things were about to pick up when a lot of those who spent their lives in England came back to retire here," says Pauline. "There was a time in the 1980s when on a Friday, pension day, the pub would be absolutely filled to capacity. But many of those elderly people have passed away and there were no young people to take their place — things can get very quiet around here now."

However, in the last few years new houses have been built on the outskirts of the village, with Ballyheane becoming a commuter suburb of Castlebar, which is four miles away.

With business building up again, Pauline says the biggest change she has seen in the pub trade is the change in the price of the pint: when she started working in the bar, a pint of Guinness cost 17p!

P. McMANUS

Patrick McManus, High Street, Drumshanbo, Co. Leitrim

It is claimed that Paddy Mac's in Drumshanbo was established in 1795, but there are no records from the 18th century that definitively support the claim.

A description of the events of 1798 records that there was a shebeen at the ford at Drumshanbo where French troops crossed the Shannon and, according to McManus family folklore, the illegal drinking den was on the same site where their pub stands today.

Sometime in the 1850s, the premises was bought by a Paddy McManus. Little is known about the first Paddy Mac, except that he was originally from Keadew, just outside Drumshanbo, where he was probably a farmer. His son, who was also named Paddy Mac, was a much more memorable character.

When the McManuses started trading in Drumshanbo in the mid-19th century, the town was very prosperous and had been for several generations thanks to nearby iron mines and coalfields. Iron mining was at its height locally in the 16th and 17th centuries, but coalmining continued until the end of the century. The area's last coal mine ceased production in 1993, when closure of the Irish Sugar plant in Tuam that year meant it lost its chief customer, the sugar plant's electricity generators. Drumshanbo was also prosperous thanks to its thriving cattle market, which was connected to Belfast via the Leitrim, Cavan and Northern Counties Railway. After national independence, the railway line continued in operation, with many goods, including tea, sold in Paddy Mac's grocery, coming from Northern Ireland.

When Paddy Mac Jnr took over the pub from his father, he had already had a successful career as a circus ringmaster in San Francisco, where he also had his own act of performing horses. On his return to Ireland, the young Paddy Mac quickly gained renown as an outstanding horseman. Indeed, at the end of the 19th century, it was horses and not the pub and grocery trade that supplied the bulk of the family's income. Next door to the pub, Paddy Mac's had a shop selling a wide range of equine supplies, including saddles, harnesses and Col. Jones's patent horse medicines. To the rear of the pub there were extensive stables where teams of horses were kept to be rented out to farmers, to ply for haulage and to fulfil Royal Mail contracts. The hounds for the local hunt were also kept at the rear of the pub.

At the start of the 20th century, the business was further expanded to include plant hire for local public works, as well as agricultural plant such as horse-drawn mowing machines.

The second Paddy Mac also took an interest in local politics when he returned to Ireland, perhaps as a substitute for life in an American circus. He was a Parnellite and served as a county councillor for the National Party. Famously, during a council meeting in Carrick-on-Shannon in the early 1900s, a fire broke out in the building next door to the council chamber. Seeing that two children and a nanny were trapped on the third floor, Paddy Mac rushed into the burning building and saved all three. His active life with horses proved to be a healthy one and he was in his nineties when he died in 1932.

The pub then passed to his son, Jimmy McManus, who ran the pub with his sister Margaret McManus and for a time the pub was known locally as "Maggie Mac's".

In 1957, the pub passed to Jimmy's son, Patrick McManus, the third "Paddy Mac" to hold the licence. Their son "Paddy Jnr.", born in 1979, also works regularly behind the bar.

The nationalist political tradition continues, with Paddy Mac's being a Fianna Fáil pub, where visitors have included Bertie Ahern, Mary O'Rourke and Brian Lenihan.

There is live music in the bar regularly and the pub is particularly busy during the Tóstal festival held in June and the Joe Mooney Summer School for traditional musicians in July.

MELLETT'S EMPORIUM
Joe Mellett, Market Street, Swinford, Co. Mayo

Mellett's Emporium has been in the same family since Stephen Mellett acquired it when he came to Swinford in 1797. The word "acquired" is used because it is not known if Stephen bought the property or whether its owner, Lord Brabazon, gave it to him as a present. The year Stephen came to Swinford, he married a Ms Durkin and it is believed that the premises may have been given to him as a present by the landlord for whom he had previously worked as a rent collector.

Certainly, the Brabazons were wealthy enough to make such a gift. As well as owning a vast amount of land in north Connaught, the family had accumulated an immense fortune by fraud. Sir William Brabazon, who died in 1551, had been a vice-treasurer of Ireland and had served three times as lord justice. He played a prominent, and dishonest, role in Henry VIII's dissolution of the monasteries when the English king seized church lands to increase the English monarchy's wealth. It wasn't until after

his death that it was found that Sir William had also used the dissolution of the monasteries to make himself extremely rich, pocketing hundreds of thousands of pounds worth of rents from the confiscated Irish lands!

When Stephen opened his doors for business, the premises was divided into two halves: to the front was a general store, selling everything one might need from cradle to the grave, while at the rear was the bar, which also had a small snug used mainly by women drinkers.

The year after Stephen became vintner, 1798, is known in Irish history as "the Year of the French" because a force of 1,019 French soldiers landed at Killala Bay to aid an Irish rebellion against English rule. In Esker, two of the French troops were killed and Stephen was asked to undertake the funeral arrangements and to supply coffins for the two bodies.

In 1801, Stephen added an emigration office to the bar and grocery, selling ship passages to England, the United States and Australia. This developed into a travel agency in the early 20th century. The agency was closed in 1995, but steamship company advertisements still hang in the bar today.

Following Stephen's death in 1840, his son Michael, who was born in 1806, took over the pub and its license. The following year Michael also became Swinford's postmaster, with the post office next door to the pub. After 25 years, he ceased working for the Royal Mail and the premises was sold. In 1983, the family bought back the property and it is now home to Mellett's Newsagency.

During the Great Famine, it was recorded that Michael did much to provide relief to its victims in north Mayo.

Michael and his wife, Mary Campbell, had three children: PJ, Michael Jnr and Marie. PJ was known locally as "The Shah" and was owner of Mellett's Hotel, a building that is now home to the Swinford branch of the AIB bank. PJ's wife, Mary Meade, died in suspicious circumstances in 1910. When the police exhumed her body to perform an autopsy, PJ disappeared, never to be seen again, leaving three children behind him. The youngest, Marie Mellett, drowned in October 1918, one of 504 people to die when the *HMS Leinster* was torpedoed while travelling from Kingstown (Dun Laoghaire) to Holyhead.

Following Michael's death in 1884, the pub and grocery passed to his son Michael Jnr, who in 1902 added auctioneering to the family's businesses. Michael Jnr also constructed the building that is home today to Mellett's Auctioneers and Estate Agents, though originally it was leased out to a dressmaker called Sissy Doherty and between 1960 and 1981 it was home to a laundrette.

At this time, the family also had a mobile wholesale business supplying goods to grocery shops dotted around Mayo and Sligo.

Following Michael Jnr's death in 1916, the businesses passed to his son Joseph A. Mellett, who was born in 1870. Joe had two lucky escapes from shipwreck, as he was due to have been aboard the *Lusitania* when she was torpedoed off the Old Head of Kinsale in 1915, and was also to have been aboard the *HMS Leinster* when she was torpedoed in 1918.

Under Joe, the pub, grocery and auctioneering businesses continued to thrive, but he also added politics to the family's interest. Standing as a Cumann na nGaedheal candidate, he became the first of three generations of Melletts to be elected as a county councillor.

Following Joe's death in 1931, his son William Mellett took over the family's businesses. It was William and his brother, Dr Kevin Mellett, who gave the pub its strong rugby sporting links with both men playing for the Ballina team. Kevin, who was an Irish army officer, also played rugby for the Connaught provincial side. While William continued the family's licensing, auctioneering and political traditions, he wound up the undertaking business. However, the Melletts say they never throw anything away and the pub still has a number of coffins stored out the back that are for sale!

William's wife Bea Roddy had her own business sideline: she was a matchmaker who helped make many a marriage from the small kitchen behind the bar counter.

Following William's death in 1992, his son Joe Mellett became licensee. Joe can claim to be a sixth generation publican, a fourth generation auctioneer and a third generation county councillor. Like his father, Joe is an active member of Fine Gael and he was elected to Mayo County Council in 1999. Monthly Fine Gael cumann meetings are held in Mellett's bar.

Today, Mellett's pub is an emporium in name only as, since 1988, the building no longer includes a general store or grocery counter. However, the pub today is flanked by Mellett's Newsagency on the left and Mellet's Auctioneer and Estate Agents on the right. Since 1984, a branch of the Irish Permanent Building Society has also been housed in the auctioneering premises.

As said before, the Melletts claim never to have thrown away anything that might possibly be valuable. As a result, the pub is filled with antiques, memorabilia and historic ephemera. Among the items *not* on display are ledger books dating back to 1820.

A new stone façade was added to the bar when it was refurbished in the 1980s, but many original features were retained. Among the articles of interest are the remains of an old beer dispensing system featuring mahogany pump handles and pewter taps. When this system was installed originally is not known, Joe A., who was born in 1870 and died in 1931, told his family that he had never seen them in use. According to Joseph, the current licensee, the system used lead piping to bring the beer to the barroom taps from barrels kept in a storeroom outside. He says: "It was an extremely modern system when it was installed, but can you imagine the taste of the first pint in the morning after the beer had been lying all night in the lead pipes?"

THE MILLER'S INN
Denis Scanlon, Bunnanadden, Ballymote, Co. Sligo

This pub now known as The Miller's Inn was established as a licensed grocery and post office by a young local woman, Mary Madden, shortly before her marriage to another local, John Scanlon, in June 1883.

Together they ran the business for 19 years until Mary died, aged 44, childless. Two years later, in 1906, John remarried and had nine children with his new wife, Henrietta Hunt. As the family grew, the business prospered, helped by its location opposite the parish church.

During the Troubles, after an unsuccessful search for an IRA man on the run, British soldiers threatened to return to burn the pub down. But overall, the pub was unscathed by the Troubles, apart from the occasional looting by Black and Tans.

The licence next changed hands in 1947, on the day John's eldest son, Charles Scanlon, married Teresa Harrington. They ran the pub together, with the help of their four children, until 1985 when it was handed over to their youngest, Denis Scanlon, three years after his marriage to Betty.

They gave up the post office and the grocery and expanded the pub. Now, at a comfortable squeeze, the L-shaped combination bar and lounge holds 200 customers. Denis also put his identity on the pub in its new name, "The Miller's Inn", which comes from the nickname he had before becoming licensee when he was with NCF, the local farmers' co-operative.

The licensed trade has changed much since the times of Denis's father and grandfather. One of the first major changes he noticed was the arrival of Double Diamond. "The rep had talked my father into taking a case of the stuff and he was doubtful that he would sell much of it," says Denis. "I was only a boy, but I was put in charge of it while my parents were out. The next thing, two fellows came in and, I don't know if they were friends of the rep or had just met him outside, but they asked for a bottle of Double Diamond each. Then they had another two bottles and another two bottles. The two of them drank the whole case in one night. We knew we had a winner. We sold lots of it once, but don't stock it at all now. It was a lovely ale."

MORAN'S OYSTER COTTAGE

Willie Moran, The Weir,
Kilcolgan, Co. Galway

One of the most famous and oldest pubs in Ireland, Moran's Oyster Cottage was saved thanks to a spontaneous act of generosity, a wild Irish salmon and a "thank you" party.

Moran family records date back to before the end of the 18th century and the pub has been in the Moran family since at least the late 1700s, when a man named Daniel Moran married Mary Neiland. Her family owned the weir and may have been selling alcohol and other provisions before Daniel's arrival.

At that time, Kilcolgan was more or less the same size as it is now, with 14 houses. In its heyday as a port serving the fertiliser and fuel (seaweed and turf) markets, this tiny village had four pubs that were regularly overflowing with people. The Morans enjoyed a good living from the pub for over a century as it was passed from father to eldest son. After Daniel, the pub passed to Thomas (born 1811), then to Michael (born 1830), to Thomas (born 1870), to Michael Moran (born 1907) who is still alive today.

As you can see, the family followed the custom of naming first-born sons after the boy's paternal grandfather. But this generation's Thomas Moran died and the current licensee is his brother Willie.

In the 1930s, Kilcolgan became a ghost town when new roads allowed freight to travel by lorry along the north and south Galway coasts. The port was redundant, with the only income being provided by small scale salmon and lobster fishing and work on the state-owned oyster beds. There are 700 acres of oyster beds off Kilcolgan harbour and, because of their national economic importance, to avoid pollution there has been very little development in the village.

One by one, Kilcolgan's three other pubs closed down as publicans decided that paying an annual licence fee was not worth the effort. According to Willie: "By the 1960s, the bar wasn't trading at all. All that was in it was a bottle of Guinness, a bottle of Sandeman and a bottle of whiskey". In 1960, he was offered £1,000 for the licence — half the price of a new house — but he wouldn't sell. The licence had been in the family so long and he didn't want to be the one to let it go.

"It was about this time that my father was out salmon fishing on the river when a student named Al Byrne, up on holiday from Dublin, said to him 'I would love one of those fish, but I couldn't afford it' and my father made him a present of the salmon there and then. Al Byrne went on to become very big in Guinness's. He was down in Clarinbridge [five miles away] on company business in connection with the Oyster Festival, where Paddy Burke, the publican in Clarinbrige, said to him 'I must take you to this little pub in the middle of nowhere'. Paddy took Al to Moran's bar and as soon as Al walked in the door he recognised Michael, who had given him a salmon years before. There and then Al announced, 'At next September's Clarinbridge Oyster Festival, Guinness's will hold its private party here, we'll arrange a keg'."

Moran's were to provide the food and did so using local oysters and brown bread baked by Willie's mother Kathleen. In the Guinness party were journalists who went back to Dublin to write how they had found this "unspoilt pub".

"It was then the penny dropped and we moved to providing seafood," says Willie. "My mother used to bake 20 tins of brown bread every morning. While we have expanded the menu to include oysters, wild salmon and prawns, my big secret is 'keep the menu simple and do it well'. We now employ 12 full-time staff all year round and 50 in the summer.

"The downstairs of the old cottage is now part of the pub, with two of the old downstairs bedrooms now used as snugs.

"We got another big boost thanks to the IDA [Industrial Development Authority] who brought over a *New York Times* journalist, R.W. Apple, in the 1970s to write about the potential of Galway as a site for American multinationals to build factories. They took this journalist for lunch here and, when he went home, he wrote a front page article about Moran's of Kilcolgan with hardly a word about factories. That article was syndicated to newspapers all over the States and it really put us on the map, people would arrive here with their press clippings! A whole range of celebrities have eaten here, from Paul Newman to the Emperor and Empress of Japan."

MORRISSEY'S

Aidan Morrissey, West Bridge, Loughrea, Co. Galway

Claiming to date back 250 years and to be the oldest pub in Loughrea, Morrissey's has been in the one family for just over 100 years.

The pub has been in the Morrissey family for four generations now. The current licensee, Aidan Morrissey, is the great-grandson of Edward Morrissey, who bought the pub as a going concern in the 1890s.

Unfortunately, little of the family's history was recorded before the death of Aidan's father Patrick Morrissey in 1986. All that is known is that after Edward died, the pub passed to his son, Edward Jnr, and then to Edward Jnr's son, Patrick. Patrick's widow Eileen held the license briefly, before it was passed on to her son Aidan, the current licensee.

Although Morrissey's was primarily a pub, there were groceries sold on the premises until the 1960s. Until 30 years ago, the pub benefited from its location next to Loughrea's fair green where cattle and sheep were traded. According to Eileen, on fair days the pub was packed from morning to night with farmers either waiting to sell their livestock or enjoying some of the proceeds of their livestock sales. In some cases, farmers would have walked their livestock some distance to the fair and were often "too tired" to do their dealing outside the pub and would instead bargain with the cattle jobbers inside the bar.

The exterior of the pub features ornate plasterwork and the interior features some fine oak panelling, both of which date back to the late 1800s. Much of the furnishings inside are original, in the vernacular style, giving the pub a slightly "rugged" look. The pub still has its original snug, where women drinkers were accommodated, and the glass cabinet, used still today to store spirit bottles, is over 150 years old. As a result, Morrissey's is today a fine example of a traditional Victorian pub.

O'BOYLE'S

Patrick O'Boyle, Laught, Moylough, Co. Galway

Claimed to be one of the oldest pubs in Connaught, O'Boyle's of Laught has been in the one family for five generations and at least 200 years — though documentary evidence providing dates of when the pub was established is not available.

The current licensee is Patrick O'Boyle; his father, Thomas — known as Sonny O'Boyle — was born on the premises in 1899 and lived to the age of 102. Sonny's father, John, was also born on the premises and it was John's father, Augustine O'Boyle, who gave the pub its current name when he married one of two sisters belonging to the Bodkin family sometime at the turn of the 19th century. Bodkin is the name of an old family of Galway merchants and it is said that the two women had inherited the grocery and bar from their father and that he, in turn, may have inherited it also.

Originally comprising two adjoining thatched cottages, O'Boyle's was a grocery and hardware store that sold "everything from a needle to an anchor" during the 19th and early 20th centuries. O'Boyle's was particularly renowned for their hard-cure bacon, which was supplied to them from a factory in Claremorris that is now long gone. According to Patrick: "Hard-cure bacon was a great deal more expensive than normal soft-cure bacon, but we would have been selling three or four sides of bacon a week."

During Sonny's time, the only alcohol sold on the premises was whiskey and Guinness, which came in two forms, double stout and plain. Barrels of Guinness were kept by the fire, so that the drink when served would have a frothy head because it was warm, with the barrels also serving as fireside seating. During those days, the pub comprised a bar and a tap room, where the Guinness was bottled. Older customers still refer to the modern lounge as "the tap room", even though it is much larger than its predecessor and has been built to take advantage of the view over Summerville Lake, known locally as Laught Lake, which is famous for its coarse fishing, particularly pike.

Before the lounge was built, women did not enter the pub at all, says Patrick. "As a boy, I was given the job of taking lemonade and biscuits out to the women who would be left outside sitting in a cart, often in the rain with nothing to cover them but a rug thrown over them."

According to Sonny, on a number of occasions he "had to run out the back door" when the Black and Tans arrived at the premises. These stories weren't given much credence by the family until Sonny produced proof of compensation paid to him for beer and whiskey lost when the rampaging auxiliaries ransacked his shelves and cellar.

After Independence, O'Boyle's became very much a Fianna Fáil pub and Patrick says that cumann nights were "very big occasions that would go on to three or four in the morning". On such nights, the pub never had any problems with unexpected "after hours" raids by the Gardaí. Indeed, Patrick says: "The practice was that whenever there was going to be a raid, we would get a phone call a week or so in advance telling us which night the Gardaí would be coming. They didn't seem to mind late-night drinking, but they were always very strict about Sunday opening. When we had the grocery, there was one time when a Garda came in and we had a customer who, as well as buying her messages, was enjoying a glass of Lucozade — didn't he take a drink out of the glass to make sure there was no alcohol in it."

The O'Boyle family survived a more serious run-in with the law, caused by the fact that the pub and the family home are in two adjoining buildings. Patrick's mother Delia was a national school teacher and someone complained to the authorities that she was breaking the Department of Education's regulations by living in a pub. "An inspector came down from Dublin," recalls Patrick. "But no action was taken against her, because she wasn't living over the pub, she was living in the adjoining building and that was the loophole that saved her job when she was informed on."

As well as the grocery, the O'Boyles were involved in the rabbit trade, collecting conies caught by local farmers. Patrick says: "I don't know who bought them or where they went, but a lorry would come for them once a month." The grocery business, which included supplying a homemade remedy for cattle and sheep diseases made by Sonny, ceased in the 1970s. The rabbit meat business, needless to say, ended long before that.

Today the pub is the family's second source of income and, being closed on Wednesdays, trades only six nights a week. Patrick's main job is as a secondary school teacher, teaching business studies. He says: "As a business, the pub isn't worth keeping, but family pride in it won't let me let it go."

THE OLD STAND

Donagh Tighe, Ballymote, Co. Sligo

The Tighe family have been in the licensed trade since the early 1890s when Thomas Tighe, a returned emigrant, leased a pub in Ballymote. Originally a tenant farmer from outside the town, he emigrated to better himself. Not only did he prosper in the United States, but on his return to Ireland he was sufficiently successful as a vintner to be able to buy his own pub-cum-grocery in Ballymote, transferring his licence to the new premises.

Thomas bought The Old Stand as a going concern, its name coming from the fact that it had previously been an official stop on the coach route between Dublin and Sligo. As such, we can say that the pub bought by Thomas had been in business since before September 1862, when Dublin and Sligo were connected by rail.

At the time Thomas bought his new pub, Ballymote was enjoying its heyday. The new railway line had increased Ballymote's importance as a market town, but it was also an important administrative centre for the county and was, at the time, the second largest town in Sligo. A great deal of the town's prosperity was due to its biggest employer, Murray's Coachworks, whose carriages, traps and drays were sold to clients throughout Ireland and the UK. However, Murray's went into a quick, though not inevitable, decline because its owners failed to appreciate the threat posed to their business by the arrival of the motorcar. The number of pubs in the town illustrates its economic decline: in the 1930s, Ballymote had over 30 licensed premises; today it has only 10.

In the 1940s, the pub was passed on to Thomas's son, Denis Tighe, a time-served barman who had completed an apprenticeship and worked for 12 years in the licensed trade in Dublin, including time spent at The Parliament House and with the Mooney chain of pubs. Denis and his wife Kathleen renovated the premises, converting the grocery into a lounge. His knowledge learned in Dublin was put to good use, as Thomas was a whiskey bonder and many of the bottles of Jameson sold elsewhere in Sligo and Leitrim bore the name "Thomas Tighe" on their labels. His pub was also noted for the quality of its Guinness stout.

In 1976, the pub was inherited by Thomas's son, Donagh Tighe, who extended and refurbished the pub in the 1980s. Much of Donagh's refurbishments reversed changes made by his father; for example, the original 19th century bar counter was reinstalled. The pub's interior features mahogany wood, leaded and stained glass and hand-finished mirrors and the pub was also given a new façade in the traditional idiom. More of a restoration than a refurbishment, the work was of a sufficiently high standard to win an architectural award from Sligo County Council.

RABBITT'S BAR
Murtagh Rabbitt, Forster Street, Galway

This pub in Forster Street, Galway, was founded with the proceeds of the San Francisco gold rush. Cormac Ó Coinín was a '49er with gold in his pockets when he returned to Galway from the United States. The pub and grocery in Forster Street was not his first enterprise. Originally, Cormac ran a flourmill in Quay Street but that was destroyed by fire, leading him to set up his grocery and pub in 1872.

He chose well the location of his new business, known as *Tigh Cormaic* or Cormac's House, for it was the only pub immediately east of Eyre Square at a time when the square still hosted annual fairs and weekly livestock markets on Saturdays. It was also the last pub in Galway for those leaving the city in the direction of Oranmore; as a result, Cormac's primary source of income was from farmers buying groceries and household goods after selling livestock or farm produce on the market.

In addition to the pub and grocery, the business had stables to the rear accessed via a stone archway, where horses, ponies, traps and drays were kept. Cormac was also a shareholder in the Galway Omnibus Company and he may have kept some of the company's horses on his premises.

The large area to the rear of the pub was also used to keep pigs. According to family folklore, on more than one occasion, Cormac's pigs went hungry because he gave their food away to those who were begging for food on the streets, something that indicates that poverty remained high in Galway for decades after the Famine.

Following Cormac's death, the pub passed to his son Peter Rabbitt, who used an English-language version of his family's surname. In 1934, he made major alterations to the premises, increasing the drinking space by moving his family's living quarters upstairs. Peter ran the pub until his death in 1942, when his wife Sarah became licensee. Following her death, her son John was licensee for a number of years and played a major role in returning the family business to profitability. After John, the licence passed to his brother, Murtagh Rabbitt, in 1955.

Murty has seen major changes in how the pub was run. When he was young, the pub had an early morning licence to cater for those with market business in Eyre Square, with the pub's doors opening at 9.00 a.m. In those days, the bar's floor had sawdust scattered on it to deal with the wetness and dirt brought in to the pub on farmers' boots. With a livestock market in Eyre Square, the streets of Galway were much dirtier then than they are now.

As well as bottling Guinness, as a boy Murty was one of the first in Galway to bottle Smithwick's beer and he claims to be the man who first served Smithwicks to the Galway Chamber of Commerce.

During the 1970s, the range of goods sold by the grocery gradually decreased, with the pub no longer stocking bread after 1984, but loose tea is still sold there. The pub now also has a restaurant attached, serving traditional Irish food, and an off-licence opened in 1997. The pub is now run by Murty's son, John Rabbitt, great-grandson of Cormac Ó Coinín.

THE RUSTIC VAULTS
Conal Murphy, Vicar Street, Tuam, Co. Galway

Probably one of the best-known pubs in Connaught, the Rustic Vaults in Tuam is an architectural gem. The pub probably dates back to the arrival of the railway in Tuam in 1861. It is still the closest pub to Tuam's railway station and is frequented by railway staff and passengers alike.

It has been in the one family since it was bought in August 1884 by Michael Walsh, a local businessmen, who purchased "the leasehold of the premises known as the Rustic Vaults, Bar and Grocery" from Mrs Ellen Mulry, who had been widowed that year.

As well as already owning several other properties in Vicar Street, Michael was proprietor of the Tuam's Connaught Arms Hotel, so he had no difficulty in having the license for the Rustic Vaults transferred to his name. Shortly after purchasing the Rustic Vaults, Michael married Winifred Flanagan of Corofin and the couple went on to have two children, Margaret (Madge) and Eugene. After Michael's death in 1902, Winnifred was proprietor until 1923 when she passed the Rustic Vaults on to Madge and her husband William Quinn.

They were a colourful couple. William was an acclaimed tenor and Madge took an interest in the arts. It is she who is responsible for the Rustic Vault's much-loved good looks. Her redesign in 1925 included the installation of the

Connemara marble shopfront, the large front windows topped by stained glass, the terazzo floor and the polished granite bar counter.

When William died at an early age in the 1930s, he left Madge with nine children to rear on her own. Luckily, the pub supplied a steady income thanks to its favourable location. Its proximity to Tuam Cathedral and the Cattle Mart meant mass-goers and farmers were regular customers. During the sugar harvest, before the sugar factory was closed in the 1980s, business boomed. The pub even benefited from being close to the Grove Hospital — though that closed in early 2001.

All of Madge's children — two boys and seven girls — worked in the bar at some stage in their life, but following her death in April 1958, the pub was left to Freda, Maeve and Fionnuala Quinn — Madge's three daughters who were not married. The three women are still well remembered for their strict house rules: "No rude words, no singing and no raised voice arguments".

The last of the three to die was Fionnuala, who passed away in July 1997. With the pub being left jointly to Madge's surviving children, the other family members' shares were purchased by Therese Quinn Murphy who became sole proprietor. Her son, Conal Murphy, is the present owner and licensee of The Rustic Vaults.

Today, trade is still brisk, despite the decline in rail use and the loss of Tuam's sugar factory. The pub is a favourite of members of The Saw Doctors rock band, something that has helped trade and make the Rustic Vaults internationally known. Conal explains: "Ten years ago, The Saw Doctors recorded a television programme in the pub for Channel 4 and we have had visitors because of it ever since."

TEACH UÍ SHIORADÁIN

Cathal Sheridan, Milltown, Tuam, Co. Galway

On the main road between Claremorris and Tuam stands a large maroon and white building, Teach Uí Shioradáin, the first pub in Galway when you leave Mayo on the N17.

North Galway is footballing country where local rivalry with Mayo is high. Few people know this as acutely as Cathal Sheridan, Teach Uí Shioradáin's current licensee who is also a former captain of the Milltown team.

According to Cahal, the pub has been in his family for six generations. Nothing is known about his great-great-great-grandfather who, according to the family, ran the pub as a shebeen in the early 19th century. Efforts to learn more about him have been thwarted, not just because the national and county records were destroyed during the War of Independence and the Civil War, but a fire in the local church at the turn of the century also led to parish records being destroyed.

Little is known about the next proprietor also, except that he was named James Slattery, and that his daughter Mary married Anthony Sheridan, a local national school teacher, in 1895.

Mary Sheridan is listed as licensee in the 1901 census, partly because, as a teacher, Anthony Sheridan was barred from running or owning a licensed bar. The 1901 census records Milltown as a village of 13 houses, two of which were pubs. Today, Teach Uí Shioradáin is the only pub in a village of 30 houses or so. The pub and family house were contained in a single-storey thatched cottage until 1920, when it was replaced by a new two-storey building which, though expanded, is in use today with the Sheridan family living above the pub.

Following Mary's death in 1936, the pub passed to her son Charlie Sheridan who ran it until 1970 when it was passed to his son J.J. (James Joseph). It was J.J. who gave the pub its current name, Teach Uí Shioradáin, which, in English, means "Sheridan's House".

Since 1995, the pub has been run by Cathal Sheridan. Inside, it has all the accessories of a modern pub: pool table, jukebox, gaming machines, dart board, Sky Sports television and even Internet access. A large function room has been added to the building, making Teach Uí Shioradáin a centre of community life today.

WALDRON'S
Gerry Waldron, Athleague,
Co. Roscommon

This pub in Athleague, Co. Roscommon, has been in the same family since at least 1877 when the licensee, as listed in Slater's Directory, was James Johnson, a spirit dealer. Notably, the directory also lists a Martin J. Waldron as a spirit dealer and grocer, but that listing refers to a different premises. In fact, the current licensee, Gerry Waldron, can trace his family tree back to two different licensees who were operating in Athleague in the 19th century.

James Johnson's daughter Kate married a Martin Carrick and their daughter Anne, who was born in 1877, the year *Slater's Directory* was published, went on to marry Michael J. Waldron's son Ralph. As a result, at one stage there were two Waldron pubs in Athleague, though the second of these has long since been demolished.

At some stage in its history, probably during James Johnson's tenure, this premises was home to a bakery, as well as a drinks counter. For years there was a 6'×9' fireplace in the bar, but it was removed in 1993 to create more room for drinkers.

Ralph Waldron and his wife Anne ran the pub until 1936 when it was passed to their son, James Joseph Waldron, who reported that during his lifetime he had never seen the bakery in operation.

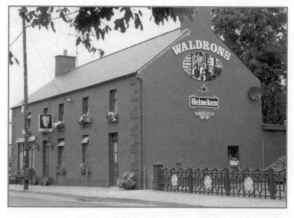

In the same premises as his pub, James ran a drapery business and, until the mid-1960s, you could have a pint there while trying on a new pair of trousers.

James and two of his sons, Tommy and Ralph, were keen hurlers who played for both their local club and the Roscommon county team. Today Waldron's is considered "The GAA pub" in Athleague with plenty of sports photographs and GAA memorabilia decorating the walls.

Local sporting rivalry is fuelled by the fact that although Waldron's is in Roscommon, one part of the parish, on the other side of the River Suck, is in County Galway.

The pub is now run by Gerry Waldron, who has been licensee since 1975, following the retirement of his father James, who died in 1981, and his mother Bridget, who died in 1992.

According to Gerry, the first draught sold in this pub was not Guinness, but Watney's Ale, though it did not remain on sale for long.

Up until the 1970s, Waldron's benefited from extra trade when horse fairs were held in Athleague in July and September. The pub still benefits from the livestock trade with workers from the local Kepak factory drinking here.

The pub was extended in 1982 and refurbished in 1993, when the bakery fireplace was removed, but this remains very much a traditional Irish country pub.

THE WOODFIELD INN

Nuala Rafter, Beltra, Co. Sligo

According to family folklore, the Rafters have been running an inn at Beltra, Co. Sligo, since 1775, but there is little precise information available about the family's history.

The inn originally stood on the seashore and was a "waiting house", where travellers passing along the north of the Ox Mountains would wait for the tide to recede before journeying across the sands of Ballysadare Bay. Indeed, the Beltra's name in Irish, *Béal Trá*, is best translated as "strand entrance".

Over the years the coast has crept further and further away due to land reclamation schemes, so the pub is no longer on the shore. Before the main N59 road was built, all passenger and freight traffic between Sligo and north Mayo would have passed the Rafter's door. Red Hugh O'Donnell passed this way with his troops during the Nine Years War during the 16th century, and 1,100 years before that Ireland's patron saint would have passed along this route going to and from Croagh Patrick.

Today, the layout of the Woodfield Inn is very much the same as it was two centuries ago: it has a small one-room bar with bed-and-breakfast accommodation upstairs. While the pub was refurbished in 1993, the last major change to its structure was in 1959 when the thatched roof was replaced with slate.

This is a busy pub during the summer months, with the bar's customers overflowing into The Woodfield Inn's beer garden.

Today, the bar is run by Carol Rafter, but her mother Nuala, who is 80 years of age, is the current licensee.

Nuala has been licensee since 1996 when her husband Patrick Rafter died; before then, she and her husband ran the pub together for nearly 60 years. Before them, the licensee was Michael Rafter, who died in the late 1930s. Before then, the license was held by Michael's father, Thomas Rafter, who is believed to have held the license in the year 1900.

Family-Owned Pubs of Leinster

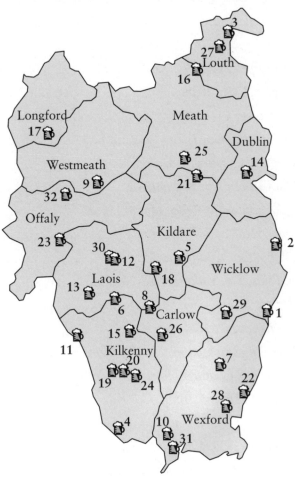

T.J. BIRTHISTLE

Thomas Birthistle, Main Street, Arklow, Co. Wicklow

In the 1860s, 5 Main Street was a saddlery and harness makers run by one Samuel Whitmore until in 1870 it was purchased by George Manifold who ran a grocery and beer retail business from the premises. This was bought in 1881, by Thomas Birthistle who is the first person recorded as holding a licence to sell alcohol from the premises.

In those days, purveyors of alcohol were also required to sell tea — because it was a beverage — and Birthistle's tea ranged in price from one shilling to two shillings a pound in 1891.

A picture of Thomas and members of his family, taken in the 1890s, hangs in the bar today. He was a prominent local politician who in 1887 became a member of the Arklow Town Commission, a forerunner of today's Urban District Council. As a land leaguer, he was instrumental in taking over the administration of Arklow from the control of the Carysfort estate.

His son, also named Thomas, born in 1900, inherited the business, which continued to include a grocery until shortly after the Second World War. One of the main reasons for the grocery's closure was the restrictions imposed on it by rationing.

In 1966, the pub passed to the third generation, though the name Thomas Birthistle is still on the licence. Tommy runs the bar with his wife Josephine; in 1988 they added the "Lazy Lobster Restaurant" to the business.

BYRNE'S IRISH HOUSE
Simon Doyle, Kilcoole, Co. Wicklow

Originally part of the Duke of Leinster's estate, this pub started life as a coachstop-cum-farmhouse in the late 17th century.

The property has been in the possession of the Byrne family since about 1840 when it was bought by a Daniel Byrne of Laragh — the exact date is unknown,

but the deeds of sale described the property as "a farmhouse with licensed shop". Hence, Byrne's began its licensing history not as a pub, but as a licensed grocery, but alcohol would have been served as a matter of course to travellers staying in the coachhouse.

Under Daniel Byrne, the coaching business continued. A certificate recognising it as an official Bianconi coach stop survives and at one stage the building was structurally adapted for the coaching trade. On the front of the building there was a platform where passengers could emerge from coaches without dirtying their feet on the unpaved roads. Passengers then ascended to a first floor entrance via a flight of wooden steps that led to a dining room. To the rear of the building there were also stables where coach horses were kept overnight.

In the 1870s, the pub passed on to Daniel's son James, who was active in the Gaelic League and it is from his time that the pub became known as "the Irish House", as James Byrne was an active promoter of Irish language and culture.

In 1908, the pub passed to James's son Daniel, who ran the pub with his wife Maria (nee McGrainer). When Daniel died in 1928, Maria became licensee, with her daughter Isabella also working behind the bar. When Maria died in 1949, the pub was left jointly her son Patrick and Isabella, who changed her surname to Byrne after she married.

Patrick Doyle never married and, following his death, his share of the business was left to Isabella. She was licensee and sole owner of the pub until 1968, when she left the business to her son, Patrick Byrne.

Even before taking over the licence, Patrick started making improvements to the pub — a new lounge was added in 1967, after Patrick bought the farmhouse next door, Ballelis House. Since then, he has also added a function room and a new lounge to the pub. Though Patrick still takes an interest in the pub and you will find him working behind the counter, the business is now owned by his sons, Simon and Ciarán, with Simon being the licensee.

Patrick remembers the days when he was given the job of bottling up to 300 bottles of Guinness and Smithwicks every week. He says that when draught Guinness was first introduced in the pub, his customers weren't that keen on it. He says the brewery ended the practice of "home-bottling" by publicans through imposing higher hygiene standards. "The first condition was that you had to have flushing water; then they insisted that the bottling area be completely tiled," he says. "In any case, you wouldn't do it today: you had to steep the bottles, wash and dry them, fill the bottles, cork them and then stack them up. Once you had done that you had to sell them within three weeks. I used to bottle two firkins of draught plain stout a time — that is two to three hundred bottles. Today, I haven't got one bottle of stout on my shelves — I don't stock it anymore."

The pub is closely linked to Kilcoole GAA Club, with Patrick being the club's honorary president for the past 20 years.

BYRNE'S

Loretto Byrne, 10 Hill Street, Dundalk, Co. Louth

Built and opened as a licensed grocery store in 1895, Byrne's Public House is a Dundalk landmark.

The pub fits in well with the local landscape too, mainly because most of the surrounding red-bricked houses were built by the pub's founder, James Gosling. No doubt these houses also provided custom for his business venture. James's newly purchased property also included farmlands and dairying, which provided a large part of his annual income.

The pub in Hill Street (named after a former landlord and not the incline leading to the nearby railway bridge) would have been one of the first in Ireland to be established with a licence transfer; according to family folklore, the licence originally applied to a public house in Knockbridge, several miles outside Dundalk.

James died in 1910, leaving behind eight children. Unusually for the time, he chose to leave his entire estate to his daughter, Mary-Anne Gosling. When she married, the pub's name changed to that of her husband's surname. He was Michael Byrne, a GNR engine driver, whose locomotives would regularly have crossed the nearby Dublin–Belfast railway bridge.

Early in the marriage, Michael died and Mary-Anne was left on her own to run the pub and raise two sons, Michael and James. In 1962, Michael inherited the pub, while the farming land went to James. Michael made substantial changes to the bar bearing his father's name: the grocery was closed and a lounge bar installed.

"The lounge really opened up the start of females being in the pub; it was the breaking of new ground in the business," says John Byrne, who runs the pub, though his mother Loretto has been licensee since Michael's death in 1973. Even though she celebrated her 80th birthday in June 2001, she still has a final say in major business decisions.

Having grown up in the pub, John can vividly remember the lounge's original furnishings and can give testimony as to the changing fashions in Irish lounge bar decor. He says: "It was first renovated in 1969. But we made major changes in 1980 when it was extended and we brought in carpeting, velour seating and dark woods. It sounds horrible, but we thought it was luxury. In 1991, we put in a beer garden and brightened the place up. It now has conservatory-style glass, a mixture of stone and wooden flooring and furniture is in light-coloured woods."

Another recent major change is that substantial space is now given to an off-licence, reflecting an increased local trade for wine and, especially during the barbecue season, chilled canned beer. "In the 1960s, the only demand for off-licence sales would have been a Baby Powers," says John who reckons that, if current trends continue, by 2006 the off-licence will account for over half of revenue.

Part of the frontage was remodelled to accommodate the off-licence, but this has been done in a traditional idiom to match the surviving Victorian facade. Inside, the walls are decorated with vintage photographs of local scenes. Pride of place is given to a portrait of Georgie Forty Coats, a famous Dundalk character.

The pub attracts a strong soccer following, not least because John is a director of Dundalk FC.

COMERFORD'S

Seamus Comerford, Main Street, Mooncoin, Co. Kilkenny

A pub that has been in the one family for over 200 years is remarkable enough, but what distinguishes Comerford's of Mooncoin is that one name, James Comerford, has been on the licence for seven generations.

The first of this long line of James Comerfords was born in 1731 and became licensee shortly after he married Frances Cummins in 1778. According to family tradition, the pub was in her family before the marriage, but it is not

known how long there has been an alehouse on the main crossroads in Mooncoin.

As well as having a pub licence, the business included a grocery counter until the end of the 1950s.

The first James Comerford died in 1807 and the pub passed to his son James, born in 1782. After the second James married, two Comerfords ran the pub, as his wife Bridget had the same family name.

In the 1840s, Comerford's became an official stop on the Bianconi coach service running from Waterford to Carrick-on-Suir and Clonmel. As a result, the family were able to replace the original single-story thatched cottage that housed the pub with a new substantial two-storey building. The pub is seven miles from Waterford city and teams of horses were changed here. To the right of the pub today there is an archway which coaches used to reach the pub's stables and courtyard.

In 1849, the licence passed only briefly to the third James Comerford, as he died aged 29 in the same year as his 67-year-old father. Before his death, the third James had fathered four children by his wife Ellen, nee Aylward. Ellen is believed to have been licensee for at least the next 16 years, as the fourth James Comerford to hold the licence was only two years old when his father died.

By the time he died in 1891, James Comerford the fourth had nine children with his wife Johanna Rowe. It was during his lifetime that the Comerfords began to be identified with nationalist politics, something which may have resulted in harassment from the local police. Politics aside, it didn't help that the pub was less than 100 yards from the police barracks and on several occasions the Comerfords were prosecuted for trading outside licensed hours. In the 1880s, James Comerford was charged with trading on Christmas Day, a day when pubs are closed all day by law. Constables heard noises from within the pub, but were refused entry into the premises — the refusal in itself was a licensing offence. In court, under oath, the accused admitted that the constables heard activity in the bar, but that this was no more than the family "making Christmas puddings". The judge accepted the explanation and the case was dismissed.

The fifth James Comerford was born in 1870 and had six children with his wife Margaret Power. He was the first treasurer of the Mooncoin GAA club and the pub has had close links with the hurling club ever since. Indeed, the pub sits halfway between the GAA grounds and the police barracks.

At the end of the 18th century, the Comerfords also became coal importers, taking advantage of Mooncoin's location on the banks of the River Suir.

In 1946, following his father's death, the pub passed to James Comerford the sixth, who was born in 1900 and had three children by his wife Catherine O'Shea before his death in 1955.

The current licensee is the seventh James Comerford to own and run the business, although normally he is known as Séamus, the Irish version of the name. Born in 1944, Séamus reckons he may be last in the line of James Comerfords to be pub licensees. His son James, who was born in 1970, has worked behind the bar in the past, but he currently works as an accountant in Boston, Massachusetts.

With regret, Séamus and his wife, Rene Kinsella, understand why none of their four children wishes to continue in the family business. "There are easier ways of making money — we work between 80 and 100 hours a week, including every weekend, as they are your busiest periods," says Séamus. "There was a time when it gave you a half-decent living, but there are better opportunities now. Throughout the generations, the Comerfords have known good times and bad times; they always looked as though they were prospering."

Seamus reckons there are some 30 pubs in Carrick-on-Suir and only one of them has been in the same family for two generations; of the 80 or so pubs in Waterford City, he reckons that only about five of them would have remained in the one family since the 1950s.

As well as sitting on an important local crossroads, Comerford's has benefited from its location opposite the Catholic parish church. "We get business if there are christenings, first communions, confirmations and especially marriages, as they have a drink here before moving on to the hotel reception. Of course, funerals are very big drinking events — the saying here is that you 'bury him decent' by having a few drinks.

"If I was buying a pub in rural Ireland, the first thing I would look for is whether it's attached to a church. Sunday would be my busiest day of the week, because there is business throughout the day here on a Sunday."

Another peculiarity of the local trade is that, among the older generation, bottled beer is preferred to draught, with about 850 pint bottles sold every week. Many of the long-standing customers start their night out with a call for "a half and a bottle", i.e. a measure of whiskey and a bottle of Guinness.

Séamus says he remembers a time when Strangman's Black Jack Ale, brewed locally in Waterford, was the local favourite in the 1950s. He also remembers seeing corpses laid out in the pub's storeroom during the time when the pub was regularly used for post-mortem inspections, which usually involved victims of accidental drownings in the River Suir.

After the law was changed in 1962, post-mortems in pubs became extremely rare, something that coincided with another development in the licensed trade: the arrival of a female market. "Women would not be seen in this pub at all when I was a boy in the 1950s," says Séamus. "We had what we called a tap-room and some of the more adventurous ladies — 'shawlies' — they would come in there for their beer."

The pub has been extensively refurbished, renovated and extended since the grocery counter was closed in the 1950s. Besides a pitch pine ceiling above the bar and some grocery shelving, nothing of the original 18th century interior survives.

Central heating provides the warmth today; in Séamus's youth the bar was heated using cast-iron stoves. He remembers: "When you switched out the lights in the pub, the stoves were so hot that they would glow red in the dark. Old men would spit on them and it would make a sizzling sound."

O. CONNOR
Pat O'Connor, Ballitore,
Athy, Co Kildare

This pub in Ballitore is owned by the O'Connor family, but there is no apostrophe in the name above the door. This is because the pub was founded by "a staunch nationalist", Owen Connor, who added the "O" prefix to his children's surname.

Owen served his apprenticeship in the drinks trade in Athy and then served as an "improver" in Dublin before becoming a fully qualified barman.

Sometime about 1870, he set up business in Ballitore, buying the building occupied by the pub from an Owen Finn who is recorded in Mary Leadbetter's book, *The Annals of Ballitore*, as "a respectable shopkeeper" who sold hardware and drugs. Like many in Ballitore, Owen Finn was a Quaker who would not have sold alcohol for general consumption.

Members of the Society of Friends came to Ballitore in the 17th century after fleeing persecution in England. Today, the old Quaker preaching house is a museum and Mary Leadbetter's house is home to a library.

Indeed, O. Connor's Pub was once home to a famous Quaker school founded in 1726 by Abraham Shackleton, grandfather of Mary Leadbetter. Among the distinguished pupils who studied at the school were Edmund Burke, James Napper Tandy and Ireland's first cardinal, Archbishop Paul Cullen. Both Abraham Shackleton and his father were born in the premises now occupied by the pub.

At the time Owen bought the business, it was a well-known hardware store, but he had no interest in that business. He secured a licence and was very successful in the alcohol trade — so much so that he was the only member of his family not to be left anything in his father's last testament. According to William Connor's will, dated 22 November 1876, "my son Owen Connor, being settled in Ballitore, does not want any".

As well as running a pub, Owen took a great interest in politics and represented Ballitore on the Baltinglass No. 3 District Council until that body was dissolved in 1918. He played a major role in making Baltinglass the first district council in Ireland to introduce compulsory education and was successful in having many labourer's cottages erected in and around Ballitore. In the 19th century, Ballitore was an important commercial town with a large tannery employing many people and providing drinking customers for O. Connor's Bar.

By the time of Owen's death in 1931, his son Joseph O'Connor had been running the business for nearly a decade. Joseph's mother Kate Connor was a schoolteacher, who by the rules of her profession was banned from living in the pub. As a result, she lived in the town's schoolhouse and it is here that Joseph was born.

As well as being a publican, Joseph was a qualified carpenter and also worked as a part-time rate collector. He used his carpentry skills to refurbish and extend the pub; both the pub's mahogany interior and its shopfront were installed by him in 1927, with the wooden panelling being bought second-hand from a pub in Lucan that had gone out of business.

The current licensee, Pat O'Connor, became licensee following Joseph's death in 1955, though Pat, who is now aged 74, has worked all his life in the pub. In 1982, he extended the premises by converting the family kitchen and sitting-room into a lounge area.

He says: "The biggest change in my time has been the arrival of women in the pub. When I was 16, there were only two old women who would drink in the bar. They would sit behind the door and whenever anyone came in they would hide their bottles of porter beneath their aprons!"

Pat and his wife Sally still work behind the bar, but most of the work is carried out by their sons Joseph and Brian.

In recent years, the main pub game played here is darts, but there are still many customers who play rings here, with one customer, Pat Shaughnessy, being a former all-Ireland rings champion.

DRURY

Michael Drury, Church Street, Ballinakill, Co. Laois

After being evicted from the Valleymount House estate in 1790, tenant farmer John Lawlor turned licensed grocer, trading from a small thatched cottage on a plot of land in Ballinakill.

At the time, Ballinakill was an industrial town, its main source of income coming from iron ore mining. The town was established in 1640 and by the end of the 18th century was the second largest town in County Laois with a population of 8,000 in its heyday. Today there is little industry in the area and Balli-nakill's population is about 400 people.

The new pub had to be an extremely orderly house from the day it was established in 1790, as the local sheriff lived next door. When the sheriff's house was sold, the pub still had to follow the straight and narrow, as next-door became the parochial house of Ballinakill's parish priest.

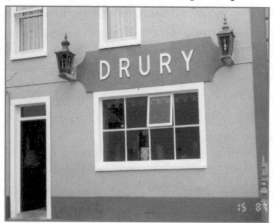

Following John Lawlor's death in 1823, the pub passed to his son Denis "Dinny" Lawlor, who was licensee for the next 60 years, finally handing it on to his daughter Mary and her husband John Drury on their wedding day in 1883. They followed the family custom of passing on the license to their son when he married, with James Drury becoming licensee when he married Mary Bergin in 1927.

When the new couple took over the business, James added a butcher's stall to the family business, which already comprised a pub, grocery and a drapery. The butchering trade ceased in the 1950s, with the grocery and drapery business going when a new lounge was built in 1968.

James and Mary ran the pub together for 50 years until their son Michael Drury becoming licensee in 1977.

Michael remembers a time when the pub sold Guinness only in bottles, with Smithwicks and Perry being the two beers on draught. Michael describes Perry's as "a good strong beer, much darker and stronger than Smithwick's, and tasting a bit like McArdles". He also says that before his father's time, there was a brewery at the back of the pub producing Dempsey's Ale, another draught beer long gone. Some of the old brewery outbuildings and stables still stand at the back of the pub.

Michael is extremely proud of his licensing heritage and the fact that, apart from the lounge, all of the bar's décor is original, with much of it dating back to the time of his great-great-grandfather. He says: "In this part of the country, we still bring down our shutters whenever a funeral is passing. It's something that has always been done and which we continue."

In more recent years, Drury's has become a soccer club and currently sponsors the strip of Timahoe, the local FAI first division team.

DUNBAR'S
Tom Dunbar, Ferns, Co. Wexford

Many people visit Ferns to view its walls, as the Wexford village is considered to have some of the best-preserved medieval fortifications in Ireland. Drinkers at Dunbar's in Ferns can't help but be impressed by the walls either: they are four foot thick. According to local legend, the walls of the pub are made from stone that was originally used by the Normans to build Ferns castle. Dunbar's is one of the oldest buildings in Ferns today.

It has been in the one family since at least 1871, when Martin Dunbar, a member of a prosperous Wexford farming family, bought it. According to family folklore, before Martin bought the property, it belonged to two of his cousins. At the time of  the purchase, Martin also owned several houses in Ferns and was owner of The Angler's Rest, a pub in the nearby town of Bunclody.

It is believed that alcohol was on sale at the store when Martin took possession of it, but it is not known when the business first became licensed. During the last decades of the 19th century, the business prospered, helped by being an official coach stop on the Bianconi service between Dublin and Wexford.

Although Martin sold the pub in Bunclody at the turn of the century, he remained licensee of Dunbar's in Ferns until his death 1915, when his eldest son Tom took over.

Tom was to see a man shot dead in the pub, during the War of Independence, after a customer refused to drink with a Black and Tan. Even more disconcerting, the victim, a local baker, was also named Tom Dunbar. He was shot twice inside the pub, taken outside and shot once again while he lay in the street. The British officer was never brought to justice, says the current licensee, who is also named Tom Dunbar, in memory of both his grandfather and the man who was murdered.

By the time the pub passed to the third generation in the family, the business was in decline. Tom, the current licensee, remembers the difficulties his father Martin suffered as he tried to keep the business afloat during the 1940s. Tom says: "They were tough times, when we only just about survived." At the end of the decade, Martin decided that the grocery business was no longer profitable and turned the whole premises over to the licensed trade. In the early 1950s, Martin bought the first television and installed it in the bar.

"This was in the days before RTE, so it was just BBC," recalls Tom, who as a boy remembers the TV set being placed in "the annexe" next to the bar. "There wasn't much on in those days, but I do remember all the kids in the village coming round to the house to watch *The Lone Ranger*. I say 'watch', but the reception was so bad that it was like staring at snow!"

Until the 1970s, Tom says it was an extremely rare sight to see a woman drinking in the bar. "They weren't banned from drinking in the bar," he says. "It was just the social convention in those days. Women were allowed into the snug and the kitchen — but, until the 1970s, that was it; that's when a lot of things changed."

Tom's father Martin died in 1972 and he started helping his mother, Rosaleen, behind the bar soon after. Thanks to Tom's previous exploits on the local soccer and rugby clubs, the pub now has a strong sports following. Despite his involvement in "garrison games", Tom is fonder of Gaelic games than anything else. You will find purple and gold flags decorating the pub exterior any time there is a major Wexford hurling or football match taking place.

THE GLENSIDE
Brendan Fitzpatrick, Killeshin,
Co. Carlow

Rather unfortunately, the centenary celebrations of the Glenside pub in Killeshin in 1996 did not pass unnoticed: the police were called and the current licensee ended up in court.

The court case was reported in *The Carlow Nationalist* under the heading "Celebrating Pub's 100", recording the fact that the police raided the premises at 5.25 in the morning to find the pub crowded and a birthday party in full swing.

"I wonder if the patrons of 100 years ago had the same stamina as the patrons in question today," asked Mr Justice Terence Finn when licensee Brendan Fitzpatrick was summoned before him. Then, rather kindly, in honour of the anniversary, the judge told the publican: "And I wonder if you could give an undertaking that such an occurrence will not happen for another 100 years." After the undertaking was solemnly given, Brendan was fined a modest £50, but he is still unable to testify to the staying power of the Glenside's customers at the time when it was bought, in 1896, by his grandfather, Michael Fitzpatrick, from a local family called Shortell.

Located on a busy road between Carlow town and the mines of the Leinster coalfield, the Glenside became a popular stopping point for carters, known at the time as "car-men", who bought coal from the mines for sale in Carlow and beyond. At one stage, there were over a dozen working coalmines in the county, but the last mine closed in the 1970s. With the mines went the car-men. They had been a constant feature inside and outside the Glenside, as their horse-drawn drays would be parked outside the thatched pub.

During the War of Independence, the Glenside's ambience could best be described as "tense". Most of the pub's locals were Republican sympathisers and many were members of the IRA, but the Glenside also served the soldiers and police stationed at the barracks nearby.

"We were lucky to have come through the early 1920s without the thatch on the roof being set alight," says Brendan. "My grandfather never knew who might be drinking in the bar. There might be a Republican sitting at the counter having a drink and an hour later there would be a Black and Tan sitting in the same place. And the Black and Tans were never shy of burning anyone out."

Following Michael's death in 1940, the pub passed to his son Patrick, who held the license for the next 35 years.

During the 1939–45 Emergency, the business had to deal with food shortages and rationing. Apparently, the biggest headache was the rationing of cigarettes, which, Patrick used to say, caused conflict among customers every bit as bitter as the war in Europe!

"When a publican got a new carton of cigarettes, my father said, it was both a blessing and a curse," says Brendan. "A blessing because in their scarcity it was great to get them, but a curse because they were so scarce that people would almost kill for a cigarette and there would be terrible trouble in the bar."

When Brendan took on the license in 1975, he had already been working in the pub full-time for six years and also had 10 years' experience working in pubs in Ballyfermot and Dún Laoghaire. By 1969, the thatch roof was gone and a new lounge added. During the 1970s, the Glenside was on the showband circuit and the lounge was extended twice in that decade to accommodate the growing numbers of dance fans. At one stage, the Glenside was one of the biggest licensed music venues in Co. Carlow, but now it hosts live music only sporadically and the pub, though big, has been dwarfed by the arrival of "superpubs" in Carlow town in the 1990s.

While the pub has been renovated extensively, there are some relics on display from the "old days". Among the exhibits is an 18th century musket with retractable bayonet that was found hidden in the thatch when the pub's roof was replaced in the late 1960s.

Brendan's 18-year-old son Patrick Fitzpatrick is already working behind the bar and it is planned that he will eventually become the fourth generation in the family to be licensee of the Glenside.

GONOUD'S
Jody Gonoud, Tyrellspass, Co. Westmeath

Tyrellspass in Westmeath has long been a place where travellers between Dublin and Galway break their journey. It is a pretty town containing a good mixture of formal Georgian buildings and vernacular buildings from the 18th century, among them Gonoud's Bar, which has been trading for at least 250 years.

The pub has been in the one family since about 1900 when John Gonoud became licensee. He had owned a grocery across the road, but moved over to the other side of the street when he married a widow woman by the name of Mrs Monaghan.

John had the reputation of being a character. He was never seen without a bowler hat on his head and it was rumoured that he even wore it in bed. During his time, the business included a grocery, millinery, a drapery and an undertaking business. Grocery items were delivered by horse and cart to the surrounding area, with payment usually made with eggs, hens and rabbits, which John sold on to dealers in Dublin.

Near Tyrellspass is Belvedere House, which is now open to the public. In John Gonoud's time it was an orphanage run by Lady Belvedere. At the turn of the century, the Honourable Sybil Atkinson wrote: "During the last 12 months, I visited the orphanage and with Lt. Boyd Rochford went into the question of new serge for the children's dresses. We thought that we might have been able

to get material equally good at a cheaper rate than what the matron was paying, however on getting patterns from different houses in Dublin we found that any serge less than 10/= to 12/= per yard was inferior to what the matron was ordering through Gonoud locally."

During this time, Tyrellspass hosted regular fair days and many a pig or a calf ended up being sold inside Gonoud's bar. The pub also benefited from the fact that it was a recognised bus-stop on the Dublin to Galway route and a sign for Ireland's first ever public bus service, the IOC — Irish Omnibus Company — still hangs on the pub wall.

When John Gonoud died in 1943, the business passed to his son Joe, who was born in 1900 and had been working behind the bar for several years. Joe had helped his father to develop the travelling grocery with the purchase of a lorry from the local bottling company, P&H Egan.

This lorry carried more than groceries in its time. It gave James Daly a lift to Mullingar station the day he joined the British Army; later, the lance corporal would be executed by firing squad in India for his part in the Connaught Rangers' mutiny in 1916. The lorry also carried home the bodies of two young republicans, Patrick Geraghty and Joseph Byrne, who were executed by firing squad in Portlaoise prison in January 1923.

Joe was licensee until his death in 1972 when the pub passed to his son Jody, who runs the pub today with his wife Caroline and his children Tracey, Gordon and Trevor John.

Jody is very proud of his licensing heritage and has many stories to tell about the pub. For instance, he says: "As news about President Kennedy's assassination was announced in the bar, the local sergeant entered and took the names of everyone present to charge them with drinking after hours.

"For many years, on the two days prior to Ash Wednesday, the then King of the Tinkers, Davy Joyce, would ask that he and his clan be served, guaranteeing that there would be no trouble from anyone. There never was and after the two days' drinking, the whole clan would give up the drink for Lent."

A distinguished visitor was Mel Gibson, who made Gonoud's his regular when taking a break from filming the movie *Braveheart*.

Today, this is a pub with strong GAA links. When Tyrellspass won the county championships for the first time in 1999, their jerseys were sponsored by Gonoud's and while Westmeath has never won an all-Ireland, the pub has hosted both Sam and the McCarthy Cup, which were brought to the pub by the Offaly team.

HART BROS.

Declan Hart, Campile, New Ross, Co. Wexford

Hart Bros. is one of two pubs listed in this book where a family has not actually held the pub's licence *continuously* for over 100 years.

The pub was bought in 1884 by Matthew Hart, who was originally from Kilcock, Co. Kildare. A long-serving RIC officer, he was stationed nearby at Ballybrazil Barracks when he bought the pub from local landlord Robert Barron. Aged 49, Matthew was taking early retirement from the force, as by law RIC officers were prohibited from owning licensed premises.

It was after Matthew died that the pub and the premises left the family's hands. On the old man's death in 1896, the pub went almost automatically to Matthew Jnr, the eldest son in a family of three boys and five girls. But Matthew died without children and his widow re-married, changing her surname and the licence's name to "Henehan". However, she was widowed a second time, again without children.

It was about this time, in the 1930s, that Hart Bros. became a temporary Garda barracks, with police business being conducted in the same premises as the bar for over six years until a permanent Garda barracks could be built.

In 1941, one of Matthew Snr's other two sons, Joe Hart, decided to buy the pub and grocery back into the family. "Mrs Henehan's brother-in-law, my grandfather Joe, bought the premises off her for about £2,000 in 1941," says Declan Hart, great-grandson of the pub's founder.

Declan adds: "Joe never ran the pub, he was a farmer. But he put his son, Joe Hart Jnr in it. My father was the licensee until it passed on to my brother Joe in 1987 and the two of us run the pub together."

While "the structure" of the original building remains the same, today petrol pumps stand outside Hart Bros. and the grocery counter has been moved to separate premises next door. It is not surprising that the family pub is supported by income from the grocery and petrol sales as the pub is one of three licensed premises in Campile, a parish of barely 2,000 people!

HAYES

Richard Hayes, Main Street,
Urlingford, Co. Kilkenny

The history of Hayes pub, and modern day Urlingford, can be traced back to the 1750s and the building of a new coach road between Dublin and Cork.

The town was an early monastic settlement, but Urlingford took on a new importance in the Georgian era when the new coach road was built. Indeed, the town's modern-day Main Street grew out of the navvies' tented village, with road labourers building the pub, which has been in the possession of the Hayes family for over 100 years. The canvas village, on the outskirts of the original town, became the main focus for business in the area because the road-building scheme was substantially delayed by Fennor Hill, a granite obstacle outside Urlingford, which required months of chiselling and blasting before a route could be cut through it.

Halfway between the Republic of Ireland's two largest cities, coach travellers would over-night here and this pub was an official stop on the Bianconi coach route. Even today, Urlingford is an important middle-point for motorised transport, with Bus Eireann drivers swapping coaches here so they do not have to travel the whole distance between Dublin and Cork.

The name Hayes appeared above the door in 1851, when Richard Hayes married into the family. As well as being a supplier of alcohol, the business was a general providers that included a grocery, drapery and an undertakers. Urlingford at that time was an important commercial centre in north Carlow with its own linen starching mill, a woollen mill and a distillery.

Richard Hayes' first wife and child died while she was in labour and it wasn't until his third marriage that he had a son and heir, the first of seven children, who was also named Richard. The second Richard Hayes lived until 1932 with his wife Mary, nee Maher, running the business until 1954, when it was taken over by their son Jimmy and his wife Mary, nee Brennan. Mary ran the business in Urlingford, while Jimmy managed a butcher's shop in Mullinahone. Following Jimmy's death in 1979, the business was run by Mary until 1983, when the couple's son Richard took over.

Inside the pub today, you will find mirrors advertising Ross's Royal Ginger Ale — a Northern Irish brand from the turn of the century which is no longer in production. Hayes claims to be the first pub in Urlingford to supply Guinness on draught in the early 1960s — before then, like most other pubs in the town, the only drink on tap was Smithwick's, brewed nearby in Kilkenny. Indeed, during the 1950s, Hayes was selling 14 firkins (126 gallons) of Smithwick's a week and hardly any Guinness. According to family lore, when, after much persuasion, Jimmy first agreed with Guinness to supply draught stout, he was only managing to sell two pints of the stuff a week and it took more than 18 months for Ireland's favourite pint to gain general acceptance among Urlingford's drinkers.

Other drinks that were supplied here once included Perry's Ale, which was brewed in Rathdowney, and Dunphy's Whiskey, another brand that has disappeared.

Situated on the Kilkenny/Tipperary border, Urlingford is a place of great hurling rivalry. After any match played between the two counties, Urlingford is a great place to watch coat trailing and flag waving as GAA fans drive through the town with their car horns blaring.

Ironically, given that Hayes pub and Urlingford town can trace their roots back to a road-building scheme, the town now faces a new challenge as it is bypassed by the Dublin to Cork motorway.

HUME'S

Noel Hume, 106 Main Street, Portlaoise, Co. Laois

Originally a delph, china and bric-a-brac shop when it came on the market in 1862, Hume's became a public house thanks to the efforts of the parish priest of Stradbally, Co. Laois, Fr George Hume, the great-great-grand-uncle of the present owner, Noel Hume. Fr Hume had sufficient clout locally to ensure that his brother Robert, who had bought the premises, obtained a licence to sell intoxicating liquor.

Robert married Winifred Creamer of Ballyroan, Co. Laois, a young widow of a tenant farmer. According to Hume family history, on the same day that Winifred received a receipt for rent due, she was also given notice to quit her farm. For six years, Robert and Winifred built up a thriving business and had five children, until one day Robert died suddenly outside the pub. Winifred continued to run the business and raise her young family, opening up the shop and bar. As well as normal trade, twice a month on fair days she would open up for business at seven o'clock in the morning.

Following Winifred's death in the early 1900s, the pub passed to her son Arthur. By this time, Hume's was also a general goods store. By the 1940s, Winifred's grandson, who was also named Arthur, was licensee. He regularly spoke of "the hard times" between 1940 and 1960s, when farmers brought unpackaged "country butter" and eggs to the shop where pig meal, chicken feed and other foodstuffs were sold.

Following Arthur's death, the licence passed to his wife Maureen, who was licensee until 1976. Maureen, aged 93, still comes down to the bar on her birthdays and other special occasions, but her son, Noel Hume, is now running the business.

Noel, the fourth generation involved in the pub, has been a publican for over 40 years and says he owes an extreme debt of gratitude to his wife Rosaleen who is "a publican, diplomat, cook, psychiatrist and mother".

HYLAND'S
Sean Hyland, Ballacolla, Co. Laois

The history of this pub can be traced to the 1880s, when the licensee was a Mary Whelan, who was born in the 1860s and is believed to have started a bar in her farmhouse kitchen sometime in the 1880s. However, her great-grandson Sean Hyland, who is the current licensee, believes that her family may

have had a license before then as there is no record of any other licensed premises in the district.

An illegal drinking den did operate in Clough in competition to Hyland's during the 1930s, however, with a local woman, known as Mag Bob, serving drink in her kitchen without approval from the law. Following Mag Bob's death, her house was demolished to allow the local cemetery to be extended — one consequence of this was that, for many years afterwards, abstemious local citizens refused to have their relatives' remains buried in the part of the cemetery once occupied by the illegal shebeen!

Mary's daughter Margaret, who was born in 1894, started helping her mother behind the bar at an early age, but she moved away from the family home when she married a Nicholas Hyland in 1913. Nicholas was considerably older than his 19-year-old bride and did not enjoy good health, so in 1933 the couple returned to the Whelan family home. Nicholas died shortly afterwards, leaving Margaret to rear their nine children on her own, while she helped her mother in the bar.

When Margaret's eldest daughter, Mary Hyland, reached the age of 14, she joined her mother and grandmother in working behind the bar, going on to serve drinks for the next 69 years. Both Mary and Margaret Hyland were long-lived, with Margaret living to her 94th year and Mary living to 83.

Indeed, as well as caring for Margaret in her old age, Mary ran the pub single-handedly until she reached her 80s, when she asked her nephew, Sean Hyland, to help her in the bar. At Mary's funeral in 1996, most of the hundreds of mourners were male. Sean reckons that 99 per cent of Mary's customers were men as she did not approve of women drinking and it wasn't until her later years that she would serve "unaccompanied women". A few years before her death, when two women walked in and ordered pints, her reaction was "What is the world coming to?".

During the post-war era, the two most popular drinks served in the pub were Perry's Ale and Jameson whiskey. Indeed, the pub won an award from Perry's for selling more of their ale than any other pub in the country and, according to legend, Hyland's sold more Perry's ale than all the pubs in Rathdowney, home of the Perry's brewery.

When Perry's ceased trading in 1996, Guinness became the main house beer, with Mary using a system of transferring the stout from one glass to another to produce what was considered to be the best pint in Co. Laois.

During the era of the bona fide traveller legislation that allowed those who travelled more than three miles to drink out of hours, a local man, Dan Guilders of Kyledellig, escaped prosecution for "posing as a traveller" in a notable court case. Guard Frank McMahon found that the kitchen of Dan's house was barely less than three miles away from Hyland's pub and therefore he was not legally entitled to drink in Hyland's outside licensed opening hours. However, Dan insisted that the legal measurement was the distance from where a person had spent the previous night — when a measurement was taken from the pub to Dan's bedroom, the distance was found to be three miles and one yard! According to local legend, following the ruling, another local man, Paddy Kirwan of Kilbreedy, started sleeping in another bedroom of his house so that he could drink in Hyland's out of hours.

Sean Hyland has been licensee since the death of his aunt and he runs the pub today with his wife Marian. They have demolished the old premises and replaced it with a more substantial pub. Next door to the bar, the couple also run a bed-and-breakfast known as The Foxrock Inn.

"Hyland's has served the area well, since its beginning well back in the last century," says Sean. "The family has had good times and bad, but has always conducted its business in a proper and proficient manner."

JOHN KAVANAGH'S
Eugene Kavanagh, Prospect Square, Glasnevin, Dublin 9

This pub is one of Dublin's hidden gems, located on a quiet square by a now little-used gate into Glasnevin cemetery.

The pub's first licensee was John O'Neill, who was owner of the Prince of Wales Hotel on the North Wall and who originally used the premises on Prospect Square as his family residency.

However, he converted part of his home into a pub in 1833, a year after Glasnevin cemetery opened its gates to receive the dead for the first time. Daniel O'Connell is said to have played a major role in securing the pub's good fortunes in its earliest years, because he campaigned for a new road to what was then the cemetery's main gates, so that funeral processions would not have to pass via a tollgate. The pub returned the favour by mainly stocking O'Connell's Ale.

John O'Neill was licensee for almost a year when he handed over the business to his son-in-law John Kavanagh in 1835 after he had married Suzanne O'Neill.

Remarkably, John and Suzanne had 25 children. Three of their sons served in the Union Army in the American Civil War, with all three being mentioned in despatches for bravery after the Battle of Gettysburg. In 1867, one of the three war heroes, Joseph Kavanagh, briefly returned to Ireland, but was forced to return to America, where he spent another 10 years, after being targeted by Dublin Castle as a Fenian activist.

When Joseph returned again in 1877, he was no longer regarded as suspect and was free to become the pub's new licensee. Shortly after he took over, the business suffered a loss in trade when the original cemetery gates were closed and new gates were opened on the Finglas Road. Ever after, the main funeral business went to Hedigan's on Prospect Road, a pub that features in James Joyce's *Ulysses* and which has been in the same family since 1904. In a bid to attract customers, Joseph added a shooting range and a skittle alley to the premises, but these were not long-term successes.

In 1907, the licence passed to Joseph's son John H. Kavanagh, but he died at a relatively young age in 1920 and the licence passed on to his wife Josie. During her tenure, the bar was known by locals as either "Josie's" or "The Widdow's", two nicknames that remained current until the 1950s.

In 1943, the licence passed to Josie's son John M. Kavanagh, who ran the business with his brother Fintan. During the 19th and 20th centuries, the pub included a grocery counter, which remained in operation until the 1950s. Today, behind the bar you can still see the drawers where tea, snuff, tobacco and spices were stored.

The current licensee is Eugene Kavanagh, a stepson and nephew of John M. Kavanagh. Eugene was eight years old when his father, Michael Kavanagh, died and he spent two and a half years in an orphanage until his mother, Ellen (Nellie) Edgeworth, married her dead husband's brother.

During the 1950s and the 1960s, the pub suffered trading difficulties, because of the general economic situation in Ireland and the pub's out of the way location. "We were not the only pub to suffer," says Eugene. "One of the reasons that there are so few old family pubs in Dublin is that a lot of publicans could no longer afford to pay their staff. Running a pub became too much hard work."

As John M. Kavanagh grew older, the workload started to become too much for him and the pub's opening hours were reduced to evenings only. His sons took their turns helping him when the bar was open, but they were limited in the assistance they could give because each of them had their own full-time jobs. In 1973, Eugene quit his job in Guinness's and bought the pub from his family to try and make a go it himself.

"Luckily, my father's lack of business enthusiasm meant that the pub wasn't gutted during the formica and plastic era in the 1960s," he says. "It is still a lovely old pub in its original condition." While the grocery counter is gone, most of the interior décor is original, including the bar counter and a partition that once separated the drinking area from the grocery.

Gradually, the pub began to be rediscovered and as the local economy improved so did business, with Eugene adding a lounge, which is twice the size of the bar, in 1980.

Today, the pub is known widely as "The Gravediggers", a nickname that Eugene says was coined by workers at the newly built Glasnevin Industrial Estate in the 1970s. "Lately, semi-yuppies have taken to calling it 'The Diggers'," he adds. "I have never used either of these names to promote the pub. Indeed, I have never promoted the pub; my policy is to serve quality drink at a reasonable price and hope that word-of-mouth will bring more customers here.

"If the pub was used by gravediggers, there are not many of them about now. When the cemetery first opened, it had nine acres and 60 gravediggers; today it is 79 acres and a dozen gravediggers with a JCB. We now get customers from all over; at the weekend, over 50 per cent of our customers are women."

Looking to the future, Eugene hopes that one of his six children will take the licence on after him. He says: "If it doesn't stay in the family, it will never be sold. I will set up a trust to run this pub, if I have to. I can understand why my sons and daughters wouldn't want to take it on, as the work is hard and long. My main aim every night is to get to bed before daybreak, but you cannot sell heritage."

LARKIN'S
Kathleen Larkin, Cainsbridge, Coolcullen, Co. Kilkenny

The reputation of Larkin's of Coolcullen extends far beyond Co. Kilkenny's borders: this is a pub where the older crowd step it out on the dance floor.

The pub has been in the Larkin family since at least 1895, when the building was bought by James Larkin, great-grandfather-in-law of the current licensee Kathleen Larkin. It is believed James had occupied the building and had run a pub there before he purchased the premises.

The pub then passed to James's son Michael. It passed from Michael to his wife Margaret Larkin, then to the couple's son James and from him to his son John Larkin, who died in 2001.

Shortly after John and Kathleen married in 1963, Smithwick's became the "local brew", mainly because John worked at Smithwick's brewery while Kathleen ran the pub. "We pushed Smithwick's quite a bit," says Kathleen, "as you have to look after your own."

Today, you still won't find "designer beers" behind the bar. "The big sellers are still Smithwick's and Guinness," says Kathleen. "Other beers would just sit there and go off."

Another part of John's legacy is the large extension that was added to the pub in 1979 and which has been hosting showband and country and western dance nights ever since. The lounge's dance floor can accommodate more than 200 people and the dancers are usually members of "the older generation". In a reversal of the normal situation, you find the younger crowd in the bar while their seniors are in the lounge.

"This is not just a pub," says Kathleen, who has been licensee since John's death. "It's a meeting place where people from all over and all ages meet. They come to the dances from Carlow, Kilkenny and Kildare. I couldn't count the number of marriages that have been made in here and I'd hope to see at least one more — my own son who is now 31 and works behind the bar!"

MULDOON'S
Fergus Muldoon, Drumconrath,
Co. Meath

This pub in Drumconrath has been in the Muldoon family since 1898 when it was bought by Paddy Sharkey, an adventurous entrepreneur.

In 1885, at the age of 14, Paddy stowed away aboard a ship that was heading for the United States via Liverpool, but he was discovered as the vessel crossed the Irish Sea and put ashore in Merseyside. In Liverpool, Paddy became an apprentice barman in a pub in Great Howard Street and was promoted to bar manager very shortly after he served his time.

In the mid-1890s, he returned to Ireland and bought a pub in Dromin, near Dunleer, the first of four licensed premises that he would own. He also bought a pub in Hunterstown, near Ardee, before purchasing this premises in Drumconrath in 1898. Later, he would sell his pub in Dromin and use the proceeds to buy the Blackrock Hotel in Blackrock, Co. Louth. The beers sold in these pubs were local brews, notably McArdles draught stout and ales produced by the Castlebellingham brewery and Cairns of Dundalk.

Previously, the pub in Drumconrath had belonged to the Halpenny family, some of whose descendents still live in the locality. While the business was chiefly a pub and grocery, until the 1940s the business was classed as a "commercial hotel", because it provided stabling and accommodation for travellers when Drumconrath was on the stagecoach route between Derry and Dublin.

As he prospered, Paddy Sharkey needed to hire staff to run his various businesses and so it was that Tom Muldoon became manager of the Drumconrath pub in 1916. When Tom married his boss's daughter, Annie Sharkey, in 1920, Annie became licensee and the Muldoon family name has been above the door ever since.

Shortly after their marriage, Tom and Annie set up a ballroom above the pub which accommodated up to 120 dancers, with music usually supplied by Tom on the violin and Annie on the piano. "There are still people who come into the pub and say that their parents or grandparents first met in our ballroom," says the couple's son Fergus Muldoon, who has been licensee since 1974.

The pub was next-door to an RIC barracks and Fergus claims that relations with the police were always good, with the exception of the Black and Tan period. "One night, the Tans woke my father up and told him they wanted food for 70 people and he said he would not be able to provide food at that late hour," says Fergus. "So the Tans set up a machinegun on the road opposite the pub and asked him if that changed his mind and my father said it did. Food was supplied, but it wasn't of the best quality. Ever since that incident at gunpoint, we have been a republican family."

During the War of Independence, the RIC barracks was attacked several times by republicans. On one occasion, the barracks was set alight, threatening the safety of the pub next-door. Villagers rushed to put the fire out, with most of them forming a human chain to throw water on the fire. However, Fergus says: "One of the pub's employees didn't join the fire chain, he was working on his own, throwing buckets on the fire — later, it was learned that it was paraffin, not water, that he had in his bucket!"

The Second World War was one of the most lucrative periods in the history of the pub and Drumconrath, as local employment was boosted hugely by turf-cutting operations to provide fuel for the Irish army during the Emergency. During this period, as well as a pub and grocery, Muldoon's also had petrol pumps, an animal feed mill and an undertaking business.

In common with many other pubs, Muldoon's suffered trading difficulties in the post-war economic slump of the 1950s, but Fergus says his parents rarely had a customer who failed to clear their weekly or monthly accounts. He says: "I don't want to name names, but I know a family of seven sisters, who had 80 children between them, and I can say that each of them cleared their accounts regularly. Other pubs went out of business because people couldn't pay their debts, but that was not the case here; we had excellent customers."

By 1970, the Muldoon's grocery, petrol pumps and animal feed businesses had all ceased trading. It was in this period that Fergus became particularly active in politics. He was elected as a Fianna Fáil county councillor in 1979 and served on the county council for 14 years. He was also the first Meath man to be elected to the party's national executive, the Fianna Fáil Committee of Fifteen. He says: "My biggest achievement as county councillor was to provide a good water supply and a sewerage system for this area! The infrastructure that was put in place has allowed Drumconrath to grow."

Part of the growth in the town can be seen in the fact that the Muldoons were able to return to the grocery business in 1998, when Fergus's son Dermot opened a shop close to the family pub.

The family's licensing tradition extends beyond Meath into County Louth. In Ardee there are two pubs named Muldoon's — one run by Fergus's brother Brian, the other run by his cousin Enda. In Dundalk, there was a pub named Muldoon's run by Fergus's uncle Paddy.

"We are obviously a licensing family," says Fergus. "And I hope our pub in Drumconrath will continue into the next generation of our family."

NALLY'S CORNER HOUSE
Ronnie Nally, Ballymahon, Co. Longford

Nally's Corner House has been a Longford landmark since 1884 when James Joseph Nally purchased two single-storey thatched cottages and built a new three-storey building on the site.

On the bottom floor, the front part of the building contained a grocery, with a licensed bar to the rear. Apparently, Joe, as he preferred to be called, had no difficulty in being issued with a licence. He already owned a pub in Athlone and, according to his grandson, current licensee Ronnie Nally: "At that time, if you were the holder of one license you could open as many pubs as you liked, providing you were experienced in the licensed trade."

Even in the 19th century, one of the most important elements in ensuring the success of a business was location and Joe had chosen his business location well. Situated on the corner of Main Street and the road to Edgeworthstown, Nally's Corner House has always enjoyed a steady passing custom. Horses were accommodated in stables to the rear of the pub and travellers would warm their hands on the bar's pot-bellied stove.

Guinness arrived in Ballymahon by canal from Dublin with the cargo being ported half a mile away from the town centre at Ballybrannigan, where the canal ticket office has recently been restored.

Joe married a local woman, Elizabeth Mulvihill, in 1890 and together they had five children. During the War of Independence, Joe's eldest daughter, Katie Nally, played a major role in the love affair between Michael Collins and Kitty Kiernan. Collins took enormous risks to meet his lover at a time when he was the most wanted man in Ireland. He would meet Kitty secretly upstairs in Nally's garret, with Katie acting as an all-night protector, keeping watch for any sign of a raid by the RIC or the Black and Tans.

Following Joe's death in 1936, the pub was inherited by his eldest son, Hughie Nally, who added undertaking to the business. Hughie also laid the foundations for Nally's strong sporting links by founding Ballymahon Rugby Club, which in 1931 made it to the final of the Provincial Towns Cup. Despite the GAA's ban on "foreign games", Hughie was also active in Gaelic sports and four of his sons played for Ballymahon GAA in the senior club championships during the 1970s.

Hughie died in 1982 and the pub was run by his widow Kathleen until 1988 when Ronnie took over. Ronnie is proud of his family's business heritage and hopes that either his son Marc or daughter Kate will continue it after him. He is an active member of the Vintners Federation of Ireland and for the past 12 years has been chairman of the County Longford Licensed Vintners Association.

Recently, he has set up a pub golf society, which Ronnie says is "great creating a sense of community", particularly among those who have moved away from Ballymahon and who use the golf as an opportunity to return home.

O'BRIEN'S

Frank O'Brien, Emily Square, Athy, Co. Kildare

This Athy pub is one of the few licensed premises in Ireland that still retains its original grocery counter — you must pass by shelves of household goods before you reach the bar hidden behind some stained glass panelling.

O'Brien's claims to be the oldest pub in Athy, though it is not known exactly how long it has been in operation. It has been in the one family since 1875, when Stephen O'Brien moved from Dublin to Athy with his wife and the first of their seven children.

Previously, Stephen had run a tea importing business in Dublin's Dorset Street, but in Athy his business sign declared that he traded in "Tea, Grocery, Fuel, Wine, Spirits and Wholesale Bottlers". As well as bottling his own stout and bonding his own whiskey, Stephen also manufactured and bottled mineral water.

In Athy, Stephen quickly became a part of the local community and at one stage he successfully ran for election as an independent councillor. At the turn of the century, Athy was a prosperous town, which benefited the O'Brien's trade. The grocery's customers also included the Duke of Leinster and records of then Lord Walter's accounts in the 18th century still survive.

In 1919, the business was passed on to his son, Francis, who was better known as Frank O'Brien, or Frank Snr. Frank was a keen sportsman, with a particular love of Gaelic games. The mahogany-panelled walls are decorated with hurling photographs and, behind the bar, there is an extensive collection of sporting reference books, which are regularly consulted to settle disputes about sporting records.

There are also plenty of general history books in the library, reflecting the interest that the current licensee, Frank O'Brien Jnr, has in local history. He has been licensee since 1970 and is extremely proud of his pub's heritage. In 1998, Frank Jnr played a central role in organising the events commemorating the rising of 1798 and he also played a major role in the restoration of Michael Dwyer's Cottage. One of the biggest changes over the years has been in prices — according to the grocery's sales ledgers from 1934, a family could once buy a week's supply of bread, sugar, butter, tea and jam for a couple of shillings.

Though the family parlour was converted into a new lounge, the original character of the bar and grocery has been preserved.

O'DWYER'S

Leo O'Dwyer, Kells, Co. Kilkenny

This pub and grocery was bought by Michael Marnell in 1894. As well as selling Guinness and spirits, he also sold foodstuffs and a wide range of household goods. Both Guinness and whiskey were bottled on the premises. The business thrived and was expanded when Michael bought the house next door, converting it himself into a hardware and farm machinery store.

He was helped by his wife Mary Kate and later by his daughter Delia, who started working in the business in 1928. Michael died that year and the two women carried on working in the business together until Mary Kate's death in 1948, when the entire business was left to Delia.

The business was expanded further shortly after that when Delia invested in petrol pumps — a move that required Delia to recruit a non-family member as employee. But sticking to her past experience, her assistant was also female. When Delia died in 1960, the business was left to her brother Richard Marnell who ran the pub, grocery and petrol pumps for three years before transferring the ownership to his daughter Colette, wife of Leo O'Dwyer, the current licensee.

Colette and Leo added a lounge to the pub in 1980 to cater for parties and musical nights and the grocery and petrol pumps are also still in operation.

KATE O'GRADY'S

Charley Malzard, Stoneyford, Co. Kilkenny

Named after the woman who ran it at the start of the 20th century, Kate O'Grady's in Stoneyford, Co. Kilkenny, has been in the one family for at least four generations.

Records show that Michael O'Grady, who died in 1879, was an innkeeper in Stoneyford. According to family tradition, Michael used local millwrights from the mills along the River Nore and the Kings River to erect the building.

The bar's pitch pine interior and entrance porch date back to the late 19th century and were installed by carpenters who were ostensibly working at Flood Hall, one of the large estate houses nearby. Both the bar interior and the shopfront are now subject to preservation orders.

Little is known of Michael O'Grady or his son Martin and the type of establishment they ran. It is thought that they offered some limited lodging facilities and the pub-cum-grocery was known as The Lamp Hotel, even though by the time Martin's daughter Kate inherited it at the end of the 19th century, it rarely took in guests.

Kate proved to be an enterprising woman — perhaps because she had worked for some time in the United States before she returned home to Ireland to run her father's pub.

Long before lounge bars arrived, Kate purchased an old mill building to the rear of the pub and turned it into a hall for balls and musical entertainments. These were hugely popular events in their time. One 1921 cricket club dance in particular, which was attended by most of the local landowning gentry, is celebrated in a song that includes the verse: "The room was loaned for this event, that truth to you I tell / by the sporting Kate O'Grady from the well-known Lamp Hotel".

In addition to the pub and dancehall, Kate owned a hotel in Waterford which was run by her sister Mary. Like the property in Stoneyford, the Waterford business was known as The Lamp Hotel, but unlike its Co. Kilkenny namesake, the Waterford business relied on paying guests for its income.

And indeed, there were some who didn't pay their bills at The Lamp Hotel. A credit note survives from 1922, which is signed by a "Capt Power" and is headed "North Tipperary Batt. Flying Column", with the text, "Please give the bearer two bottles of best Irish whiskey and charge same to above account".

In 1901, Kate sold the hotel in Waterford after her sister May married a Channel Islands man named Alfie Malzard and moved to Jersey with him.

However, May died soon after bearing her second child and her two children, a boy and a girl, were sent back to Ireland to be raised by Kate.

Despite her sporting reputation and her substantial business interests, Kate never married and on her death in 1937, the pub passed on to her nephew Alfred Malzard, who was born in 1903 and died in 1986.

In 1948, the Irish Tourist Board forced Alfred to change The Lamp Hotel's name, after the board ruled that the pub didn't have the accommodation facilities necessary for the description "hotel". Forced to take his aunt's sign down, Alfred re-named the pub after the woman who fostered him and the pub has been known as "Kate O'Grady's" ever since.

The current licensee is Alfred's son, Charley Malzard, who has been working in the bar since leaveing school 50 years ago. He says the biggest change he has witnessed in Irish drinking patterns has been the end to daytime drinking. He says: "In the 1950s and '60s, we would have farmers hammering at the door before morning opening. Often on a Monday morning, they would tell the wife the tractor had developed a fault and use that as an excuse to come into town. The drink-driving laws put a stop to all that — or else the tractors have got more reliable! These days, during the day we are mainly a tourist facility for people who want to use our toilets!"

Nevertheless, Charley is proud of the pub, its heritage and its continuing reputation for music. Twice in recent years Kate O'Grady's has won the Kilkenny Singing Pubs competition — despite the fact that the pub has no organised musical entertainment. "It's just a thing we have always had," says Charlie. "Our customers have always enjoyed singing ballads. It's one of those places where you will hear a grand old song, if you ask one of the right regulars on the right day."

O'KEEFFE'S
Thomas O'Keeffe, The Harbour,
Kilcock, Co. Kildare

When this business was bought in 1850 by Thomas O'Keeffe it was trading as a pub, a grocery, a drapery and a hardware store run by the Harte family under one thatched roof. The original business had been positioned to take advantage of the Royal Canal with the stretch between Dublin and Kilcock opened in 1796.

It was thanks to the Royal and Grand canals that Guinness became Ireland's first national brewery. Harte's also benefited as wholesale suppliers of porter to the surrounding district. Kilcock, then a predominantly unionist town, was attacked by rebels during the 1798 rising with Harte's being looted in the process; records survive showing that the business later received compensation from the British government for the loss of 5,000 barrels of beer.

As well as supplying Guinness, Harte's would also have supplied an ale manufactured by a brewery that once operated in Kilcock and whiskey made in a distillery in the town. At the start of the 18th century, Kilcock was a major industrial centre with a brickworks and a clothing mill.

Guinness and Harte's were among the few ventures which benefited from

O'Keeffe's disguised as "The Green Ribbon" for the RTE television drama Home Ground

the building of the Royal Canal which, because of a lack of other freight traffic, never became a commercial success. Before the canal finally reached Mullingar in 1820, it went bankrupt in 1814. When the Midland Great Western Railway bought the waterway in 1846, it was used mainly by the company to build the railway line alongside it, more or less taking away all of the waterway's freight and passenger traffic.

Nevertheless, under Thomas O'Keeffe the pub and general store standing by Kilcock Harbour continued to prosper. A turn-of-the-century photograph depicts Thomas, his wife and four of their children outside the premises at a time when it still bore a thatched roof. The family are well dressed, the second youngest child is in a pram and there are flowerpots on all the windowsills.

Following Thomas's death, the pub was inherited in 1926 by his son Patrick O'Keeffe. Patrick kept his father's name above the door, but he replaced the thatched roof with slate.

In 1975, Patrick's son became the second Thomas O'Keeffe to have his name on the licence. Thomas has made considerable changes to the pub, converting the old family parlour into a lounge and adding a second lounge to the rear, so that the pub can now accommodate 300 people comfortably. The façade has also been remodelled with larger windows installed and there are tables and chairs outside so that visitors may enjoy the good weather by the canal-side, when there is good weather. The original bar, however, is still more or less in its original condition and, unlike the two lounges, it doesn't have a ladies toilet. Today, food is an important part of the business, with a carvery bar during the day and an à-la-carte menu in the evenings.

THE REAL UNYOKE

Bernard Murphy, Ballyhought, Blackwater, Enniscorthy, Co. Wexford

The Real Unyoke has been in the Murphy family for five generations and was founded by Charles Murphy after he had been evicted from Ballyorley, near Boolavogue, following the 1798 rebellion. History records that it was Charles who unhorsed Lieutenant Bookey at the opening skirmish at The Harrow. Ironically, given that Charles would later become a publican, Bookey was the worst for drink when he charged alone into a crowd of insurgents. Charles unseated him with one blow of his pike handle and when Bookey fell to the ground, he was despatched by others among the rebels, at a spot known today as "Bookey's Stream".

The Murphys were lucky to escape with only an eviction. Many, who were suspected of rebel sympathies, were summarily executed in the brutal military suppression that followed the 1798 rising. Homeless, on the road between Oulart and Wexford, the family found a deserted cottage and took shelter there. The local landlord, a man named Adams, not only agreed to let the property, but also allowed Charles to run a public house there.

Situated at the end of a long climb on a main road, the premises became known as "The Unyoke", because it was there that farmers and carters unyoked their wagons to "rest and bait" themselves and their horses — "bait" being a local word for "to feed".

As well as carrying traffic from Oulart to Wexford, the R741 was a main route for transporting grain to Castlebridge. The pub also benefited from being located close to a lime kiln — an important source of fertiliser.

The pub run by Charles and his son Bryan was tiny. Its main business came from the kitchen, but it also comprised a parlour and a bar, which accommodated fewer than six people at a time. However, business was steady by day and by night. According to the Murphys, The Unyoke once had a 23-hour licence — one of only two in the country — but it was lost in the 19th century in a fire at Wexford County Hall and the family could only replace it with an ordinary seven-day licence.

When Bryan died, aged 99, in 1908, a newspaper wrote: "No man was better known or more highly respected throughout a great proportion of North Wexford than the deceased, Mr Bryan Murphy."

The business then passed father-to-son to John Murphy and then father-to-son to Charlie Murphy. The pub was then passed on to Charlie's nephew, the current licensee Bernard Murphy, a great-great-great-grandson of the 1798 rebel. It was Charlie who added the word "real" to the pub's title, after a nightclub also calling itself "The Unyoke" opened locally. The nightclub burnt down, but The Real Unyoke is still open for a drink and a bait to eat.

While the original bar and fireplace are still in place, the pub has been significantly expanded. The parlour, with a thatched roof, also remains in place though it is not currently in use.

THE RIVERVIEW INN
James Dempsey, Cadamstown, Birr, Co. Offaly

This is a pub whose exact foundation date is unknown. It had been run for at least a generation by the Ryan family when a Board of Works engineer, Thomas Dempsey, originally from Balivor, Co. Meath, married Bridget Ryan in the 1860s.

The pub was inherited by their son James Dempsey, who was born in November 1870 and whose his name can still be found today on the exterior walls of this 200-year old building, written in primitive, but long-lasting, concrete. James's brother, Msgr Timothy Dempsey, born 1867, served in the United States where he won renown as a champion of the poor and homeless in St Louis, Missouri.

James married twice. His first wife was Elizabeth Digan of Tullamore, Co. Offaly, with whom he had five children. After her death, he married one of his barmaids, Annie Elizabeth Fagan of Ballymahon, Co. Longford, with whom he had another 14 children — giving him 19 children in all. There was at least 15 years of an age difference between James and his second wife, though this was not unusual at the time. Not surprisingly, she outlived James by 40 years after he died in 1928.

Annie enjoyed a great local reputation for holiness, something which worked to her advantage. According to the Dempseys, whenever the pub was raided by police after official closing time, Annie would order all the customers on their knees so that when the Gardaí were allowed in, she could claim that they were there for a prayer meeting rather than late-night drinking!

Another story told is that the pub survived being burnt down in a Black and Tan reprisal during the Troubles, thanks to a coincidence. One of the British auxiliaries had a mother whose maiden name was Dempsey and, for that reason alone, he stopped his colleagues from razing the pub to the ground.

One of Annie's sons, Tim, was active in the old IRA and was a wanted man with a price on his head. He fled to America where his uncle and namesake, Msgr Tim, paid for his education, with the former rebel becoming a stockbroker and, eventually, a very rich man.

Following Annie's death in 1968, the pub was taken over by her son Augustine, known as Gus, who ran the business with his wife Breda until he died in 1986. Breda is still active in the business. At first she ran the pub with her son Tim, but he has moved on to new pastures, and the pub's licence is now in his brother's name, James Dempsey. James was a priest of the Hamilton Diocese in Ontario, Canada, until 1999, but now he is a publican, working behind the bar with his wife Elizabeth. "There are a lot of similarities between being a priest and a publican," says James. "Both sometimes require the patience of a saint!"

The stables attached to the original coaching tavern have long since been demolished and the grocery business, which also included farm supplies, ceased operations in the early 1970s. The bar has been serving draught Guinness since the early 1960s; before then all beers — Guinness, McArdles, Phoenix Ale and Smithwicks — were only supplied in bottles. According to Breda, in the 1950s the bar was selling 100 dozen bottles of beer a week, a large part of which was off-trade to farmers living in remote parts of the Slieve Bloom mountains.

It was James who changed the name of the bar to "The Riverview", in honour of the pub's fine view of the Silver River. James says: "It's a lovely spot, in what I believe is the last unspoilt scenic area in Ireland."

Looking to the future, James and Elizabeth's daughter, Bridget, was born in September 2001 and her parents hope that she will continue the family business into the next generation.

THE SALMON POOL

Martin Walsh, Mill Street, Thomastown, Co. Kilkenny

According to family folklore, the Walshes have been running a pub in Thomastown since 1709. While this claim cannot be confirmed with documentary evidence, there is a listing in *Piggot's Directory*, under the heading "Inn Keepers and Publicans", for Edward Walsh, Mill Street, in 1824.

Certainly, beer was being consumed on the premises before then — the Walshes' property includes an outhouse that was once a brewery. Thomastown had a long tradition of brewing. The town was home to an important monastery whose monks would have drunk weak beer, instead of water, for hygiene reasons. The brewery building, which is at least 200 years old, can be seen from the bridge overlooking the fishing spot that gives The Salmon Pool its name.

Historical records list Thomas Walsh as the owner of a "pub, grocery" in Thomastown in 1845, and his son Joseph is listed as owner in 1884. Joseph died in 1911 and his widow Alice was licensee until 1927, when the licence passed to her son, Thomas Walsh, grandfather of the current licensee Martin Walsh, who runs the pub with his brother Gerard.

Walter Walsh, who was licensee from 1963 to 1999, was a great innovator. In 1967, he extended the pub, giving Thomastown its first public lounge and its first ladies' toilet! Walter also introduced live music — which is very much a feature of this pub today.

SHAW'S
John Shaw, Summerhill, Co. Meath

When this pub was founded in 1902 as a spirit grocers and hardware store by John Shaw, who came from North Meath, it was the second licensed premises to be established in the village. John's wife Rose Cluskey came from a family of publicans who owned The Warrenstown Arms six miles away.

John died in 1943 and the pub was run by Rose until 1955, when she died. It then passed to the couple's son and daughter Patricia and Jim Shaw, with a second son, Bill Shaw, inheriting The Warrenstown Arms. Bill Shaw died in 1945 and his wife Nora died in 1949, leaving their son John Shaw an orphan. He was sent to Summerhill to be reared by his aunt and uncle and he eventually inherited their pub in 1976.

According to John, who is still the licensee today, old ledgers from the Second World War years show how marginal the business was during the 1940s, with many bills being unpaid by the grocery's customers, many of whom were farmers affected by the land war with Britain.

191

Shortly after taking over the pub in 1976, he closed the grocery and the hardware store. In 1978, the drinking premises was extended, so that where once the pub held 50 people it now holds 300. He says the main spirit drunk in the pub in its early days was whiskey and water. If customers ordered gin, it was usually accompanied by orange as a mixer, with gin and tonic not becoming fashionable until the 1950s.

The pub has a close link with Summerhill GAA and Bill Shaw was a member of the first Meath team to win the national football league championship in 1933. Inside, the pub is decorated with vintage GAA photographs as well as pictures of racehorses. The pub runs a racing syndicate that was particularly successful with Sheila na Gig, a mount the syndicate part owned.

In days gone by, the busiest days of the year were fair days in September and October. "They were the equivalent of a major sporting occasion today," John says. "In those days, the local publicans helped one another: when there was a fair in Summerhill, publicans in Dunboyne and Kilcock would send down members of their staff to help us out and our staff would be sent to help them out when it was their fair day."

SMYTH'S

Michael Smyth, Newtown, Bagenalstown, Co. Carlow

According to records at Carlow Museum, members of the Smyth family ran a business in Newtown in 1745, but family records date back only as far as 1815. In the early 19th century, John Smyth and his wife Elizabeth (née Burn) are listed as publicans in parish records. Since then, the pub has passed from father to son, with Robert Smyth becoming licensee in 1830 followed by Patrick Francis Smyth in 1860.

It was Patrick who started Smyth's long-standing tradition for musical evenings, taking out newspaper advertisements for evenings featuring the music of Handel and the songs of Thomas Moore.

Following Patrick's death, the pub was run by his son John, who was born in 1872. John trained as a barman in Dublin where he was involved in the nationalist movement, becoming a founder member of the Gaelic League. He and his wife Anne also had a strong interest in classical music. They built a large hall attached to the bar and ran nights of music by Sibelius, Mozart and other classical composers.

Following John's death in 1951, the pub was run by his wife with the assistance of their son Michael, who became licensee in 1972. According to Michael: "The musical nights were a great success once. We could seat 350 people and by 8.30 p.m. there wasn't a seat available in the house. Today, the large lounge is rarely used,  despite the fact that it now has a first class grand piano. The younger generations aren't as interested in classical music evenings. People say to me, 'Why don't you get a pop band in?', but it would be too much trouble."

For those who like sing-songs, particularly those involving music hall ballads, they are a weekly occurrence at Smyths. Held on Saturdays and Sundays, Michael has been advertising his musical evenings on the front page of every edition of *The Carlow Nationalist* newspaper for over 35 years. When, as part of commemorations marking the new millennium, *The Nationalist* reproduced an edition from 1900, Michael was delighted to see that the front page featured an advertisement for a music night placed by his father 100 years ago.

SORAGHAN'S

Desmond Soraghan, Prospect, Dundalk, Co. Louth

According to genealogical records, John Soraghan, who was born in 1770 and who died in 1853, ran a public house on this spot on the Dundalk to Ardee road. His son Thomas, who died in 1889, is reckoned to be the first member of the family to have held an alcohol licence. It then passed to Thomas Soraghan, who died in 1920 when the licence passed to his son John, who died in 1941. The licence was then held by John's wife Mary until her death in 1965.

The current licensee, Desmond Soraghan, has been working in the bar since he left the Christian Brothers School in Dundalk in 1939, and he is now aged 77. Like his father before him, Des is a member of the Pioneer Association of the Sacred Heart, a Catholic organisation whose members pledge not to drink alcohol.

Des vividly remembers the war years when Guinness was in short supply, so that when stocks were low it was replaced by stout brewed by McArdle's, the Dundalk brewer usually associated with ale. "During the war, you couldn't get metal caps, so the McArdle's stout was bottled here on the premises using corks," he says. "McArdle's stout kept condition in the bottles for three days, after that the corks would start popping out and we had terrible trouble with them. Guinness has always been the regular drink here."

A Fianna Fáil pub, regular visitors to Soraghan's included Frank Aiken who was TD for North Louth. Another man who supped pints here was the late Cardinal Tomás Ó Fiach, former Archbishop of Armagh.

The pub's capacity was doubled shortly before Christmas 1999 when the premises was extended. Des claims the pub can now accommodate 100 people comfortably. Today, though Des remains licensee, his wife Dora is very much involved in the management of the pub, while day-to-day matters are dealt with by their sons Thomas and Desmond.

THE SYCAMORE HOUSE

Declan Doyle, Killurin, Enniscorthy, Co. Wexford

This Wexford pub is unusual in that, since its foundation in 1870, it has had a name other than that of its licensees. That is perhaps a good thing, for in four generations of the one family, three different surnames have adorned the licence.

The pub is named af-ter five sycamore trees that once stood outside the premises, which was established by local man Nicholas Redmond in the year that the Dub-  lin–Wexford railway reached Killurin. Though the mainline still runs past the village, it no longer has its own railway station.

When Nicholas died in 1908, the pub and grocery passed to his niece Mary-Anne Carley, with her husband, Dick Doyle, becoming the licensee. Killurin has a strong hurling tradition and Dick was a noted hurley maker. As a result, the pub became an after-match haunt of members of the Glynn-Barntown club.

195

Originally a two-storey thatched building, the upper storey was made higher when a new roof was installed, but inside the pub the wooden ceiling is original and the timber floor dates back to 1922.

Following Dick's death, the pub passed to his daughter Dorrie Doyle. When she died in 1967, the pub was left to her son Declan who is the current licensee and who runs The Sycamore House with his wife Mary.

Today, this is a traditional Irish pub, with no television, pool table or juke box to interfere with quiet conversation.

TALLON'S

Elizabeth Dolan, Stratnakelly, Tinahely, Arklow, Co. Wicklow

Now a welcome resting place for weary hikers on the Wicklow way, Tallon's bar started life in 1798 as a coaching house on the main postal route between Shillelagh and Hacketstown, two South Wicklow garrisons that had gained importance following the rising of that year.

By 18th century standards, this one-room bar is large and its bare stone walls retain plenty of the building's original character, though the front awning is a more recent addition.

As it was handed down from father to son, alcohol would have been supplied, as a matter of course, to travellers stopping overnight or refreshing themselves and their horses. However, the oldest surviving documentary proof of trade in alcohol is a stock list belonging to James Tallon, who died in 1882. Not only would he have been a witness to the Famine, his business would change forever because of it. Lower in the valley, a coaching road — still known locally as "The New Line" — was built using Famine relief labour.

After James's death, the pub was run by Lawrence Tallon, who died in 1896, leaving the pub to his wife Elizabeth, who died in 1932. It was then run by their son Edward Tallon, who saw business pick up because of the "bona fide" licensing laws which allowed drinkers from nearby Tinahealy and Shille-lagh to drink here to their hearts' content long after official closing time. When the bona fide dispensation was scrapped, Edward, who died in 1963, saw a de-cline in business. For many years, the pub's only customers were local farmers and the odd, rare hiker.

The current licensee, Elizabeth Dolan, Edward's daughter, says that while ale from wooden kegs was sold in the pub during the 1920s, during her youth, and much of her adult life, the only beer sold came in bottles, be it Guinness, Smith-wick's, McArdle's or Time and Phoenix lagers. Indeed, the pub even bought its Guinness pre-bottled from Donoghue's Wholesalers in Enniscorthy. Draught Guinness is a very recent introduction, only having come on tap here for the first time in 1993.

TREACY'S
Tom Treacy, The Heath, Portlaoise, Co. Laois

According to family folklore, this pub four miles outside Portlaoise was founded in 1780 by a John Treacy and it has belonged to the family for seven generations since. However, family records date back only to 1880 when Patrick Treacy was licensee and was charged with serving a customer who was drunk.

At that time, and for decades afterwards, the British army kept a garrison at the Heath. Patrick was charged with serving a member of the Queen's Rifles while drunk, but the case was dismissed after defence counsel argued that, although the soldier left Treacy's in a severely intoxicated state, there was no evidence that he had consumed alcohol there; it was quite possible that the soldier had wandered in the door drunk and wandered back out again.

After Patrick's death, the pub passed to his son John Treacy who was licensee until the mid-1920s. The pub then passed to John's son Willie, who ran the bar with his wife Mary. Following Willie's death in 1955, Mary continued as licensee until her death in 1974. The pub is now licensed to her son, Tom Treacy.

During Tom's tenure, the pub has been extended three times — in 1975, 1982 and 1987. Where once the original bar held a maximum of 50 thirsty troopers, the pub now caters for up to 200 people.

It's very much a sporting pub with close links to the local GAA club and to the Shannon Rugby Club. As a result, Gaelic and rugby photographs adorn the walls. When Laois won their first every All-Ireland minor title, the players' jerseys were sponsored by Treacy's.

The front of the pub is very much as it was in 1780 and it also retains its thatched roof — indeed, it is estimated that the thatched roof is 375 years old, indicating that the building pre-dates the arrival of John Treacy in 1780. Inside, the original bar retains its low ceiling and some of the original mud walls. In 1989, a restaurant, which is open throughout the year, was added to the premises.

VINE COTTAGE BAR

Margaret Walsh, Saltmills, New Ross, Co. Wexford

The Vine Cottage Bar has been in the same family since 1894, but the name pre-dates the arrival of the Walshes and Costelloes and the original licence pre-dates this pub's very scenic, and historic, location.

The pub overlooks Bannow Bay, scene of the first Norman landings in Ireland in 1169, but the area was inhabited by Vikings long before then. Only a short walk away stands the ruins of Tintern Abbey, which was founded in 1200

by William, the Earl Marshall of Pembroke. Named after the monastery in Wales from where its original Cistercian inhabitants came, it was known as Tintern De Voto (of the vow) because it was built as a result of a promise made by the Earl when he was praying for his life while caught in a storm off the Wexford coast.

As with most monasteries, a village grew up around the Abbey, which continued under Cistertian rule until the mid-16th century, when the Abbey and its vast estates were granted to Sir Anthony Colclough, whose descendants lived in the Abbey until 1959.

The earliest record of an inn in Tintern is found in a baptismal register for the year 1759 where a child's father is listed as "George Boyce of Tintern, Innkeeper" and the Boyce family continued as licensees until 1894.

But before the pub was sold, it was moved. At the end of the 18th century, the Colcloughs thought it would be better if the village was moved away from the Abbey where the family now lived. So between 1810 and 1820, the entire village left their old homes and houses in Tintern to new estate buildings in Saltmills. It is believed that The Vine Cottage's name dates back to this period, as vines were planted in the pub's new grounds. Those vines had withered in the ground by 1894 when Jeremiah Boyce sold the bar and grocery to William Costelloe, grandfather of the current licensee Margaret Walsh.

In 1936, the licence was transferred to William's daughter, Lally Costelloe, and her husband Thomas Clegg. During their time, the pub underwent several physical changes and some policy changes too. Lally's daughter Margaret, who became licensee in 1981, still remembers a time when women were neither served nor granted admission into the bar. Even when the policy changed, Margaret says: "My mother would comment that 'such-and-such a woman was in the bar last night' — she frowned on women being in the bar for some time."

Over the years the bar has been extensively renovated and refurbished. In 1960, the ceiling of the old bar was raised to give more air and light to customers, while in 1999 an upstairs seating area with large windows overlooking Bannow Bay was added. During the most recent refurbishment, a beer garden was also added to the premises and, as a result, there are now vines growing once again at Vine Cottage.

While this is a lovely pub for visitors to stumble upon, the pub relies on a local trade and card playing is a regular part of an evening's entertainment here.

M.H. WHITE

Mary White, Main Street, Clara, Co. Offaly

White's Lounge Bar has been in the one family since P.J. White founded it in 1858. For over a century, the business comprised a bar, grocery and hardware shop — the bar was to the left of the front door and the grocery and hardware counters were to the right. Following P.J.'s death in 1902, his son Michael Henry White became licensee and there has been an M.H. White behind the counter ever since.

The first M.H. White died in 1921 and the pub passed to his son Michael Henry who ran the pub with his wife Mary until he died in 1977. Mary remains the licensee, but the pub is now managed by her son, the third M.H. White to work behind the bar.

In 1964, the hardware and grocery were converted into a Mace Supermarket, but that venture lasted only until 1968 when the supermarket was replaced by a modern lounge bar.

Though the pub exterior has had larger windows installed, the frontage still features railings that were once used to protect the original windows from being broken by livestock on fair days.

In the past, the biggest trading day was the second Friday of the month, when a fair was held in Clara and the pub opened at 8.00 a.m. Clara was also very much an industrial town and Friday, when the workers got paid, was known as "a big supper night" when children would get a fish-and-chip supper and parents would enjoy a few pints. This Friday night trade has suffered following the closure of the local Goodbody jute-bag factory and the local Ranks flour mill.

The original bar contains many of its 19th century features, but two 36-inch screens have been added to cater for the bar's soccer fans. The lounge bar is more spacious and features luxury seating and background music. Both lounge and bar have large open fires.

Mary says it is still a hard trade, though it is much easier now than it was in the days of hand-bottling and wooden barrels. She says her son is very like his father and "seems cut out for the trade". She says: "He has the dedication and is always spending money to improve the pub."

Family-Owned Pubs of Munster

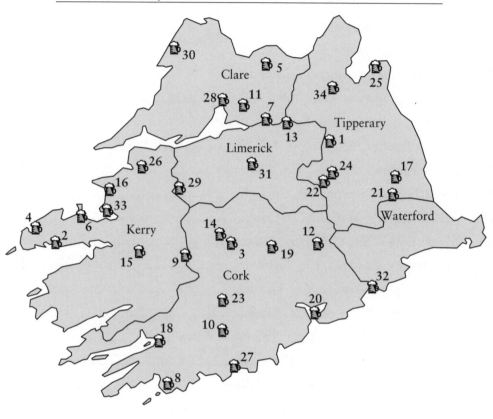

ARMSHAW'S
Liam Armshaw, Cappawhite,
Co. Tipperary

This fine pub in the pretty village of Cappawhite in Co. Tipperary has been in the same family since 1 November 1897 when it was leased by William Armshaw for £3 a year.

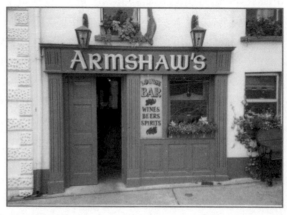

Little is known about William, except that it is said he was descended from a north of England family, with the first Armshaw, believed to have been a medical school drop-out, arriving in Ireland in the 1640s.

Apparently, the 50-year leasehold was a sublet, with the Armshaw holding being part of a much larger estate that had been leased in 1872 by William's landlord, Denis Ryan, for "the perpetual rent of one hundred and thirty six pounds and ten shillings, late currency, and three couple of fat hens".

In those days, Cappawhite was noted for its fair days which were often accompanied by organised faction fights, where teams of men would lay into one another with cudgels and sticks — sometimes because of a genuine argument, sometimes for sport. Indeed, the phrase still survives: "A fair in Cappawhite is no place for a man with a thin skull".

As well as being a licensee, William made shoes and boots, as cobbling was a family trade that was continued by his son, who was also named William Armshaw. The second William Armshaw became licensee when his father died, in his late seventies, in 1930. Five years earlier, the Armshaws had terminated their 50-year lease early, by buying their holding outright for the sum of £42 in 1920.

As well as shoe-making, the second William Armshaw was also a seller of radios. He never married and, following his death in 1966, the pub passed to his sister Kathleen. She also never married and following her death in 1976, the pub passed to her next of kin, James Armshaw, a first cousin.

Apparently, by this stage there was only one branch of the Armshaw clan left in Ireland, all the rest having either died out or emigrated. Indeed, James was the only member of this branch of the family to marry and have children: four sons and seven daughters. Like many in the family, James was a shoemaker by profession, but he had no interest in running the pub. As a result, he immediately sold the business to one of his sons, who by happy coincidence is also called "William Armshaw", though he uses Liam, the Irish version of the first name.

Once installed as licensee, Liam renovated the pub, but maintained its original character sufficiently to win a regional award for best traditional shop front in the Tidy Towns competition. Inside the pub, one of his biggest innovations was the introduction of draught beer. Liam is also a founder of the Cappawhite Street Theatre Group, which re-enacts faction fights, including on one occasion staging a re-enactment of a fight on the streets of New York. Today, Armshaw's is one of four pubs in Cappawhite. When Liam became licensee in 1976 there were 10 licensed premises in the village and once there were 27 in total.

ASHE'S

Thomas Ashe, Main Street,
Dingle, Co. Kerry

Ashe's has been a licensed bar since 1900, but like many traditional Irish pubs, originally it was a licensed grocery. It was founded in 1850 as O'Connor's drapery and general store, with the founder, John O'Connor, a local businessman, taking out a spirits grocer's licence shortly afterwards.

According to Kate Ashe, great-great-grandniece of John O'Connor, originally alcohol sales were very much "a sideline", provision of alcoholic refreshment being secondary to the other business interests.

When John died in the late 1870s, his wife Mary continued running the shop for four years before passing on the deeds and the licence to her nephew, John Kennedy, who was born in America and had returned to his parents' "old country".

In 1926, John Kennedy retired and handed over the business to one of his three daughters, Hannah, and her husband James Gregory Ashe, the bar's name being changed to Ashe's. As well as running the pub, James was a manufacturer of soft drinks and he also became an agent for Guinness. Indeed, the Ashes are still the local distributors of Guinness products for the whole of the Dingle Peninsula.

James's son, Thomas Ashe, who had been born on the premises, took over the licence in 1941 and ran the bar with his wife, Kate. They converted the drapery section of the store into a new bar and their kitchen into a lounge, simply replacing the Aga cooker with a fireplace. The lounge still contains all the original kitchen cupboards.

Kate was licensee of the bar until she passed on the running of the business to her son Thomas in 2001. She has documentation outlining the history of the premises from 1881. According to an old rent book from that time, John Kennedy paid a ground rent of £2 annually to the local landowners, the Moriarty family. The Ashes continued to pay ground rent until Kate and her husband bought out the lease in 1946.

The bar had become famous in the area during the early 1950s in part because of Thomas's success in sport. He played for Kerry in the 1953 All-Ireland final and also collected a number of Munster championship medals. An even greater spotlight was put on the pub in 1970, when one day the film director David Lean walked in, bought a pint and told Kate that he was going to be making "a big

Many pubs bottled their own Guinness — but Ashe's had an Irish-language label

film" in the area. Kate says: "I didn't believe him when he said that, I thought it was the drink talking!" However, later that year, Lean began filming *Ryan's Daughter* and the cast and crew made Ashe's their local, with Kate becoming the caterer for the movie.

"There weren't many cafes open in Dingle at the time," says Kate. "I remember one of the crew came in when I was cooking Irish stew. David Lean asked if the cast could have some and before I knew what was happening I found myself making soups, stews and sandwiches for the whole time they were filming."

Kate was not star-struck at meeting Robert Mitchum and the other cast members, however, because Gregory Peck's mother was a member of the Ashe family and Gregory had previously visited the bar for a pint.

Dingle had always been a prosperous town because of its fishing port; however, since the filming of *Ryan's Daughter*, the town has become a popular tourist destination. Kate says long-distance members of the Ashe clan from America come into the bar because of the name outside. Kate has recently passed on the running of the bar to her son Thomas, but she still pops in to help out when things are busy. "I have to," she says, "the older generation still like me to pull their pints!"

BARRETT'S

Edmond Barrett, O'Brien Street, Kanturk, Co. Cork

Founded as a grocery and bar in 1852 by William Barrett, a local farmer and active member of the Land League, this pub has been trading in Kanturk for a century and a half. In 1907, the pub passed to William's son Edmond and then, in 1955, passed to the founder's grandson and namesake William Barrett, who though born in 1927, is still active in the business.

According to William, in his father's time the pub had no toilets of its own — instead the family bathroom was used, with customers accessing it by walking through the Barrett's kitchen every time they went to the loo!

The bar and grocery were on the one premises until the family bought the building next door, allowing the bar to accommodate a greater number of customers and providing space for dedicated gentlemen's and ladies' conveniences. The grocery is now mainly an off-licence, though it still also sells ice-cream and bottles of Calor gas!

Outside the bar, a brass rail runs across the window, which William polishes at 10.10 a.m. every day. Too ornamental to be a protection against stray cattle on mart days, William, says: "We installed the brass rail when we refurbished the pub as a traditional symbol of publicans, like a red and white pole outside a barber's shop."

William is extremely proud of the fact that the pub is a family-run business and that a Barrett is always behind the bar. Though his son Edmond has been licensee since 1993, William takes his hand at the pumps everyday: "Every morning I wake up, I look forward to going to work. I love it, because you are working with people. When there are only three or four people in drinking, the great skill of a good barman is getting all of them talking to one another."

This is a GAA bar with dozens of hurling and Gaelic football photos on the walls. As well as the red and white colours of Cork, the green and white flags of Kanturk are flown out the windows on match days. Not only did William play for Kanturk, he also coached the team that won five Duhallow club titles in a row and one country championship in the 1960s.

TIGH BHEAGLAOICH
Rita Begley, Baile na nGall, Tralee, Co. Kerry

This pub on the Dingle peninsula is a well-known traditional music venue today, but it was only a small licensed grocery when Michael Begley, grandfather of the current licensee, bought it in 1901.

This is a Gaeltacht area, so while the village appears on most maps as "Ballydavid", it is known locally as Baile na nGall (literally, "The Village of the Strangers") and the Begleys refer to themselves by their Irish name "Beaglaoich".

Michael Begley was born in 1873, the son of a small farmer, and is remembered by his family today as "Seana Bheaglaoich" (literally, Old Begley). He quit school early to work as a farm labourer. It wasn't until after he emigrated to the United States at the age of 18 that he completed his education, studying at night school while working on building sites. In the US, Michael made his fortune as a bricklayer and met his wife, Margaret O'Donnell from Liscarney, Co Kerry. After the couple had their first child, Helen, they returned to Baile na nGall with enough funds to buy the licensed grocery from a man named Tom Johnson, who sold it to them for £700.

As well as running the grocery, Michael set up a business exporting salt fish to the United States. He bought mackerel and herring from local fishermen and salted and packed them in barrels in a shed he built in Murreagh, the next townland. However, the business was hit by the outbreak of the First World War and Michael was unable to find a buyer for his fish. With a growing family — he and his wife had 11 children, seven of whom survived — he faced financial difficulty. Michael decided to risk the U-boat menace himself and travelled to the US with his fish, selling it when he reached New York. While the war continued, he stayed in America, working again as a bricklayer.

Eventually, he returned home to find that his fish factory had been converted to a dance hall! As a result of the conversion, the local clergy, who viewed dancing as immoral, denounced Michael from the altar. At one stage, the priests went so far as to raid "Shed Bheaglaoich" and drive all those inside out into the darkness. Michael lived with the clerical censure, and is said to have even enjoyed the notoriety it gave him and his dance hall.

When "Seana Bheaglaoich" retired in 1941, his pub-cum-grocery was taken over by his son, Jim, who until then had been a Garda. Born in 1913, Jim Begley joined the Gardaí in 1933, but was obliged to leave the force when he became a licensee.

Shortly after taking over the licence, Jim demolished the old pub and grocery and built larger premises that included a new lounge. The grocery counter remained in place until poor profits led to its closure in the mid-1970s. He also demolished his father's shed and constructed a purpose-built dance hall in Murreagh in 1955. Thanks partly to the dance hall, the 1950s and '60s were a boom time for the pub: because the dance hall was unlicensed, people would drink in the pub until closing time, then would travel on to the *céilí* taking place in the dance hall. As well as traditional music, the pub and hall also thrived during the showband era, with the hall hosting acts including The Cadets, DJ and the Kerryblues, The Mexicans, Dermot O'Brien and many more. Today, the hall is little used except during the summer when it hosts *céilithe* for secondary school students visiting the area to learn Irish.

Meanwhile, Begley's Pub has become known throughout the world as a premier Irish traditional music venue, thanks mainly to the prowess of Jim's brother Breandán Begley, the noted accordionist. Breandán's son and daughter Séamus and Máire have become internationally famous, since they recorded their first album, *An Ciarraíoch Mallaithe* (*The Accursed Kerryman*) in 1972.

In 1992, when Jim retired, the pub was handed on to his daughter Rita, the current licensee. A year after she took over the licence, the pub suffered a disaster when it was completely destroyed by fire. However, a new much larger building was constructed comprising a pub, guest accommodation and a seafood restaurant.

BOHAN'S BAR
Seamus Bohan, Feakle, Co. Clare

It was a brave move to establish a business in Feakle, Co. Clare, when Michael and Anne Fitzgerald opened a grocery, bar and tailors in the town in the 1890s.

At that time, the land war was at its height in Co. Clare. Falling prices for agricultural produce meant tenants were unable to pay their rents. Seven miles away, the infamous Bodyke evictions had taken place in 1887, when 28 families were forcibly ejected from their homes. Publicity surrounding the evictions, which took nearly three weeks to complete, led the British government to tackle rack rents and to introduce measures that would give Irish peasant farmers ownership of their lands. The Land League urged peaceful means of protest during the Bodyke campaign, but many of the dispossessed peasantry took the law into their own hands and joined a secret agrarian society, headed by the mysterious Captain Moonlight, to attack landlords' property, particularly their livestock. These attacks, known locally as "moonlighting", in turn prompted reprisals, creating a spiral of violence.

In these troubled times, the Fitzgeralds were fortunate to remain in business. One reason they might have survived was Michael's physical stature: at 6 feet 6 inches in height, he would have been a giant of a man at a time when many of the local population would have been malnourished.

The couple had three children, but their two sons, like their father, died of arthritic fever and in 1927 the pub was inherited by their daughter, Bridget.

During her time as licensee, the pub comprised a small bar, a snug across the hallway from the bar and a kitchen which had a serving hatch connected to the pub. And though she wasn't a tailor like her father, she continued the drapery business, selling ready-made suit lengths.

In 1932, Bridget married Michael Bohan, but she remained the licensee because of Michael's job. He was a policeman, one of the first 1,200 recruits to join the Garda Síochána when it was founded in February 1922.

The licensing laws, which remain in force today, forbade Garda Bohan from being on the premises while on duty. As a result, once he married, Michael was transferred from Feakle to Ennis. For the next 22 years, until his retirement in 1954, Garda Bohan lived permanently in Ennis, cycling the 18 miles home once a month to spend the night with his wife and family.

These visits home usually coincided with the village's monthly fair when cattle and sheep were sold by local farmers, says the current licensee, Seamus Bohan, son of Michael and Bridget. He says his father's presence was often needed. "Farmers, if they sold cattle, would have a few drinks, but their capacity for drink would have been small, as their food intake wouldn't have been great and they wouldn't have been used to consuming alcohol," he says. "As a result they would get drunk very easily and as a follow-up, invariably fights would take place, especially with regards to civil war politics, particularly as de Valera was the local TD."

Following Michael's retirement at the age of 52, he and Bridget ran the pub together until Michael died in 1972, when Seamus became more directly involved in running the business. Following his mother's death in 1980, he became licensee.

Seamus demolished the old bar, snug and kitchen in 1981, replacing them with a larger, more modern, building, able to accommodate 50 people, but decorated in an "old world" style, furnished with rope chairs and an open fireplace. In 1990, he added a function room that can accommodate up to 250 people and which is one of the main venues during Feakle's Traditional Music Weekend, which is held on the weekend following the August Bank Holiday.

According to Seamus, the pub did not have Draught Guinness until the 1970s. Before then, the black stuff was bought from wholesale bottling companies: Hassett's in Ennis or Twoomey's or O'Byrne's who were based in Limerick. Limerick's Guinness arrived from Dublin by barge via the Grand Canal and the Shannon. Seamus says: "An old boatman, Dinny Weir, told me it was very pleasant work: they had a way of loosening the hoops on the barrels and getting at the stout inside during the journey. After they had their sup, they would tighten up the hoops again and no one knew the barrels had been tampered with. On another occasion, during a storm, one of the barges broke free and ended up running aground in Whitegate where the locals had a week of free drink."

Inside Bohan's, it is obvious that this is a strong GAA pub, with photographs of the local Feakle hurling team dating back to 1910 and portraits of the All-Ireland winning teams of 1914 and 1932. Pride of place is given to a hurley that has been autographed by those who served on the Clare team between 1973 and 1980, when it was managed by Seamus's brother, Fr Harry Bohan, who has also been a major force in Irish rural redevelopment.

BOLAND'S

Raymond Boland, Main Street, Castlegregory, Co. Kerry

Boland's in Castlegregory is a large bar and lounge popular with the town's young people. There has been a pub on the site for over 200 years and it has been in Mary Boland's family for about 150 years.

Her grandfather, John O'Callaghan from Abbeydorney, was the licensee until it passed to his son, Michael O'Callaghan. Up until the late 1960s, there was a grocery and a bakery attached to the business, but they are now gone. Fol-

lowing Michael's death, the pub passed to Mary, whose married name is Boland. Now aged 70, she became licensee when she was 32. Two of Mary's sons, Raymond and Val, work in the bar, with Raymond being the current licensee.

Much has changed since Mary began working behind the counter in 1950. She says: "In those days, beer was sold in bottles. We did not have kegs. It was mainly Guinness, Bass and whiskey, which people drank and we stocked. Now there are so many different drinks on sale."

BROWNE'S

Gerard Browne, Parteen, Co. Clare

This pub in Co. Clare was founded at the end of the 19th century by Delia Browne, grandmother of the present licensee. The current owner of the pub, Gerard Browne, reckons the pub was established "circa 1885".

In those days, the family's main source of income was farming, with the pub providing additional revenue.

In the early days, the bar-cum-grocery was based in a front room of the family house, which was more than enough for the level of custom provided by local farmers and the passing trade travelling along the road between Killaloe and Limerick. Being located three and a half miles outside Limerick, the pub also benefited to some extent from the out-of-hours "bona fide traveller" trade.

During one of de Valera's famous general election campaigns in Clare, the Fianna Fáil leader called to the pub for an election rally. After giving a speech, Dev bought a drink for every man present — however, he never paid the bill and the amount, 3s/6d, remains outstanding on Browne's old accountancy books.

During the 1920s the pub experienced a major boom in trade thanks to the building of the Ardnacrusha hydroelectric scheme, the first major civil engineering project in the state following the Civil War. Between 1925 and 1929, more than 5,000 labourers and engineers were employed on the Shannon scheme, with Parteen being the nearest town to the site where a massive dam and an eight-mile long canal was being built. A souvenir from the period, a painting by a German engineer who worked on the project, still decorates one of the walls of the pub.

From its earliest days, Browne's has had close links to the GAA; Delia's husband, William Browne, was a founder of the famous South Liberties hurling club in Limerick. An old joke told in the pub is that during the Ardnacrusha years, Parteen was the only GAA club to field a team of hurlers where the players spoke four different languages: English, Irish, German and "bad".

Following Delia's death in 1939, her son John became licensee. His brother-in-law, James Gleeson, had been killed in the Meelick Ambush during the War of Independence.

John's son Gerard Browne has been licensee since 1968. Shortly after taking over, Ger extended the pub and closed the grocery counter. Improvements in transport and the pub's location on the outskirts of Limerick meant that the shop counter was no longer profitable.

CAHALANE'S
James Cahalane, 20 Bridge Street, Skibbereen, Co. Cork

Travellers have taken their rest in Cahalane's Bar in Skibbereen for over a century. Immediately outside the pub is the town bus stop, but long ago it was where the Skibbereen postal coach halted.

The pub has been in the family since "Auntie Maloney" took the licence on 27 March 1898 — but it is not clear if she only took possession of the licence or if she bought the premises. For many years, this pub was a "tied house", part of the Beamish and Crawford brewery and permitted only to sell Beamish stout. The pub was also an important distribution point for Beamish in West Cork, as the brewery kept carts and horses here, with the stables behind the pub and access provided by the little lane that runs to the back of the present building.

Little is known about Auntie Maloney, except that she was born Mary O'Sullivan and was a returned Yank who had made her fortune in Boston. After her death, the pub was inherited by her son Bill Maloney, who died childless in 1953. The pub then passed to Auntie Maloney's niece, Nora O'Sullivan, who ran the pub with her husband John Cahalane.

The pub is now being run by Nora's son James, who has been licensee since 1984. Because of its location, the pub is busy throughout the year with tourists from the four corners of the world. But it is the week before and after Christmas when this pub is at its very busiest, filled to bursting with returnees. For many from Skibbereen, a pint in Cahalane's is part of the visit home.

CAHILL'S

Ann Cahill-Buckley, Rathmore, Co. Kerry

Cahill's Bar first opened its doors for business as a licensed general store in the 1890s. Local tradition fixes the opening year as 1896, "the year of the runaway bog" when that Christmas eight people from the one family were killed in a landslide at Gneeveguilla.

The pub's founder, Denis Cahill, had been a farmer with a reasonably large hillside holding in Aunaskirtane, a townland two miles to the south of Rathmore. With his family of six children grown up, the farm was passed on to the eldest son, Denis Jnr, while Denis Snr bought a site for a new home and shop in Rathmore, which at the time was more commonly known as Shinnanagh.

Eventually, the pub and shop also passed to Denis Jnr, who ran it with his wife, Catherine O'Sullivan. The business was expanded and at one stage included a corn mill, petrol pumps and a travel agency, which mainly specialised in providing emigrants with one-way steamship tickets to the United States.

The couple had six children, with the pub passing to the eldest, Vincent Cahill, who ran it with his wife Joan O'Riordan. During their time, the corn milling business declined and eventually closed, as did the travel agency. In their place, the pub was renovated and extended.

Before the alterations, the pub had two snugs, rooms to one side where women would be served from the bar via a sliding shutter. The larger of the two snugs was known to patrons as "the gluepot". The room is said to have got its name from its convivial atmosphere — once you slipped into the snug, it was very difficult to slip out!

The licensee today is Ann Cahill-Buckley, daughter of Vincent and Joan. Ann married Frank Buckley in 1976 and the couple have a daughter named Joanne, who they hope will maintain the family's licensing tradition.

DESSY'S BAR
Nora Hennessy, Ballineen, Co. Cork

The licence for Dessy's Bar in Ballineen has been in the family for over 100 years, but the surname on the licence has changed three times in that period.

The current licensee is Nora Hennessy, aged 74, but the bar is run by her son, Desmond, who gave the pub its current name. Nora's grandfather, Dan  Enright was licensee in 1892 when he died, but Nora claims it had been held by Dan's father before him and that the licence has been in the family since at least the early 1800s.

Following Dan's death, the pub passed to his son Thomas, who died in 1911, aged 55. The pub went to his only child Johanna, who married Daniel T. Lordan, who became the licensee. Daniel was quite an entrepreneur, as well as growing tobacco for cigarettes, running a milk farm, raising pigs and growing flax, his main source of income was auctioneering.

His daughter Nora, who has been licensee since 1968, boasts that Dessy's has always been an independent house. The other pubs in Ballineen and Enniskeen, the village next door, were all tied houses, owned by either Murphy's or Beamish and allowed sell only those brands of stout. As well as selling Guinness and Murphy's or Beamish, the pub also sold Farm House Cider, which was a premium brand in its day.

Nora well remembers the days when the family pub bottled its own Guinness — at one time, she spent two days a week, every week, washing empty bottles for re-use. She also ruefully remembers the days when porter was dispensed from wooden kegs and half-tierces. She says: "There was a real skill in putting in the tap — you had to make sure there was just enough paper wrapped around the tap to seal it, not too little and not too much. There was one keg of Guinness that we kept at an awkward angle and, because I was a *ciotóg* [left-handed person], I had to approach it backwards and bent over, looking at it between my legs. One time I got the paper wrong and the Guinness burst out with such force that it went up my dress and out the neck. Another time, I was putting the bung in a half-tierce of Beamish when it exploded, with 16 gallons of beer going all over the place. There are men still today who remember that night, because it was free drink all night."

In her father's time, as well as growing tobacco, West Cork was a flax growing area with the harvest exported by sea to the linen mills of Belfast. Nora says: "They were great times when a dozen neighbours would get together to bring the flax in and when the job was done they would come in for a pint. When the flax was being harvested, everyone was smiling, because it was the time of the year when the big cheque arrived and all the bills were paid. The flax was scutched at a mill in the village and the dust from the mill would put a great thirst on the workers. They would come in at their break, order a pint, drink it straight down and then order another one."

Nora became licensee when her father Daniel T. Lordan died in 1968, with the farm going to her brother. The name on the licence then changed a second time when Nora married John P. Hennessy, who like her father was a successful auctioneer.

"My husband had weekly auctions with full-page advertisements in *The Southern Star*," says Nora. "He was very well known and very successful. Shortly after he died, I received a telephone call in the middle of the night in connection with a property he was selling at the time of his death. Sitting in my bed at two o'clock in the morning, I made the deal, earning £2,500 in commission. It was a help getting over the death of my husband, Lord have mercy on him, but I never made money like that again."

In the 1960s, a lounge was built next door in what had been a shoe shop belonging to Nora's sister and, before that, the butcher's, which her father ran. "We had the first lounge in the two villages. It was built after the Lilac Ballroom opened when women started coming into the pub," says Nora. "Before that, women would only come into the snug — there would only have been a few of them, all wearing black shawls and saying they were drinking 'on doctor's orders'. The Lilac Ballroom changed all that — it was the most famous hall of the time, and people came to it from all over: Macroom, Schull and Ballydehob."

Today, despite once being the only pub in the village to serve Guinness, regulars at Dessy's are more likely to drink Beamish. Nora explains: "Beamish got a great following from the time when it was cheaper than Guinness; Guinness was 12 pence a pint, but Beamish cost only 10 pence."

P. DONNELLON
Patrick and Nancy Donnellon, Kilkishen, Ennis, Co. Clare

Only 10 miles from Bunratty Castle, Donnellon's of Kilkishen is very much a traditional pub. The interior décor dates from early in the 19th century, but many of the decorations are barely older than the brother and sister who run the pub today, Patrick and Nancy Donnellon, who are both in their seventies.

The pub was originally founded as a licensed grocery by their grandfather, Patrick Donnellon, a man who knew hardship. Patrick was the son of a tenant farmer, but they were evicted from their smallholding in Classduff, two miles from Kilkishen, in the 1850s. According to family tradition, a neighbour took them in when they were dispossessed — but the law of the time allowed the neighbour to provide shelter for no more than one night.

Somehow, the family both survived and thrived. By 1870, when Patrick married Kate Corbett from Scariff, Co. Clare, he was able to describe himself as "publican" on his marriage certificate. Family tradition has it that he established the pub as a licensed grocery in 1856, though there is no documentary evidence to support this claim.

In 1922, the pub passed to Patrick's son John Donnellon when he married Ellen Flannery. Together, John and Ellen built up the business, adding a bakery to the grocery. Today, you can still see the hole in the wall where the bakery oven once stood. The couple also expanded into the wholesale business, dealing in grain and manure.

During the War of Independence, the pub was ransacked by the British troops who took all the spirits bottles from the back of the bar — but the Donnellons had the last laugh, as the brandy and whiskey bottles contained only coloured water!

Nancy, who grew up in the pub during the war years, can remember a time when "the tea and sugar was rationed, and the drink was curtailed". She says the interior décor dates back to either her father or her grandfather's time and that she and her brother have kept the traditional look. She adds: "On the wall we have an old mirror with Francis Drake on it advertising Gold Flake cigarettes. The strange thing is that Francis Drake is smoking a tipped cigarette and, as far as I remember, Gold Flake cigarettes never had a tip."

In the old days, women used to drink in a back room. "Their husbands weren't supposed to know they had slipped in for a little drop of sherry or port," says Nancy. "So after they finished their drink they always asked for 'a lozenge' and there was a box of lozenges kept in the bar for that purpose."

Kilkishen is a village of no more than five houses, so many of Donnellon's regular customers would travel some distance to drink there. However, while the new drink driving laws have reduced the number of serious road accidents nationwide, Donnellon's, like many other country pubs, has suffered a loss of custom.

During the "bona fide traveller" era, because most of Donnellon's customers lived more than three miles away, most of the pub's drinkers were allowed remain on the premises after normal closing time. However, even when there were late-night drinkers present, the law required that the pub's shutters be put up and all exterior lights be extinguished by closing time. This lights-out rule was used by many to tell the time.

"An old customer of ours, now dead, grew up in a farm on the mountain at the back of our pub. His family, like many others, had a clock that didn't keep time well and they had no radio with which they could check the correct time. Every Saturday night as a boy, he was sent out of the house and down the road to a bridge where he could see our pub across the valley. When he saw the shutters go up at 10.00 p.m., he would run home with the news so his parents could adjust their clock and set it to go off at the right time for Mass the next morning."

While neither Nancy nor Paddy have children, they hope the pub will remain in their family after they are gone. Nancy says: "We would love if one of our nephews or nieces could continue running it."

FITZGIBBON'S
Nuala Fitzgibbon, Fermoy, Co. Cork

Recognised as an Irish jewel since the 1960s, Fitzgibbon's is a small traditional pub on a quiet street in Fermoy. As far back as 1962, Bord Fáilte, the Irish Tourist Board, was using an image of Fitzgibbon's exterior to promote Irish hospitality.

Alcohol has been traded on the premises since at least 1869, according to the current licensee, Nuala Fitzgibbon, who has a ledger from that year recording spirit off-sales. She reckons the pub was first established as a licensed grocery in about 1850.

The earliest surviving official licensing document relating to the pub dates back to 1877, and was granted to Michael Dunlea, but his wife Elizabeth Browne had the business before she married — so the pub certainly predates Michael's arrival. Records also show that as well as selling alcohol and general goods, there was also a loans office in the rear of the building, run by a Daniel Browne.

When Elizabeth died a childless widow in 1895, she bequeathed her business to her niece Margaret Fitzgibbon, but the will was contested by relatives and the pub put up for auction. It looked like the pub would leave the family, but Margaret proved to be a popular woman and none of her neighbours would bid against her. As a result, she acquired the pub for the knockdown price of £50.

Subsequently, Margaret married Richard Hobbs, whose name then appeared on the licence. The couple had only one child, Samuel, who died in infancy. So, when Margaret reached old age, she signed the property over to a nephew, Daniel Fitzgibbon, who ran the pub with his wife Mary Hyde. The couple had two sons and two daughters; the first children to grow up in the family house. Mary continued to serve in the bar until she died in 1994, but her daughter Nuala has been licensee since 1982.

While a good deal has changed outside of the bar since her great-grandaunt and uncle's time in 1877, Nuala claims, not much has changed inside the bar. Many of the shelves and furnishings are original and date back to Michael Dunlea's time, when flour, meal and salt — as well as alcohol — were sold on the premises. Indeed, Nuala says that some of the pub's interior walls are impossible to paint because they are embedded with salt from stores kept there decades ago.

On the pub's front door, there is a twisted doorknocker, which, according to local legend, was damaged during the War of Independence when the Black and Tans were run out of Fermoy.

During the 1950s, the pub also offered bed-and-breakfast facilities. Among the regular guests was Agnew McMaster, a famous Shakespearean actor, and his wife Marjorie, who was a sister of Michael MacLiammóir.

In the history of the pub, April 1946 stands out as "the time of the free drink", as that month a locally bred horse, Lovely Cottage, won the Grand National.

HERBERT'S

Michael Herbert, Sallymount, Castleconnell, Co. Limerick

Herbert's Pub on the Dublin Road, six miles outside of Limerick, was founded in 1867 as a licensed grocery by Mary Ryan, a local woman who set up the business with her mother. Mary married Matt Herbert in 1876 and the name Herbert has been on the licence ever since. As well as setting up a dynasty of publicans, the couple also founded a family that would have a strong nationalist heritage.

Since the foundation of the GAA in 1884, the family have been involved in Gaelic games. Three Herberts played on the Sallymount team that won the first Limerick County club championship and three generations of Herberts have played on Limerick County hurling teams.

The War of Independence features strongly in the history of this pub with all four of Mary and Matt's sons — Jimmy, Paddy, Joe and Tommy Herbert — serving as members of A Company of the Mid Limerick Brigade of the IRA.

During his tour of Munster in the autumn of 1915, Sean MacDiarmada, who was to be one of the signatories of the 1916 Proclamation, visited the pub and during his stay swore Paddy Herbert into the Irish Republican Brotherhood, the forerunner of the IRA.

After the Knocklong ambush in May 1919, when Seán Treacy and Dan Breen rescued Seán Hogan from police captivity, killing two RIC men in the shootout, Treacy and Breen met up with Joe Herbert, who took them to hide out on Pol's Island on the Shannon.

During Christmas week of 1920, the original thatched pub was burned to the ground by Black and Tans who were hunting Tommy Herbert and his brother-in-law Sean Carroll, commander of the local flying column. Tommy escaped the manhunt and, on the death of his mother in 1929, he inherited the pub. Following Tommy's death in 1949, the pub passed to his nephew Michael Herbert, the current licensee. In 1967, Michael was elected to Dáil Éireann as a Fianna Fáil TD for East Limerick and was active in politics until his retirement in 1981. He was also a Fianna Fáil MEP from 1973 to 1979.

During Tommy's time, the grocery continued in operation and the business also included petrol pumps, but both the grocery and the pumps were discontinued in the early 1970s. Since 1967, there has been a pitch-and-putt course adjacent to the pub.

Today, the pub is managed by Michael's daughter Bláithín, who remembers going to school one day in 1969 when suddenly a helicopter appeared and landed on the pitch-and-putt course. Fearing some kind of emergency, the family rushed over to the aircraft, but all that was wrong was that the helicopter was running low on fuel and the pilot had stopped to fill up at Herbert's petrol pumps.

Today, the pub is as busy as ever, with Bláithín describing it as "a lively, friendly establishment, with a GAA and, to some extent, political ambience".

JACK'S

Jack Collins, Scarteen Street, Newmarket, Co. Cork

L ike many a busy Irish pub in former estate villages, Jack's Bar is strategically located right in the centre of town. Newmarket is a thriving Irish village with an ancient history dating back to the Barony of Duhallow and the time when Ireland was ruled by High King's. This town was originally named Kilmacroghan and was the ancestral home of the McAuliffe clan. But the McAuliffes were dispossessed in 1620 by King James I and their lands given to Sir Richard Aldworth.

With the large North Cork estate came a licence allowing the English knight to "hold forever a Thursday market and two annual fairs; on November 11th and August 20th". The day the licence was issued to the Aldworths, 28 May 1620, marks the day that the town was named and settled.

How long the Collins family have been trading in Newmarket is unclear. But by 1824, the family was prosperous enough to afford a substantial headstone in the parish graveyard and it is thought that they had been trading in the town as butchers for some years before then. Their current premises in Scarteen Street has been in their possession since at least 1878, as a lease bearing the signature of Cornelius

Eugene ("Con") Collins survives until this day. As well as being a publican, Con was a master butcher who had served part of his apprenticeship in Wales.

On his death in 1939, the pub passed to his eldest son, Con, who continued the butchering business. As well as running his own slaughterhouse at the back of the pub, Con was an agent for English and Welsh beef buyers. The current licensee, Jack Collins, is not a butcher and admits that at least one element of his father and grandfather's craft remains a mystery to him. Jack says: "There is no back entrance to the back yard. So, unless they ran the cattle through the front hall of the house, I don't know how their system worked."

Today, Jack's Bar is a comfortable place warmed by an open fire and decorated with historical photographs and documents. "I'm particularly proud of one picture from 1932 showing a huge crowd waiting to greet Pat O'Callaghan, who won Olympic medals for hammer throwing. Certainly, they are a very well-dressed crowd in hats, collars and ties. Newmarket was a prosperous place."

Newmarket is a thriving town today partly because, during the 19th century, the Aldworth family were benevolent landlords, who had become more Irish than the Irish themselves. Richard Oliver Aldworth, who had an estate of 8,064 acres in 1870, is remembered as a landlord who charged fair rents in times of famine and economic hardship. Like most of Newmarket's population, the Collinses were tenants of the Aldworths and the landlord, rather than the central authorities, would have had most say in the issuing of trading licences.

Today, the Aldworths are remembered with affection. Jack says: "In 1917, a woman in the town was left widowed and couldn't pay the rent. Richard Oliver Aldworth told her that she wouldn't have to pay rent on her house, but could buy it outright for £20 when she had the money. Eventually, she put £20 together and went up to the house. Aldworth took the money off her and gave her a receipt, then he gave her back the £20, saying 'You need it more than me'. The woman was the grandmother of one of the bar's regular customers today."

As well as catering to visitors to this part of North Cork, Jack's has a strong base of local customers, particularly among card players who enjoy bridge here on Thursday nights and 45 on Fridays.

JACK C'S

Seámus O'Shea, High Street, Killarney, Co. Kerry

This pub in High Street, Killarney, dates back to the 1790s. It has been in the one family for 130 years and has been trading as Jack C's since 1901. The pub was bought as a going concern by a William Hayes in the 1870s, with his daughter Mary Ann Hayes inheriting the pub and licence on his death in the 1890s. While she was licensee, the pub was known as "Mary Ann's".

The day Queen Victoria died in 1901 was a significant one also in the O'Shea dynasty, as that was the day James Christopher O'Shea married Mary Ann, and also became the pub's new licensee. Known as "Jack", it was James Christopher who gave the pub its current name to differentiate himself from every other O'Shea in Kerry.

O'Shea is the third most common named in County Kerry and, at the turn of the century, there were three other businesses on Killarney High Street trading under the name O'Shea (oddly enough, all three were blacksmiths).

The year 1901 also saw the birth of the next licensee, Jack Christopher O'Shea, the son of Mary Ann and James Christopher, who became licensee in 1934 — the year he married Eileen Sheehan.

When Eileen and Jack Christopher ran the pub, Jack C's was a substantial business, having sufficient trade to warrant, during Second World War rationing, the biggest Guinness quota in Co. Kerry. The fact that it is still relatively easy to find Guinness bottles with O'Shea labels from this period testifies to the importance of the pub's off-trade during this period.

Jack's son Séamus has been licensee since 1968, running the bar with the help of his wife Joan since they married in 1970. They have a son and a daughter, John C. and Brigitte, both of whom now regularly work behind the bar.

The pub was refurbished in 1968, giving it a décor which Séamus describes as "1970s".

K.L. KIRBY'S

Michael Leane, Main Street, Ballyheigue, Co. Kerry

Records for this pub date back to 1867, when the local landlords, the Crosbie family, ordered the then licensee Michael Kirby to move his premises to the other side of Ballyheigue Main Street. It is not known how long the pub had been in operation before the order to move was given to all businesses and householders on one side of the street. The reason for the order was that the Crosbies felt that no one should occupy a building that had its back to their castle and for several decades after 1867 there were buildings on only one side of Ballyheigue Main Street.

A rent book dating from 29 September 1867 reveals that Michael was charged a rent of three pounds ten shillings a year by the Crosbie family, from whom the American crooner Bing Crosby is descended.

Following Michael's death, the pub passed to his son Patsy Kirby who ran the pub-cum-grocery until his death in June 1938. It then passed to Patsy's son Edward J. Kirby, who was known locally as "Ned". Following Ned's death in 1938 of pneumonia, his wife Nora Harty Kirby ran the business until her death in February 1968. It then passed to her daughter Noreen, who ran it with her husband Dónal Leane. Shortly after taking over the business, Noreen and Dónal closed the grocery counter and installed a lounge in the pub.

During the 1970s, a regular customer in the bar was Christy Brown, the author of *My Left Foot*, who became great friends with Dónal; the two men would have £100 bets with one another whenever Dublin and Kerry met in All-Ireland championship matches. When Christy left Ballyheigue in 1980, he presented a bronze bust of himself to the pub and it occupies pride of place above the mantelpiece of the bar today.

When Dónal died in 1986, his son Michael Leane took on the license. At the time Michael was only 18 years of age and was reckoned to be the youngest publican in Ireland at the time. He claims that the law had required licensees to be a minimum of 21 years old, but that the law was changed in the year that he inherited the pub.

While the number of licensed premises in most Irish towns had decreased since the 19th century, Ballyheigue is an exception. Originally, Kirby's was the only pub in Ballyheigue; today the town has four pubs and a hotel serving alcohol.

North Kerry, unlike the rest of the county, has a strong hurling tradition and Kirby's is part of that. Numerous hurling photographs decorate the walls and Micheal Leane played on the team which won the minor county championship in 1982. Not surprisingly, the pub is the main sponsor of the Ballyheigue hurling team.

The pub is unusual for its tradition of rings, a bar game that is played in no other pub in north Kerry and which is mainly found in pubs in Co. Cork.

Between 1987 and 1992, the bar had a restaurant attached to it, but that has now been converted into additional lounge space. The pub is now an extensive building that can accommodate up to 400 people. During the summer on Saturday night's the pub hosts "Moody Mike's Disco", named after the alleged temperament of the current licensee! On Thursdays, the pub has a big band and there are ballad sessions every Friday.

The biggest day of the year is "Pig Trotter Day", held on the day after the annual Pattern Mass, which is celebrated at a local holy well on 8 September. Each year on 9 September, the pub offers customers free crubeens; a free glass of beer is offered with every pig's trotter eaten by customers.

P.J. LONERGAN'S
Pat Lonergan, The Square,
Fethard, Co. Tipperary

The equine pictures and portraits on the wall of P.J. Lonergan's in Fethard, Co. Tipperary, tell you immediately that the pub and town have a strong link with horses. Today, one of Ireland's biggest studs, Coolmore Stud, is "just up the road" and every one of Fethard's four licensed premises have equine memorabilia on their walls.

As well as being a publican and grocer, P.J. Lonergan was also a blacksmith when he was given official permission to sell alcohol in 1833.

Fethard was for many years a garrison town and many of P.J.'s customers were English army soldiers garrisoned across the square. No doubt he, and his Lonergan ancestors, were providing food and drink to the garrison long before licensing was introduced. It is not known when the Lonergans entered the walled town, but they had been living and trading there for at least two generations before P.J.'s received its licence.

Lonergan's was a thriving business when it was handed on to P.J.'s son William. As well as being a large tavern in a garrison town, and a blacksmith to the local garrison, the Lonergans also ran stables which were mainly used for officers' horses. But after the War of Independence, in 1922, the barracks closed and the loss of 600 men was a major blow to the local economy, including Lonergan's.

Matters worsened when the Civil War broke out and "guns were sticking out the windows" on two separate occasions; the pub and town were first occupied by Republicans and then by Free State troops. A diary of that time, kept by William, still survives and the current licensee Pat Lonergan says reading it reveals the full extent of those "very troubled times". After William's death, the pub passed to his son, who was also named P.J., and the pub passed on after that to Pat, who is great-grandson of the original P.J.

Pat has two sons and a daughter involved in the pub and, with the recent birth of Pat's grandson, Kian Patrick Lonergan, at some stage later this century, it is hoped that the sixth generation of the family will be running this historic Co. Tipperary pub.

Today, the signs of Fethard's troubled past have disappeared. It is now a prosperous town with no trace of the dereliction that scarred it until well into the mid-1960s. Indeed, Fethard is celebrated as a valuable heritage site, mainly because of its superbly preserved 1,200-year-old town walls, a part of which runs along the back of P.J. Lonergan's beer garden.

Another memento of the past can be seen in the rear courtyard: an anvil taken from the forge of the blacksmith's that used to be on the site. Meanwhile, the tradition of serving good food continues, with the composer Andrew Lloyd Webber and the singer Luciano Pavarotti among those to have experienced Lonergan's ample welcome.

DENIS LUCEY'S

Denis Lucey, New Street,
Bantry, Co. Cork

One licence has served the Lucey family in three different premises since the business was founded in 1892 by Mary Anne O'Sullivan, who came from farming stock outside the town, but moved to Bantry to set up a grocery and pub on the town square.

In 1896, she married Daniel Lucey and the name "Lucey" has been on the licence now for three generations at three different addresses — the first on the Square and the other two at premises opposite one another on New Street.

In 1922, the pub was inherited by the couple's son, Jeremiah Lucey, who, in addition to managing the pub and grocery, also ran two horse-drawn taxis and a hearse. He was also a butter agent and a main agent for Kyper's Whisky, with the spirit sent in kegs from Scotland for racking in bottles stored on his premises.

After Jeremiah's death, his wife Margaret was licensee until 1979, when their son Denis Lucey started running the business.

The pub bottled its own Guinness with a special machine to do the job and labels provided by the brewery. According to Denis, the worst part was handling the scalding bottles when they were washed.

Before the 1950s, the pub supplied two types of Guinness. On the premises, the Guinness was 4X strength supplied in bottles or on draught. But if a farmer wanted a keg to provide refreshment after a thrashing, or if kegs were needed for a wedding or a wake, a weaker brew, Double X, was supplied, usually in nine-gallon firkin barrels.

ALBERT LYNCH'S
Denis Murphy, 17 O'Brien Street, Mallow, Co. Cork

The building housing this pub was originally part of a Church of Ireland school for the Cloyne diocese. The school's most illustrious pupil was William Smith O'Brien, who was born into a wealthy Anglo-Irish family and who was elected as a Conservative MP for Ennis. A supporter of Catholic emancipation, O'Brien was radicalised by his experience of Westminster and went on to become a Young Ireland revolutionary, leading the unsuccessful rising of 1848 in the Widow McCormack's cabbage garden.

Today, the street on which Albert Lynch's Pub stands is named after O'Brien. After the diocesan college closed, local landlord Sir Denham J. Norreys of Mallow Castle bought the building and then leased it to a Daniel Relihan, who became the pub's first licensee on 1 September 1851.

In 1875, the lease was acquired by Denis Browne who took over the licence on 22 June that year and the license has been in the same family ever since. Though Denis was licensee, much of the daily work was done by his sister Barbara. In January 1910, the Browne family agreed to sell the lease to Barbara's husband Albert Lynch and the pub still bears his name today.

Albert was an astute businessman who bought the pub to ensure his family's financial security. Previously, he had been a successful cattle breeder and dealer, but his farmlands were not his — he had a life tenancy on the Longueville Estate and there was no guarantee that his family could continue farming there after his death.

Albert used the pub's location across the road from the town's "Fairfield" and next door to Mallow Courthouse to great effect. As well as farmers and cattle-dealers, his clientele included criminals and rogues, judges, lawyers and policemen. He used the extensive college buildings to the rear of the pub to store fodder and animal feedstuffs, and he was one of the few people in the town supplying hay and grain to farmers on market days. As well as having weekly cattle and sheep sales, Mallow had both monthly fairs and seasonal "old fairs" such as the Runaway Horse Fair in May, the Gooseberry Fair in July and a major public fair on New Year's Day.

Before the pub was renovated, the public toilets were at the rear of the pub at the far end of a backyard — many customers wouldn't make the full journey across the yard when spending a penny, choosing out of laziness or disrespect for the law to relieve themselves against the courthouse wall instead! Albert's proximity to the courthouse didn't prevent the pub from being used as a republican safe-house during the Black and Tan war.

In 1935, the pub was inherited by Albert's daughter Ellen, who married an auctioneer from Doneraile, Dominick Murphy, who then ran his auctioneering business from premises next to the pub. Until 1983, it was Ellen — or "Nellie", as she was affectionately known — who ran the bar. On a quiet afternoon or early evening, on entering the pub you would find her sitting on an empty wooden crate by the fire waiting for her customers to arrive. She cultivated a loyal local trade among the Cork County Council workers who were based in a nearby machinery yard — when it was raining, they would shelter in the comfort of the warm bar. As well as encouraging card games, Nellie enjoyed impromptu sing-songs. She even had an advertising slogan for the county council men: "When the cold wind pinches, come for a drink in Albert Lynch's."

In 1983, the pub was passed on to Ellen and Dominick's only son, Denis Murphy, but as he has several other businesses, it is his son, Denis Murphy Jnr. who runs the business with his wife Joy. In 1997, they extended the pub, building over the back yard so that people no longer get wet when they need to go to the toilet. The original shop-front was retained, with the new premises being built in keeping with the character of the original building. As a result of the extension, Albert Lynch's can now accommodate 250 people comfortably, while once it would have held no more than 60.

The pub's clientele remain as eclectic as ever and Albert Lynch's still has a tradition of card-playing and music.

MANSWORTH'S BAR

John Mansworth, Middleton Street, Cobh, Co. Cork

Mansworth's Bar is a fine 19th century pub that well reflects Cobh's maritime heritage. When this pub was founded in 1868, Cobh had 104 licensed premises — a vast number for a town of its size. The reason for the vast number is due to the town's location on one of the best deep-water harbours in the British Isles, which led to it being home to the Royal Navy's northern fleet for over 100 years.

When the Royal Navy departed Ireland following the end of British rule here, the number of pubs in the town decreased dramatically and Cobh today has only 35 licensed premises, even though it now has a larger permanent population.

Like most of Cobh's pubs in the 19th century, Mansworth's originally had a 24-hour licence to cater for the vast number of sailors who descended on the town when the fleet was home. Shore leave was organised in shifts, depending on ships' watches, and a single battleship often had a crew of over 1,000 men.

Indeed, the pub still benefits from Cobh's strategic military importance — many crews of US warships are given shore leave here on their way to and from the Mediterranean or the Baltic.

Before Irish independence, Cobh was a unionist town because of the economic importance of the British military presence; not only did it cater for the Royal Navy, there were three military garrisons in the town. It was also a place where former British army officers retired to take advantage of South Cork's temperate climate. Cobh's allegiance to the British crown is reflected in the fact that, until 1920, it was known as "Queenstown" in honour of Queen Victoria's visit in 1849.

In bygone years, the town's pubs also benefited greatly from Cobh's importance as a trans-Atlantic passenger port — in the days of "the American wake", many an emigrant had their last drink in Ireland inside Mansworth's Bar.

As well as being Cobh's oldest pub, Mansworth's is the only pub in the town that was in operation in 1912, when some of the *Titanic*'s passengers would have had their last pint here before boarding the ill-fated liner. As a result, Mansworth's is listed on the town's "Titanic Trail" for tourists.

Another maritime disaster linked to the pub is the sinking of the *Lusitania* in 1915, when the bodies of the drowned were carried past Mansworth's door on their way to burial in the town's Old Graveyard.

Inside, the pub retains its original wood panelling and bar counter, with maritime memorabilia decorating the walls. This is a pub that never had a grocery attached or had a lounge added to it. Like most of Cobh's older pubs, the bar is small by modern standards and holds fewer than 50 people.

As well as benefiting from the *Titanic* tourist trade, the pub also benefits from its location close to St Colman's Cathedral, which was designed by Pugin and is considered to be the finest neo-Gothic church building in Ireland today. Many a wedding and a christening was toasted in Mansworth's Bar.

The pub has probably been selling Guinness since it was founded, with barrels of stout being supplied by rail on the Cork, Cobh and Youghal Railway line that opened in 1862; elsewhere on the southern coast, Guinness would have been supplied by sea.

The pub has been in the one family since 1895, when it was bought by a Miss Halforth, great-grandaunt of John Mansworth, the current licensee. Following Miss Halforth's death the pub passed to her niece, Margaret Mansworth, in 1912. It then passed to Margaret's son Edmund Mansworth in 1962. Edmund's son John has been licensee since 1982. John is proud of his family's licensing heritage and it was he who suggested the writing of this book while he was president of the Vintners Federation of Ireland in 1999 and 2000.

MCCARTHY'S
Elizabeth McCarthy, College Street,
Clonmel, Co. Tipperary

You can learn many a thing at a bar counter, but there is only one pub in Ireland that can claim to have once been a finishing school for young ladies. McCarthy's of Clonmel is located in a fine 17th century building, originally a private home. In 1737, new owners converted the house into "a finishing school for young ladies", giving McCarthy's its "College Street" address. The school closed in the early 1800s and the building was converted into a hotel, with Clonmel being an important market town, a strategic military centre and an important stop for anyone travelling between Dublin and the south west.

The hotel was bought in 1886 by Hanna Daly, the great-grandaunt of the current licensee, Elizabeth McCarthy. Almost as soon as she bought the hotel, Hanna sold it to her sister Mary McCarthy, for reasons that are not known today. Mary ran the business until her death in 1913, when it passed to her husband Martin Ryan who was licensee until 1930.

At this stage, the pub passed from Martin to his nephew Patrick McCarthy, who was licensee for the next 41 years. He was helped in the bar by his son James and James's wife Elizabeth. Come the arrival of the young couple's first child in 1964, the hotel was converted into a bed-and-breakfast (B&B) to give more room to the next generation of the McCarthy family.

In 1971, the pub was passed on to James, who was licensee until his death in 1992, with Elizabeth being the licensee since then. Today, she manages the pub and the B&B, but behind the bar more often than not you will find Elizabeth's son Robin McCarthy, the great-grandnephew of Hanna Daly and Mary McCarthy.

Today, the bar interior is modern, with a small beer garden to the rear. Elizabeth says she now regrets substantial renovations that were made in the 1970s. "The terrible thing is that I remember the time the pub was done up about 30 years ago," says Elizabeth. "At the time we had the lovely, old brass pumps in the bar, but, then, we didn't think much of them and threw them out on the rubbish without thinking about it. They're now worth a fortune, if only we'd known at the time."

The brass fittings went with the arrival of Draught Guinness and the introduction of standard dispensing pumps in the 1970s. While the new dispensers weren't as pretty, the new system made for a cleaner, dryer bar. In the days when Guinness was dispensed from wooden kegs, particular care was needed when tapping the barrel. "The first time I tapped a barrel, I nearly died," Elizabeth says. "I had no idea what would happen: when I hammered the tap in, a great big shoot of beer came rushing out and sprayed all over the ceiling. I nearly had a heart attack."

While Elizabeth describes licensing as "a tough profession", she loves being a licensee. "Of course, the pub will go down to my son when the time comes," she says. "But only when my toes are turned up!"

MORONEY'S

Gerard Moroney, Lisvernane, Glen of Aherlow, Co. Tipperary

This pub has been in the one family for over 200 years, though the name Moroney only appeared above the door since 1868. Before then, the licence was held by an Eileen O'Brien, who also owned a grocery shop that is still in operation a few doors up the street from the bar.

Eileen married Edmond Moroney in 1868 and his family name then appeared on the licence, with Edmond running the pub and Eileen running the grocery. They had a long and happy marriage with eight sons, seven of whom emigrated to the United States where they set up a very successful family bakery. When Edmond died, the son who remained,

Laurence, inherited the bar. But Laurence only held onto the licence for seven years, selling the pub to his brother Patrick on his return from America. Laurence must have had itchy feet: as soon as he sold the bar, he himself emigrated to the United States.

Patrick was licensee until his death in 1938. It passed to his son Edmond, who held it for the next 50 years. In 1988, Edmond retired and his son Gerard has been licensee since. According to Gerard, not a great deal has changed in the way the pub looks or how the business has been run since his great-granduncle married Eileen O'Brien over 150 years ago.

Gerard runs the bar with the help of his wife Kathleen, whom he married in 1987, while his sister Helen runs the neighbouring shop, which now includes petrol pumps. Helen and Gerard are both helped behind the counter and the bar by their brothers, one of whom is "Effin' Eddie", a well-known character in Lisvernane.

Eddie sprang to prominence in 1994 when a video of him commenting on Tipperary's victory over Clare in that year's Munster Gaelic Football Championship was distributed widely, with many finding his colourful bar-room commentary absolutely hilarious. The video led to numerous radio and television appearances and people still contact Moroney's from all over Europe and the US trying to get a copy of Eddie's video.

Among the other characters to have frequented the pub was the actor Richard Burton, who made this his favourite watering hole when working on a film being shot in Cahir Castle in 1978. Burton was unused to the barman's normal closing time call of "time gentlemen, please", insisting that Edmond Moroney could have all the time he wanted, as long as the actor did not have to leave.

Michael Collins frequented the pub during the War of Independence, to hold planning meetings with local volunteers. The IRA intelligence chief, then the most wanted man in Ireland, used a safe house located on the same road as Moroney's pub. One night, the house was raided by the Black and Tans and a volunteer named Gerry Kiely was killed in the ambush; a memorial to Kiely lies across the street from the pub.

Today, Moroney's is very much a social centre for locals and tourists alike. The pub receives regular custom from the Lisvernane GAA ground across the road and the pub is a starting and finishing point for hillwalkers exploring the Glen of Aherlow. The locals are a brainy bunch too: in 2000, they won the Smithwick's National Pub Quiz competition.

Inside, many of the pub's fixtures and fittings are original. Barring the pump handles installed in the 1970s, most of the furnishings date back to the 18th century.

One reason the pub hasn't changed is that, unlike many of the other pubs in this book, it did not have an extension added to it in the 1970s. "We were happy with the pub the way it was, so we didn't extend the way others have," says Gerard. "The biggest change, since I started working here, has been the disappearance of the day customer. When the main kind of transport around here was the bicycle, farmers would come in and have a few pints at lunchtime and, then, cycle home quite safely. But with cars — and tougher laws — that's not possible anymore."

J.C. MURPHY
Catherine Coughlan, Middle Square,
Macroom, Co. Cork

Now in the same family for three generations, it is believed alcohol was sold on these premises before 1870 when they were bought by John Cornelieus Murphy, whose initials and surname still stand proudly above the door.

When he bought the business, alcohol sales were only a small part of the turnover. On these premises once, you could also buy groceries, delph china, Christmas toys, newspapers and steamer tickets to the United States. In 1882, National Line one-way steerage tickets to New York were priced £6 each.

After J.C. Murphy's death, the pub was run jointly by three of his seven children, Henry, Julia and Anne. All three died childless and the pub went to

J.C.'s granddaughter, Betty Sheehan, whose mother Catherine Sheehan was the only one of the Murphy daughters to marry.

From the start of the 1950s, Betty ran the business with her husband, Eddie O'Hare, with the bar being open only six days a week. Even more strangely, the bar was not open in the evening, with the couple shutting up shop when the last *Evening Echo* newspaper was sold. They stopped trading as a grocery in the 1980s and the delph business went long before that.

Since 1997, the pub has been run by Betty's niece, Catherine Coughlan, a great-granddaughter of J.C. Murphy who returned from Australia to run the bar. Now trading seven days and evenings a week, Catherine has decorated the interior with many documents dating from her great-grandfather's time. Though at first glance Victorian, the exterior façade is a reproduction. However, the large picture window, giving light to the pub interior, is true to the original building's design.

O'BRIEN'S BAR

Maureen O'Brien, Bridge Street, Tipperary Town

As period pictures on the walls of O'Brien's Bar prove, the frontage of this pub in Tipperary town has changed little since it was opened in 1898 by James O'Brien, great-grandfather of the current licensee, Maureen O'Brien.

Originally from Kerry, James was one of several men from that county who set up businesses in the town at the end of 19ᵗʰ century. James passed the pub on to his son Jimmy, who died in 1978. Jimmy's wife, Norrie O'Brien, who was born in 1913, is considered one of Tipperary's great characters — indeed, most locals call the bar "Norrie O'Brien's".

Norrie's son Eamonn managed the bar for 20 years, and still works behind the counter, but the pub is now in the name of Eamonn's daughter Maureen.

In its first three decades, the business prospered, thanks mainly to custom from the town's large military barracks. "Half the town was living off the barracks," says Eamonn. "The English soldiers had plenty of money and regular wages. My grandfather made plenty of money and he had a contract with the army to supply vegetable provisions. Nearly every pub in Tipperary had a contract to supply the army with something, even meat or hardware. Every pub in Tipperary at that time had a second business."

When the British army left, the departure of more than 6,000 troops was a major economic blow to the town and the pubs in particular. Today in Tipperary, a town of 4,600 people, there are 33 pubs — a pub for every 139 people.

With business tight, the O'Briens had to be innovative. "We were the first in Tipperary town to have a television in a pub. It was the time of Mill House and Arkle in the Gold Cup and the pub was packed. Business was up for a few months, until everywhere else got a television!"

Eamonn, now aged 64, started working behind the bar full-time at the age of 14. He remembers in the 1950s when Guinness arrived in wooden kegs that were placed on the bar counter and emptied, not by gas, but by the force of gravity. He says: "When I started, a firkin of Guinness [9 gallons/72 pints] cost three pounds and four shillings wholesale. Now two pints will cost you €6.20 [£4.88]. There was a real skill to putting a tap in the kegs. You had to tap it in just right: hit it too hard and there would be Guinness all over the ceiling."

At that time, Guinness was generally the only beer sold in Tipperary pubs, but the manner of drinking was different. Eamonn says: "A man would always start drinking with a few whiskeys and then move on to drinking pints, if he had money in his pocket. The first new beer I remember coming in was Phoenix, which is gone now, and the next one to arrive was Harp."

Even in the 1950s, Guinness was placing a strong emphasis on quality control — not that Eamonn was impressed: "We would be given notice that one of the top brass would be coming to Tipperary next month. He would come in, taste his own stuff and then tell you it was good. Sure, what else would you expect."

"Any fool can pour a good pint of Guinness now, but at that time it was a real art. It was a totally different drink that still had live yeast in it; Guinness is pasteurised now; sure it's only glorified water."

O'ROURKE'S

Philip O'Rourke, Rosemary Square, Roscrea, Co. Tipperary

Earliest records available show that, in 1887, Margaret O'Rourke held a license to sell alcohol from her shop in Rosemary Square, but it is believed that she was a second generation licensed vintner. As well as being a grocery, O'Rourke's also provided lodgings with an upstairs bed costing 3d. When Margaret died, the pub passed to her son Philip, who also inherited a farm. Roscrea is known as "the Rasher capital of Ireland", but it also includes a beef factory and Philip became a successful cattle dealer; many a market day deal was made on the premises. After Philip's death, the pub was run by his wife Mary and their son Philip, who has been licensee since 1975.

The exterior of the pub is much the same as it was in 1887. The interior can be described as traditional, the only major change being the addition of new seating and toilets in 1985. The pub is very much part of Roscrea's community and social life, especially given its location close to St Cronan's church and Roscrea Town Hall. More than 100 people can squeeze into Phillie's and the pub has some very busy card nights, the main game being "Stop the Bus", a version of Pontoon.

The pub has also developed a rugby tradition, both on and off the pitch. The pub sponsors Roscrea RFC off the field, while on the pitch Phillie was captain of the team of 1968/69; his son, Brian, was captain from 1997 to 2000.

O'SULLIVAN'S
Eugene O'Sullivan, Ballydonaghue, Lisselton, Co. Kerry

When Denis O'Sullivan first started selling alcohol, he did so illegal, supplying poteen in a shebeen hidden away at the back of his farm. Sometime in the 1830s, he was persuaded to go legitimate and opened a licensed grocer's at his home on the Listowel to Ballybunion road.

When Denis died in the late 1890s, he was to pass on several prosperous businesses to his son, John Denis O'Sullivan, who was more usually known as "Jack". The bar was now covered by a full pub licence and the grocery had expanded to include agricultural supplies. The businesses also included a flour-mill.

The pub also benefited from the arrival of the Lartique railway, the world's first monorail, which ran between Listowel and Ballybunion between 1888 and 1928. The monorail played a major role in establishing Ballybunion as an Irish seaside resort, a development that helped O'Sullivan's pub prosper further. Carriages and locomotives were perched on the rail that ran at about shoulder height above the ground; passengers and freight had to be balanced carefully for the trains to run properly. When passengers embarked or disembarked at O'Sullivan's, the carriages would often need rebalancing.

In total, Jack employed 18 people throughout the year, one of whom was a professional cook used to feed his staff. As a result, he was able to offer hot meals in the pub, long before the practice of serving food became common in most Irish pubs.

Jack was regarded as a community leader, something that led him to be regarded with suspicion by the British authorities. During the Troubles, the pub was raided repeatedly by the Black and Tans and on more than one occasion shots were fired into the pub. The fact that Jack gave some of his land away free of charge so that locals could build houses, also made his politics suspect in some eyes.

Jack's wife, Catherine Moran, ran the grocery counter and was gratefully remembered by many locals as someone who had "connections with the tea companies" during wartime rationing, for she won renown as a person who could supply good quality tea. The family were also wholesale bottlers of Guinness, supplying bottled porter to several pubs in Ballybunion and Listowel, including the one formerly owned by the writer, the late John B. Keane.

Another famous author, Maurice Walsh, was born in the house next door to O'Sullivan's. He wrote *Blackcock's Feather* and "The Quiet Man", which was filmed as a movie starring John Wayne and Maureen O'Hara. One of the characters in the movie, Paddy Bawn, is based on a local man, Paddy Vaughan Enright, who used to be a regular in O'Sullivan's bar.

In the 1950s and 1960s, Ballybunion grew in importance as a tourist resort, catering for holiday makers from Cork, Limerick and Dublin. During the early 1970s, it became popular with tourists from Northern Ireland. Located only four and a half miles away, O'Sullivan's benefited from this trade with visitors seeking out the pub because of its old world charm. The main building is still thatched, the outside wall has hoops for tying up horses and the original bar is virtually unchanged.

More than a decade before Jack died in 1960, aged 86, his son Denis O'Sullivan took over the running of the business. Increasingly, O'Sullivan's depended on the tourist trade for their income. A new back-bar was added in the late 1960s when the meal, flour and agricultural businesses were closed down because they could not compete against the local co-op's buying power. The co-op movement was to affect trade again in May 2001, when Kerry Co-op closed Lisselton creamery and local business suffered.

Denis's son Eugene O'Sullivan has been licensee since 1983. When Eugene closed the grocery shop a few years later, other than family members, it had no permanent employees. In 1993, he added a new lounge and a restaurant by converting milling and farming buildings to the rear of the pub. Where once the bar would only hold 50 people maximum, the bar, lounge and restaurant combined can hold 300 people. Eugene is proud to say that, since August 1993, his business has employed more people than were employed by the O'Sullivans in his grandfather's time.

The restaurant, which specialises in steak and seafood, is a favourite of golfers visiting the links courses in Ballybunion and Padraig Harrington has visited the bar on several occasions. However, the Foot and Mouth crisis at the start of 2001 signalled a bad year for Irish businesses such as O'Sullivan's, which specialise in catering for the tourist industry.

Eugene says that, though the drink-driving laws are to be welcomed, they have affected trade. He also says that the extended pub opening hours have reduced Irish pubs' ability to promote community. He says: "The early drinkers still come out early and go home early, but the late drinkers start their drinking later now. As a result, you don't get the two groups mixing; you don't get the same interaction between young and old. I think the longer opening hours has had an adverse effect on an important part of the atmosphere that makes a good Irish pub."

ÓSTÁN UÍ DHONNABHÁIN

Tom, Dena and Therese O'Donovan, Pearse Street, Clonakilty, Co. Cork

Run as a hotel by six generations of one family, O'Donovan's in Clonakilty, West Cork, is now a substantial business with two licensed bars and a licensed restaurant on the premises.

The business, originally on Boyle Street (now named Astna Street) was founded by Denis O'Donovan at a time when Clonakilty was a growing holiday resort for Cork city following the arrival of a new railway line to the resort.

In 1866, the business passed to one of Denis's four sons, Thomas O'Donovan, who ran the business with his wife Catherine, with whom he had 18 children. Following an accident, Thomas had one of his legs amputated, as is apparent from the portrait of him hanging above the fireplace in the hotel reception. There is also a display cabinet containing a box holding two wooden legs — one of which was "a spare".

Thomas bequeathed the hotel to his son Denis, but he became a priest and the hotel passed to the cleric's sister Catherine O'Donovan. It was Catherine who moved the hotel to new premises in 1889, buying the site on Sovereign Street (now named Pearse Street) for £1,500 and contracting Sisk to build the new hotel while the civil engineers were also building the town's Catholic Church.

251

After Catherine's death, the hotel passed to Catherine's daughter, known affectionately as "Miss Katty". Born in 1882, she was ahead of her time and is reputed to have been the first woman in the area to wear trousers, smoke in public and ride horses using a western saddle. Whether it was because of her *avant-garde* ways or not, Miss Katty never married and, on her death in 1954, the business passed to her nephew Thomas, who ran the hotel with his sister Bernie. Thomas and his wife Mary had seven children and today three of these, Tom, Dena and Therese O'Donovan, run the business, following in the footsteps of their great-great-great-grandfather.

Over the years, there have been many famous visitors to O'Donovan's. Charles Stewart Parnell gave a public oration from one of the hotel's first floor windows, as did Michael Collins on more than one occasion. The radio pioneer Guglielmo Marconi stayed here in 1907; he hadn't intended stopping at Clonakilty, but travelling by train, he got off at the wrong station. During the Second World War, an American Flying Fortress crashed in the nearby Whites Marsh and 10 USAAF airmen were interned in the hotel for three days in 1943.

Today, inside the hotel, one of the two bars is named *An Teach Beag* (literally, small house) because it is installed inside a 200-year-old cottage.

PATRICK POWER
John Power, Clarecastle, Co. Clare

This pub has been in the Power family since 30 May 1872, when the licence was transferred from Daniel O'Brien to a Patrick Power, a farmer from Ballyea. But the licence had been in existence since before 1866, as it was acquired by transfer by O'Brien in 1866.

Patrick chose a profitable time of the year to open the pub with his name above the door, as it coincided with the start of the "Fair of Clare", one of two major fairs that ran over several days in the town each year.

As well as being a publican, Patrick, who was born in 1849, also imported coal from Whitehaven in England and exported timber from forests in East Clare that were used as mining trusses in Wales. Like most licensed vintners, he was also a general merchant, selling flour, meal and provisions. The shop was divided in half — with a drinks and a groceries counter on either side. At the end of the grocery counter there was a snug, which was used by female drink-ers. At the end of the drinks counter, Patrick had his coal office. As if this wasn't enough, Patrick also con-tinued to run his farm and took an active interest in local politics, particularly the Land League.

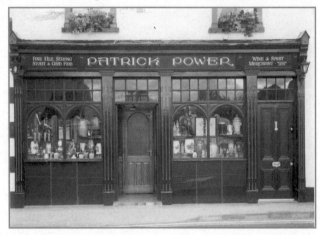

His involvement in win-ning rights for tenant farm-ers may have been the rea-son why, during the early years of the business, he was harassed by the police and was prosecuted by the local RIC repeatedly for breaches of the licensing laws.

On one occasion, in October 1882, a sub-constable McNamara summonsed Pat Power for having three men on the premises on Sunday 24 September at one o'clock. On another occasion, in 1884, he was charged with having three men on the premises half an hour after closing time. His defence was that the three had slaughtered a pig for him and that he had given them a drink afterwards — an important defence, as if the men had purchased their beer, Patrick would have been guilty of an offence. In court, the publican alleged that the officer prosecut-ing him, Constable Fitzgerald, held a "vindictive feeling" towards him. Little did PC Fitzgerald realise that at the time of the raid, there were 12 guns belonging to the Fenians hidden under the floorboards on the premises!

In 1885, his business faced a new challenge, not from the police but from the Church. Two local priests, the Rev. P. Malone PP and the Rev J. McNamara

CC, formed a Temperance Society in Clarecastle, which enlisted over 180 members at its first meeting with many more expected to join its ranks soon afterwards. According to the local newspaper, *The Clare Journal*: "The public houses are now totally avoided and a great moral change was visible to everybody. Such a society cannot fail to bring a blessing to that village." However, Patrick and his business survived this challenge too.

Patrick and Maria Power

By this time he had been twice married. He wed his first wife, Mary Murphy, in 1869, and had three sons and a daughter by her before her death in 1886. He then married Maria McNamara in 1890 and they had eight children. After Patrick's death in 1932, aged 83, the business was managed by Maria until 1945, when she passed it over to her son Bernard Power and his wife Margaret, née Ryan.

Maria did well to keep the business running, as the six years following 1932 saw the "economic war" between England and Ireland over de Valera's move to abolish the oath of allegiance and the Irish government's refusal to pay land annuities. The UK government imposed heavy duties on cattle imports from Ireland, hitting farming economies like that in Co. Clare, while the Irish government imposed duties on imports of British coal — effectively bringing the Power's coal business to a halt. Following three coal-cattle pacts between the two countries, there was a slight recovery in the local economy, but the outbreak of the Second World War in 1939 saw the local port closed and cattle exports and coal imports again halted.

However, "The Emergency" — as the Second World War was officially named by the Irish government — brought Power's an unexpected boost as the 23rd Battalion of the Irish army were stationed nearby at Dromoland Castle. Better still, Dromoland was about three miles away and thus troops stationed there could qualify as "bona fide travellers" when visiting Clarecastle and were legally allowed to continue drinking late into the night and outside of the normally very restricted Sunday opening hours.

When Bernard and his wife took over the business in 1945, many goods were still rationed or — in the case of cigarettes, tea, coffee, coal and petrol — in extremely short supply. As a result, it was decided to cease trading in groceries and to expand the pub business.

The development of Shannon Airport and the opening of a clay pipe factory nearby eventually saw the local economy improve. Many of Clarecastle's citizens were involved in the construction of the airport's runways, cycling the 13 miles to and from work. Once the airport was built, its many employees slaked their thirsts in Clarecastle's pubs after a hard cycle home. The 1960s and 1970s saw Shannon being developed as an industrial centre and, in Clarecastle itself, the arrival of the Syntex Pharmaceutical plant was a major boost to the local economy. The growing confidence in the town naturally helped the pub trade, as sporting and social events became commonplace.

While the grocery business had been long gone, the Powers continued in the coal trade until the late 1960s, when it was decided to concentrate only on the drinks business. In 1968, the pub was extended — and opened just in time for a memorable local occasion: the homecoming of local girl Eileen Slattery who won "the Rose of Tralee" competition that year.

In 1975, a lounge was added to the bar to cater for the town's growing population and Power's growing custom. As well as successfully managing the business, Bernard and Margaret also raised 11 children, six boys and five girls. Bernard died in 1978 and Margaret ran the business until she retired in 1992, handing it over to her son John who runs the pub today with his wife Eilish.

John says: "Clarecastle has changed enormously since Patrick Power opened his pub for business in 1872. The British army departed in 1922, the port trade virtually ceased in 1966, while the 'Fair of Clare' also ended in the mid-sixties. However, Power's pub still remains in the family, now managed by a third generation. The pub has also been radically transformed on several occasions since 1872, but the charm, hospitality, atmosphere and character endures to the present day."

Powers has been named Black & White County Pub of the Year five times. The pub has strong links with local cultural and sporting organisations, particularly the GAA. Inside, there is a "Memory Lane Gallery", featuring vintage photographs and memorabilia. One item of note is a tinted photograph from 1910 depicting the unloading of a cargo of flour in Clarecastle harbour with the pub's founder Patrick Power overseeing the operation from his pony and trap.

THE RAMBLE INN
Philip Enright, Church Street, Abbeyfeale, Co. Limerick

You will find traditional music sessions throughout the year in a traditional Irish pub setting at The Ramble Inn in Abbeyfeale, Co. Limerick. The current licensee, Philip Enright, has seven all-Ireland medals for *sean-nós* singing and is an active member of *Comhaltas Ceoltóirí*, the Irish traditional music association.

Enright's Bar was founded by Philip's great-grandfather, Michael Enright, sometime in the 1860s. Following his death in 1893, Michael's wife, Catherine, was the licensee until her son Philip was old enough to take charge of the business.

ness. Philip, who was born in 1888, was licensee until his death, aged 64, in 1950.

The pub then passed from father to son. Michael J. Enright ran the business for a half a century before passing it on to his son, Philip, the current licensee, in August 2000. Two of Michael J.'s greatest passions are coursing and greyhound racing and, as a result, pictures of greyhounds adorn the pub's walls. Michael J. renovated the bar in 1970 and renamed it The Ramble Inn.

Before the 1960s, Abbeyfeale hosted a cattle market on Monday mornings. As a result, most of the pubs had early morning licences, allowing them to open their doors at 6 a.m. In those days, the town had 40 pubs; today that number has declined to 30 and The Ramble Inn is one of only three pubs to have an early licence. According to Philip, those customers who take advantage of early opening are mainly factory shift-workers who clock off at 7.30 a.m. Because those with a hangover can get an early morning "cure" here, The Ramble Inn is nicknamed "The Clinic" by some locals.

Philip very much enjoys working behind the bar. "You meet great characters and you hear all the news. But best of all, the sessions are good old craic."

THE ROADSIDE TAVERN
Mary Curtin, Lisdoonvarna, Co. Clare

The Roadside Tavern in Lisdoonvarna is almost as old as the town which was once Ireland's biggest and most fashionable tourist resort.

In 1800, neither this pub nor the town existed. Lisdoonvarna literally sprang up in the mid-19th century as it was developed as an upper-class tourist resort thanks to the local mineral waters. At that time, a fashion for holidaying in spa towns was sweeping Europe and Lisdoonvarna's development was similar to that in Bath, Harrogate and Aix-en-Chapel.

"It was like the Klondike," says Peter Curtin, son of the current licensee. "It was a really upmarket place; the viceroy and all of his followers came every year for a fortnight. As well as the visitors, there were all the people who came to work as chambermaids, servants and in all kinds of trades."

The Roadside Tavern dates from this period, established by a local landlord, Pierce Creagh, owner of Rathbaun House, once a fine country manor, but which is now in ruins.

Originally no more than a licensed grocery, the pub was bought in 1893 by Christopher Curtin, a baker by trade. Shortly before buying the pub, Christopher married his wife Nora, another who had come to Lisdoonvarna looking for work. Under new ownership, the business was expanded to include a bakery. Business also benefited from another major development in 1893 — the arrival of the East Clare Railway at Ennistymon, eight miles away.

The railway made Lisdoonvarna a mass-market holiday destination, with tourists travelling from the station to the spa town via horse and trap or, from the 1920s onwards, by charabanc. With the railways came catalogue shopping and it was possible to order almost anything at Curtin's: Nora would measure you for a new suit and a month later it was ready for collection. The railway also allowed the Curtins to develop a sideline as wholesale butter merchants.

Running the bakery meant that Christopher would start working in the early hours of the morning — something which some drinkers used to their benefit with almost disastrous results. "During the Emergency — our government's name for the Second World War — there was a Local Defence Forces unit stationed guarding the coast nearby. Those stationed there used to take advantage of the fact that my father started work at two in the morning," says Peter. "They were supposed to be watching out for German submarines and Allied invasions, but on stormy nights they would come into the pub to warm themselves on the bakery oven. One particularly bad night, a pair of soldiers came in and hid their guns and ammunition in the unlit oven and then started drinking. Shortly afterwards, my father lit the oven without checking what was inside and the whole shagging thing went up! The place was nearly destroyed!"

Nora and Christopher ran the business together until 1944, when it was handed over to their youngest son John and his newly wed wife Mary. The young couple had difficult times ahead: the post-war depression years saw a decline in tourism; by the time the sixties boom arrived, domestic holidays were out of favour, with people choosing cheap package flights to the Mediterranean.

"There were other reasons for Lisdoonvarna's decline," says Peter. "In many cases, the people here then belonged to a generation that was born wealthy and they had gotten lazy. The pharmaceutical industry were also claiming to be able to produce pills to cure all ills — we know now that isn't true, but because of the claim, places like Lisdoonvarna suffered."

The arrival of mass-produced "shop bread" also hit the bakery business, which was shut in the early 1960s, with the Curtin's grocery shutting shortly afterwards. Nevertheless, the business survived and, today, The Roadside Tavern is "the only true pub" in Lisdoonvarna, says Peter. "All the rest are bars or lounges attached to hotels or guesthouses; we're the only pure pub in the town."

In the 1970s, Lisdoonvarna became noted as a place for traditional music and, during the summer, there is a *seisiún* every night. Among those who have dropped in are Christy Moore, Davy Spillane, Tommy Peoples, The Fureys and Sharon Shannon.

The resort also has developed a reputation as "Ireland's matchmaking capital", with matches most often made during September and the harvest festival. According to Peter: "Many a bargain has been struck between our four walls. It's a small cosy pub that suits matchmaking."

While you will more often find Peter behind the bar, his mother Mary, aged 80, is the current licensee. Separate to the pub, Peter set up the Burren Smokehouse in 1989 and today he exports smoked fish and cheeses all over the world. Wild smoked salmon and smoked eel also feature on the Roadside Tavern's menu, another reason for visiting this century old pub.

TÁIRNE UÍ H-AILPÍN

John Halpin, Main Street,
Croom, Co. Limerick

This small family-run pub in Croom, in the heart of the Golden Vale and on the banks of the River Maigue, was bought by Thomas Halpin in May 1900 and is now run by his grandson, John Halpin.

The pub was originally a coach house, equipped with 16 stables, a forge and a harness room and it continued to prosper with the arrival of the railway in 1860. Before arriving in Croom, Thomas Halpin was based in Limerick City, where he must have been a prominent citizen. An illuminated framed copy of his address when he left the Treaty City can be seen mounted in the bar today.

Thomas died in 1945, leaving the pub to his son, Patrick, who ran the business with his wife Esther. In those days, the pub also served as a shop, supplying locals with tea, flour, butter and all types of groceries until 1969, when the pub was refurbished.

Until his death in 1985, Patrick and Esther took their turns behind the bar with their sons P.J., Thomas and John and their daughters Maria and Breda. The youngest son, John, and his wife Phil now run the bar and are happy to continue the family tradition.

TREACY'S

Michael Treacy, The Nook, 20 North Main Street, Youghal, Co. Cork

This pub in Youghal has been in the same family since 1901, when it was bought by Michael Treacy, a local farmer. Previously, the pub had been in the ownership of the O'Mahony family, but it is not known how long it had been in operation. The pub is in the oldest part of Youghal, with Walter Raleigh's house, which dates from the Elizabethan plantations of the 1560s, to the rear of it, and thus this pub may have been in operation for several centuries.

When it was bought in 1901, it was a one-roomed bar-cum-grocery, but Michael extended it by buying four adjoining cottages and converting the former homes into drinking quarters.

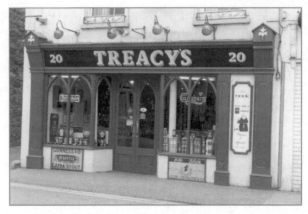

In the 1940s, Michael's son Joe Treacy became licensee. As the pub business expanded, the Treacy family quit farming; they also ceased the grocery business shortly after the Second World War. However, in 1971, Joe added a dedicated off-licence to the business. There is also a beer garden now to the rear of the pub.

Joe's son Michael Treacy is the current licensee and he is extremely proud of the pub and the central role it plays in the social life of Youghal. Treacy's is involved in sponsoring the local GAA club, the local soccer club, a local Catholic Young Mens' Society snooker club and the St Mary's Brass and Reed Band.

Michael's wife Maureen was also born into the licensed trade, as she is a publican's daughter from Castlemartyr.

As the bar has been extended, the décor has been kept in harmony with the pitch-pine of the original premises. Throughout the bar, the walls are covered with photographs of Youghal in times gone by. When the Treacys were celebrating their centenary as licensed traders in 2001, all drinks were sold at a penny a pint or a glass.

Over the years, drinking habits have changed, says Michael, with very few customers now asking for the traditional order of "a large whiskey and a pint". He says: "As well as drinking less whiskey, people now drink later in the evening. There was a time when I used to have a customer who would come in when we opened in the morning and he would order six whiskeys with a raw egg placed in each of them!"

THE WEST END
Dan O'Keeffe, Fenit, Tralee, Co. Kerry

According to local legend, Daniel O'Connell, who died in 1847, "refreshed himself" at a shebeen owned by the Cliffords on his way to electioneer on Fenit Island. But the earliest documentary proof of a public house owned by the family dates back to the 1880s when it was run by Denis Clifford, grandfather of the current licensee. That pub was based in a single-storey thatched cottage in the townland of Tallaght, but when a new railway line to the Fenit harbour was built, the business was moved a quarter of a mile to a two storey building, located beside the quay.

In 1895, the business passed to Denis's son Dan who ran the pub until 1918 when he died in the flu epidemic, which killed more people in Europe than died during the First World War.

At the turn of the century, Fenit was an important port for imports and exports and for the fishing industry, and Clifford's had a hotel licence. When licences were regularised in the 1920s, Clifford's kept their hotel licence because attached to the pub were ten guest bedrooms, the minimum required to be designated as a hotel and not a guesthouse. However, the rooms were rarely fully occupied, as there wasn't a strong tourist trade. The main guests were trawler men and fish buyers.

Following Dan's death, the pub was run by his wife Mary until 1948, when it was taken over by their son, also named Dan. In those days, the pub was stocked only with Guinness, one bottle of whiskey, one bottle of brandy and a couple of bottles of sherry. The sherry, known locally as "wine" or "tawny wine", was drunk only by women who were accommodated in a snug that has since been demolished.

Dan died a bachelor in 1979 and left the pub to his nephew, Dan O'Keeffe, the current licensee. "I was born in the pub," says Dan. "But I don't know why he chose to leave the pub to me, or whether I was blessed or cursed!" Being an O'Keeffe, it was Dan who changed the bar's name from "Clifford's" to "The West End".

Though the railway line was closed in the 1960s and Fenit port has gone into decline, Dan says his tourist trade has expanded greatly. He says: "In the 1960s, the holiday season was two weeks long — the last week in July and the first week in August — now it runs from April to October."

While the port today is still used for exports by Liebherr, a local crane manufacturer, its main source of income now comes from its 145-berth marina. To cater for the growing tourist trade, the West End now has a seafood restaurant. The chef is Dan's son, Bryan O'Keeffe, the great-grandson of Denis Clifford, who is set to inherit the licence.

YOUNG'S

Patrick Young, Latteragh,
Nenagh, Co. Tipperary

Young's of Latteragh is the pub that was built in a day. It was originally established in 1859 by John Harty, who married Anne Ryan of Borrisoleigh in January of that year. The couple were allowed open up a public house in a property rented from the local landlord on one condition: they were never to serve the landlord's wife, who was an alcoholic.

Tragedy was to befall the couple when, following a trivial dispute, John was murdered by a neighbour, Michael McGrath, on 5 October 1872. Anne continued to run the pub and raise her six children on her own, but fate then dealt her another cruel blow. The local landlord's wife became intoxicated when, through her servants, she acquired some whiskey. Without hearing Anne's side of the story and her pleas of innocence, she and her family were evicted and thrown out on the road.

But all was not lost and Anne's neighbours rallied around. The Carty family provided her with a plot of land, a stone's throw from the original pub. Furthermore, a by-law of the time allowed a family to occupy any house that was built and roofed within one day. A massive local operation was launched and the Hartys were rehoused on the same day that they had been evicted with the pub open for business again that very evening.

Since then, the business has never looked back. Following Anne's death in 1902, her daughter Kate became licensee. Kate had a reputation for strictness and for being a publican who never kept late hours. She married Patrick Young, who gave the pub its current name.

In the 1940s, the couple's son James Young became licensee. In his time, Guinness arrived in barrels from Nenagh station, pulled by horse-drawn cart. The pub also served as a grocery, but this trade died out in the early 1970s. James added a new lounge and bar to the premises in the 1960s. The original bar room which was built in a day still survives, though it is now a "spare lounge" that is rarely used.

Since 1977, Patrick Young, son of James and great-grandson of John Harty, has been licensee. For a while, Patrick named the pub *Tír na nÓg*, after the land of the young in Irish mythology, but that name never really caught on. In fact, the pub is known by two different names locally. Situated seven miles east of Nenagh and 17 miles west of Thurles, those living west of the pub tend to refer to it as "The Half Way House", while those living east of it refer to it as "Young's of the New Line" — a hark back to the days when the pub was on the main coach route between Nenagh and Thurles.

Family-Owned Pubs of Ulster

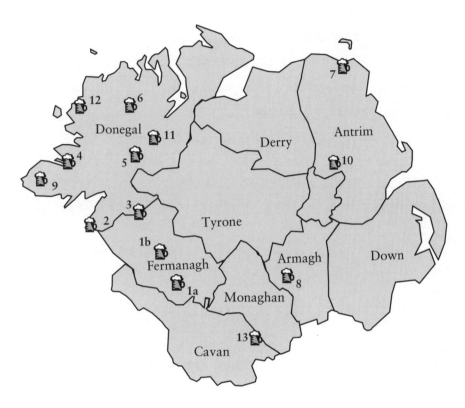

BLAKE'S OF DERRYLIN AND BLAKE'S OF THE HOLLOW
Patrick Blake, Enniskillen, Co. Fermanagh

The Blake family in Co. Fermanagh may be the only family in Ireland to have held two pub licences for over 100 years, with both pubs having been in the family since 1887.

The ownership of Blake's in Derrylin follows a direct line of succession from father to son to grandson, with each generation of licensee being named Patrick Blake. When the first Patrick Blake founded the pub it was a spirit grocers, which sold a wide range of household goods as well as alcohol. Shortly after partition, changes in Northern Irish licensing law outlawed "mixed trading" and it became illegal for pubs to also have grocery, hardware or any other non-alcohol trading counter on their premises.

The original Blake's of Derrylin

The second Patrick Blake, better known to customers as "Frank Blake", became licensee in the mid-1920s. Frank expanded the family businesses, which already included funeral undertaking, by also becoming a supplier of building, farming and hardware goods. The family business includes many of these activities still today. Following the introduction of the ban on mixed trading in Northern Ireland, the Blakes split their pub from their grocery, moving the licence to a new purpose-built building across the road in 1927.

The grocery went on to become a sizable supermarket, but the 1927 pub building was completely destroyed in 1973 — the Blakes were the target of a terrorist bombing at a time when Patrick Cooney, a nephew of Frank Blake, was serving as a Minister for Justice in the Irish government. The only consolation at the time was that no one was injured in the attack. A new pub was built on the spot, but little remains to suggest that Blake's Pub in Derrylin has a history of over 100 years.

In 1985, the pub passed to Patrick Blake, the third person of that name to hold the licence since it was founded nearly 120 years ago. His son, the fourth Patrick Blake, is "waiting in the wings" and may well maintain the family tradition into another generation.

The family's other pub in Enniskillen is one of the most celebrated pubs in Northern Ireland, partly because it retains most of its original and distinctive architectural features. The sign above the door reads "William Blake", but it is

usually referred to as "Blake's of the Hollow", because it nestles in the hollow of Church Street.

The pub has been in the Blake family since 1887 when Richard Herbert, a cousin of Patrick Blake, founded it. On opening day, "the elaborate nature of the decoration" was sumptuous enough to be recorded in a local newspaper as "quite an innovation in the trade of this town and partakes ore of the character of city establishments".

The main entrance is at the foot of a short stairs of seven steps — to the left of the entrance is a tiny snug, while to the right is a small bar, while the top of the stairs leads to a series of drinking rooms. The back bar features huge sherry casks once used for whiskey bonding, a white marble counter and an imposing set of lamps. Upstairs there is an office overlooking the main drinking area, where the pub's owners conducted their business while also keeping an eye on proceedings below. Behind the office is another drinking room and snug.

Among those to have enjoyed the pub's hospitality and décor is the author John McGahern, who said the row of snugs, the glassworks and the lamps "remind me most of first-class compartments in very old railway carriages or cabins aboard ship".

The Herberts sold the pub in 1929 and Patrick bought it for his son William and the licence has remained within the family ever since.

For generations, this was a pub noted for the quality of its wines, sherries and whiskeys and the family has not quite given up its tradition of whiskey bonding yet.

"We still have a small stock of pot still White Powers from the 1960s," says the current licensee, who is a namesake and grandson of Patrick Blake, the founder of the pub in Derrylin. "One day we will release it in numbered bottles; in the meantime, it's being kept in stock. It's extremely fine whiskey — officially, it's Power's 10-year-old, but it has actually spent 15 years in cask. It's another part of our family tradition."

One person who wants the tradition to continue is John McGahern, who says, "The whole bar is happy and as beautiful as when I was first drawn to it by its handsome front. I hope it continues forever."

BRENNAN'S
Nan Brennan, The Criterion Bar, Main Street, Bundoran, Co. Donegal

The Criterion Bar in Bundoran, Co. Donegal, first opened its doors in 1900, when the seaside resort was still in its Victorian heyday.

The first licensee, James Ward, was a "returned Yank" who had prospered in America. The fittings he originally installed still survive, including the original counter and mirrors. The pub is less smoky than most of its period, because

James gave it a high gantry ceiling. But the real historical jewel is the snug, which in 1900 (and for many years afterwards) is where women would be served. Today, the snug, which can accommodate about six or seven people standing, still has only seating for one.

According to the current licensee, Nan Brennan, her grandfather, newly married since returning from the US, had to prove he was a "respectable" person. This he did with the recommendation of four people already considered "respectable" by the licensing authorities in Co. Donegal. The local businessmen who supported his licence application include: Bob Renison, a draper; Irvine Hamilton, a jeweller; and Patrick Stevens, the owner of a nearby bakery and café.

As the pub prospered, the couple had three children: Mary, Kate and Tom. Kate left Bundoran when she married. The son, Tom, lost his leg in "The Troubles" and was an invalid whom Mary nursed, so the licence passed to Mary.

Mary's surname, and the name on the licence, changed to "Brennan" when she married a man who, like her father, was named James and had returned from trying to make his fortune in America. James Brennan, a Leitrim man, returned to Ireland in 1932 and married Mary in 1933. The pub passed to the couple's daughters, Nan and Patricia, with Nan Brennan being the current licensee. Both women are extremely proud of the Criterion Bar, which their grandfather founded at the turn of the last century.

BRITTON'S BAR

Bridget Britton, Station Street,
Pettigo, Co. Donegal

At first glance, situated immediately across the road from a customs post, you might think that that Britton's Bar was located to take advantage of the Donegal/Fermanagh border. But the bar long pre-dates partition: when it was founded by Jane McHugh in 1860, the bar's location would originally have benefited from its proximity to Pettigo Station which served the railway line between Enniskillen and Ballyshannon.

In 1895, the pub passed to Jane McHugh's daughter, Rebecca, and though she and her mother both probably sold groceries and drygoods, by the 1950s the business was known as "McHugh's Wine and Spirits Store". Rebecca did not marry and, on her death in 1956, the pub passed to her niece Elizabeth McHugh. When Elizabeth married, the pub's name changed to Britton's Bar.

Pettigo is the closest town to Lough Derg in Co. Donegal which draws thousands of pilgrims every year. This traffic is of no commercial value to the pub, however, because pilgrims are required to fast (and abstain from alcohol) on their way to and from the island made sacred by St Patrick. Nevertheless, according to Elizabeth, she once supplied two notable pilgrims, Eamon de Valera and Seán T. O'Ceallaigh, with hay. The two men were on pilgrimage together and were travelling by government car. On their way back to Dublin, they had agreed to give a lift to some fellow pilgrims, but needed hay to accommodate their somewhat dishevelled passengers in the back of their government car. Not only was Elizabeth delighted to supply the hay free of charge, she also gave the two politicians a hat full of free eggs each!

In 1963, Elizabeth's son John inherited the pub, running it with his wife Bridget, until his death in 1993. The licence is now in Bridget's name, but the bar is run by her son Pat and daughter Triona, the great-great-grandchildren of Jane McHugh.

Looking back on how things have changed since she entered the trade, Bridget remembers when a bottle of Guinness cost 10 old pence in 1956. In those days, the pub bottled its own Guinness and it took two evenings to wash all the bottles every week.

DOHERTY'S BAR
Eamonn Doherty, Ardara, Co. Donegal

Ardara Courthouse once stood where Doherty's Bar stands today. By 1855, the building had fallen into disuse and was bought by Patrick Doherty, who lived next door to it. Little is known today about Patrick, but it is thought that he was a stonemason before he started running a pub and grocery in the former court building. Patrick died at a ripe old age in 1904 and the pub passed to his son Joseph Doherty, who only held the licence for five years before his untimely death, aged 54, in 1909.

Joseph's wife Mary then took on the licence, running the pub and grocery while raising three children: Patrick, Veronica and Edward. At the time of her death in 1955, she was still licensee and had outlived her husband by 44 years and her son Patrick by seven years.

Veronica became licensee, as her surviving brother, Edward, was in Belfast where he worked in the pub trade and had a young family. However, during the Second World War, Edward sent his children to Ardara to escape the Belfast Blitz and one of these, Eddie Jnr, liked Donegal so much that he chose to remain in Ardara for the rest of his life.

While Eddie helped his grandmother, Aunt Veronica and Uncle Patrick behind the counter, like most youths in Ardara, at school he was also trained in weaving which during his youth he used a source of income. He also became involved in the local salmon fishery, with the result that at one time you could buy tweed and salmon over Doherty's bar.

On Veronica's death in 1985, the pub passed to Eddie. As his children grew older and started assisting in the bar, Eddie took up weaving again, selling tweed from a back room of the pub. That trade has since developed to such an extent that the business now includes a dedicated tweed shop in separate premises nearby.

Last year, Eddie decided to pass on responsibility for the pub to his son Eamonn, who became licensee at the age of 25. As well as being a publican, Eamonn is a keen player of Gaelic games: he is on the panel for the county team and is captain of Ardara GAA Club, winners of last year's county league and championship. On the team with Eamonn were three of his brothers, Joseph, Michael and Conal.

HARKIN'S
Francis Harkin, Brockagh, Co. Donegal

Until 1960, you could only drink standing up in Harkin's Bar, Brockagh, Co. Donegal. When built in 1895 by Daniel Coyle, the pub was a licensed grocery and had no bar licence for the consumption of alcohol on the premises. However, the law turned a blind eye, as long as customers only availed themselves of what was known locally as "a standing dram". This situation was not uncommon at the start of the 20th century; what makes it unusual is that this state of affairs continued until the 1960s.

The original premises was built by stonemasons who were in Donegal to construct bridges and embankments for the Stranorlar to Glenties railway line. According to family tradition, the building was erected within three weeks, with the stonemasons receiving a large part of their payment in poteen.

Following Daniel's death in 1901, the licence passed to his widow and left the family for four years. Details about her are not well remembered by the family today, but her maiden name was Gallagher and she had no interest in running the grocery-cum-shebeen. While remaining licensee, she let out the business to a tenant and returned to her native Creeslough, where she married a man named McFadden. Daniel's widow also found herself unable to care for his son and daughter and the children were put into an orphanage by a Fr Gallagher.

In 1905, Daniel's son Patrick Coyle came of age; he inherited the business and the licence returned to the family. However, Patrick did not hang on to the licence for long. Perhaps after leaving the orphanage, Patrick was anxious to taste freedom, so he had no interest in running the business. As a result, he sold the pub to his uncle, Barney Coyle, who was licensee for the next 20 years.

Following Barney's death in 1925, the licence passed to his daughter Margaret Mary Coyle. When in the 1930s she married James Harkin, a local farmer, the name on the licence changed, but Margaret Mary, like her aunt and cousin, had no interest in running the business. Thus, though the licence was in the Harkin name, for many years the pub was run by a Willie McGlynn and then a Johnny McGeehan.

In 1956, at the age of 21, the current licensee Francis Harkin discovered that the rent that his mother had been charging was not enough to cover the rates charged on the property. As a result, he took the licence and ran the pub himself. In 1960, he married his wife Mary. On their return from their honeymoon, Francis was immediately summoned to court charged with breaking the licensing laws. While he was away, it had been brought to the Garda's attention that the premises had no licence for the consumption of alcohol on the premises. Francis was given a £50 fine — not a wedding present he was expecting.

Francis and Mary immediately rectified the situation by securing the necessary licences to allow Harkins to become a pub, legally open for the sale and consumption of drink on the premises seven days a week. Until those licences were acquired, Harkin's was probably the oldest shebeen in existence in Ireland, having illegally sold drink for 65 years.

In 1961, the Harkins secured a restaurant licence to allow them to serve bar food and in the early 1970s, they acquired a dance licence, allowing for live music at the weekends.

The pub has been extensively renovated and refurbished several times since the 1940s. No longer a small grocery, where you could illegally sup a drink, it is now a large modern bar and thriving business; the lounge can hold 220 people with a further 40 or so squeezing into the bar.

MCCLAFFERTY'S

Charlie McClafferty, Church Hill, Letterkenny, Co. Donegal

Founded over 100 years ago by the great-grandparents of the current licensee, Charlie McClafferty, this pub in Co. Donegal started life as a grocery. As well as running a shop, bar and bakery from a tiny single-storey thatched cottage, Hugh and Sara McClafferty raised a family of eight children.

Hugh also found time for politics and was elected a Donegal County Councillor in 1908. In the early 1920s, Hugh and Sara built a new two-storey building with the old house becoming a goods store and a place where Guinness was bottled, at a time when Guinness was transported to Church Hill by rail from Dublin. The Guinness was transported from the station to McClafferty's by horse and car, but the McClafferty's business also included one of the first petrol pumps in Donegal.

As well as providing fuel to the general population, McClafferty's pumps also filled the tanks of movie stars' limousines, for nearby the millionaire heir to the McIlhenney Tabasco sauce fortune regularly played host to celebrities at Glenveigh Castle. During the troubles, RIC men were stationed at the castle and a photograph of the period shows the RIC men's vehicles parked outside McClafferty's for refuelling.

Following Hugh's death in 1940, the bar and grocery passed to his eldest son, Joseph. From the same premises, Joseph's brother Charlie also worked as a funeral undertaker. Joseph died childless in 1965, so Charlie's son Hugh inherited both the funeral undertaking from his father and the bar and grocery from his uncle. Hugh developed all three businesses, renovating the bar and shop and adding a lounge to the premises.

Hugh's son Charlie McClafferty became licensee at the age of 27 in 1977, following his father's death. "I run the bar, shop, petrol pump and undertaking," says Charlie. "The undertaking is an important part of the business and we are the only firm in Donegal still offering horse-drawn funerals. I am very proud of my inheritance and hope to continue with the work started by my ancestors over 100 years ago."

McDonnell's
Tom O'Neill, Ballycastle, Co. Antrim

This pub in the lively market town of Ballycastle was founded in 1766, when the building and surrounding site was leased by an Archibald McDonnell, who traded as a spirit grocer and provider of stabling. The importance of stabling to the business can be gauged from the fact that accommodation for horses took up three-quarters of the original site.

The property continued to be leased until 1826 when the Catholic Emancipation Act allowed the McDonnell family to buy it.

For generations, the business was known simply as "The Store", underlying how this was not primarily a place for drinking — indeed, in the 19th century, spirits were usually bought here by the gallon. The pub didn't officially become known as "McDonnell's" or, even more grandly, "The House of McDonnell", until it was taken over by Tom O'Neill in 1979, after he inherited it from his aunt Mary McDonnell.

Tom points out that the McDonnell clan motto is "Toujours Pret" or "Always Ready" and that he aims to be always ready to provide the best welcome possible to visitors.

The interior of the pub dates from 1870 and, as a result, is one of fewer than a dozen Northern Irish pubs to be listed in the UK's National Inventory of Historic Pub Interiors, which is maintained by the Campaign for Real Ale (CAMRA).

Ballycastle is home to one of Ireland's oldest surviving fairs, The Lammas Fair, which dates from 1606, and which is held on the last Monday and Tuesday in August. An edible sea-weed, known as dulse, and sticks of hard toffee, known as "yellow man" are traditionally sold during the fair and both foodstuffs are celebrated in the words of a song:

"Did you treat your Mary Ann
To dulse and yellow man,
At the Ould Lammas Fair in Ballycastle-O?"

In addition, the Northern Lights Festival is held here in May and there is a three-day traditional music fleadh every June.

MONE'S

Oliver Mone, Market Street, Keady, Co. Armagh

This pub in Market Street, Keady, was founded in 1880 by Patrick Mone, a local man from Clea, outside the town. It is not known if the pub had a full public house originally or whether it was operating under a spirit grocer's licence, but the business included a grocery counter until the 1970s. Patrick also established a funeral undertaking business, which is still in operation today.

When mixed trading was banned, Patrick solved the problem by partitioning the room with a grocery on one side and the bar on the other. After the grocery closed, the partition was removed. At that time, the family's accommodation above the bar was converted into a lounge, albeit one that had no counter serving drinks!

Following Patrick's death in 1934, the pub passed to his son Arthur Mone. Following his death in 1956, the pub passed to his son Arthur Jnr.

Until the 1990s, Keady had a weekly mart and market on a Friday, which was the pub's busiest day of the week. Today, many of Keady's younger population work in Dublin, returning to the town at weekends.

The current licensee is Oliver Mone, the great-grandson of the pub's founder. He refurbished and enlarged the pub, adding a long counter to the bar and a lounge area to the rear. The space now occupied by the pub's lounge and toilets was once occupied by stabling. Where once the pub held 50 people maximum, it now accommodates 140.

Though Oliver played for Keady GAA and Armagh's minor team, the pub has no formal sporting links. However, big match nights and major sporting events are big draws at the pub today, thanks mainly to its large-screen TV.

O'DONNELL'S

Rory O'Donnell, Meenaneary, Carrick, Co. Donegal

According to records from the Inland Revenue office in Derry, O'Donnell's Bar in Meenaneary was granted a public house licence to sell alcoholic drink on 11 November 1892. Today, this pub on the route to the Glengesh Pass is a centre for the local community, comprising a pub, grocery, post office and petrol pumps.

According to local folklore, the first licensee, Hughie "Beag" O'Donnell was a difficult man. Nevertheless, he was able to find two justices of the peace, a clerk of the peace and an RIC divisional inspector to support his application for a licence and attest to his good character.

He was also sufficiently popular to be elected as a county councillor in 1892, standing as an independent candidate. At the time, local government regulations prohibited councillors from holding an intoxicating liquor license, so the permit to sell alcoholic drink was transferred to Hughie's brother Michael.

Subsequently, in 1910, the licence passed to Hughie's wife Bridget. In all this time, Hughie continued working in the bar and he was in the pub when a group of Black and Tans arrived in his pub in 1920. The Tans were in Meenaneary hunting a local man, Peter Cannon of Crove, who was on the run. Quickly assessing that the irregular police officers were in an ugly mood, Hughie decided this was no time to be difficult. Instead, he walked out of the bar and left the troops to loot the pub.

According to records at the Donegal county museum, during Hughie's son, Michael's, lifetime, the price of drink quadrupled. In 1919, a bottle of brandy cost 18 shillings, a bottle of wine and a dozen bottles of stout both cost five shillings, a bottle of port was six shillings and sixpence and a whole gallon of whiskey cost £4! Five shillings is worth about 30 euro cents (25 pence) in 2002 — which would get you about a tenth of a pint of stout today!

Michael's son Rory has been licensee since 1990, though he has been working in the bar for over 30 years. He says that the younger crowd aren't as good with the spontaneous *craic* as their forefathers and while the pub has a television it is only switched on for big football matches and the news in an effort to maintain an atmosphere of conviviality and good conversation.

When O'Donnell's celebrated their centenary in 1992, it was a great year locally, for it also marked the first time that Donegal had won the All-Ireland Football Championship. Three local men, John Joe Doherty, Noel Hegarty and captain Anthony Molloy were on the team, so, needless to say, there was much celebration in O'Donnell's the night of that historic victory. When a celebration was held in November that year to mark the centenary, guest of honour was the late Hannah O'Donnell, a daughter of Hughie, the original licensee.

Over the years, there have been several famous visitors to O'Donnell's, including Dylan Thomas, Brendan Behan, Brian Keenan and members of the Guildford Four. Another famous visitor was Rockwell Kent, one of the first modern American painters to have his work exhibited in Moscow.

One of O'Donnell's most recent distinctions is that it is believed to be the last pub in Ireland to have been charged with breaking the Sunday afternoon closing rules. Before the passing of the Intoxicating Liquor Act 2000, every pub in Ireland not serving food could not serve alcohol between 2 p.m. and 4 p.m. With typical Irish logic, this 180-minute period was known as "holy hour". On a Sunday in November 1998, a Garda entered O'Donnell's at 3.15 p.m. and found that alcohol was being served; Rory was charged and he pleaded guilty when the case went to court.

O'KANE'S
John O'Kane, Randalstown, Co. Antrim

This pub in Co. Antrim was founded sometime in the early 1850s by John O'Kane, of whom little is known today except that he is described in a business directory of 1864 as "Grocer and spirit dealer".

At the time, Randalstown was a prosperous mill town and a centre of the Northern Ireland linen industry. After a period of economic decline in the 1950s, '60s and '70s, Randalstown has become a dormitory for commuters working in Belfast.

The current licensee, John O'Kane, is a great-grand-nephew of the pub's founder and the third person of that name to be licensee here. He says the interior of the pub has been preserved, partly because the family did not have the money to pay for modernisation and refurbishment when formica was in fashion.

As a result, the main bar retains its original mahogany counter and wall tiles and the pub is divided into a series of small drinking rooms. Today, the walls are decorated with vintage advertising posters and there is also a bottling machine on display, giving the pub an ambience that earned it the title of Bushmills Bar of the Year in 1992.

Following the original John O'Kane's death at the age of 62 in 1879, the pub passed to his son, Bernard, who is described in an 1894 business directory as "Grocer and dealer in sundries". As well as the grocery, Bernard was a spirits dealer and he also offered stabling, with buildings to the rear of the pub also being used to store livestock feed for sale when markets were held in the town.

Bernard died childless in 1924 and the pub passed to his cousin John O'Kane, who already owned a pub, The Dunsilly Arms, five miles away. John O'Kane sold The Dunsilly Arms and used the proceeds to buy out the other members of the family who had inherited a share in the Randalstown business.

Following the ban in Northern Ireland on pubs engaging in "mixed trade", John O'Kane ended the grocery business to concentrate on the pub trade. The pub then passed to John's son, Bernard O'Kane, who was more usually known as "Brian". When Brian died in 1959, the pub was held in trust until his son, John O'Kane, reached the age of 25 and was old enough legally to become a licensee.

ROSIE'S BAR

John Hannon, Drumkeen, Ballybofey, Co. Donegal

On the road between Letterkenny and Ballybofey is Rosie's Bar, built in 1892 by its first licensee, William Bonner. The year he set up his bar and grocery business, William married, so he named the pub in honour of his wife Rose Tinney and it has been known as Rosie's Bar ever since. Following her husband's death in 1905, Rose became licensee, running the pub and raising her family. During the Troubles, the pub and surrounding houses were searched regularly by the Black and Tans. According to family legend, during a raid the auxiliaries would put one of Rosie's children in their truck to avoid being ambushed.

Another family story tells how a wounded man was laid out on one of the bar's tables after he had been shot in a Civil War skirmish, but that he died as Rosie tried to revive him. Poignantly, the family story does not recall the man's name nor on which side of the Civil War he was fighting.

Following Rosie's death in 1949, the pub passed to her son John Bonner, who died in 1972. The pub then passed to his sister, Rosie Bonner, the second woman of that name to hold the license. Rosie died in 1982 and the pub passed to John Hannon, a nephew who had been working behind the bar counter since 1969, when he was 22 years of age.

The grocery business is long gone and over the years the pub has been renovated extensively. A lounge was added in 1980 and was extended four years later. The interior now is modern with a wood finish.

SHARKEY'S BAR
Michael Sharkey, Annagry, Co. Donegal

The first licensee of Sharkey's Bar was a former crochet teacher from Aranmore Island. After she married local man James Sharkey, Margaret O'Donnell set up a grocery in Annagry and obtained a licence to sell alcohol in 1888. She had chosen her location very well, situated opposite the parish church; it was said locally that you weren't baptised a Christian, married or buried, without visiting Sharkey's along the way.

The couple's son, John Dubh, inherited the business. He was an amateur photographer at a time when cameras were rare and many of his photographs are on display in the bar.

John Dubh (Black John) died a bachelor and the business passed to his nephew James Sharkey in the 1950s. At this time, as well as being a pub and large general store, the business also included a knitting factory that gave employment to scores of women. At a time of great emigration, fuelled by a global post-war recession and a continuing  trade war with Britain, the factory was a valuable source of local income.

A measure of the family's local importance is that the Sharkeys claim to have been the first in Annagry to have had electricity, the telephone, a radio and television.

Today, the pub is being run by James's sons, Michael and Joe Sharkey, with Michael being licensee since 1989. While the knitting factory is long gone and the pub interior has been refurbished and extended, the exterior remains very much as it was 100 years ago.

Annagry has a strong football tradition and Sharkey's is the place to watch a big match on TV. You can escape the telly in a recently constructed beer garden "out the back", but the best *craic* is to be had inside, with the locals by the bar or the pool table.

TRAYNOR'S

Gerry Traynor, Main Street, Shercock, Co. Cavan

Traynor's Bar in Shercock is a quiet country pub frequented mainly by an older drinking crowd. It opened for business on St Valentine's Day, 14 February 1900 when the current licensee's father set up in business for himself.

By the time he set up shop, Francis W. Traynor was an experienced barman. He had served an apprenticeship at Mary Markey's Bar and Grocery in nearby Cootehill, before moving to Dublin in 1891 to work in Peter McKeever's Bar and Grocery in Killiney, Co. Dublin.

In Killiney, he worked a six-day week, from 7.30 a.m. to 11.00 p.m., with two assistants serving under him; for this, he was paid a salary of £25 a year. With these wages, he managed to save enough to open his own bar and grocery in Shercock. The legal costs of obtaining a licence came to £2/11s/6d, with hefty paperwork adding to the costs. The bureaucracy involved in obtaining a licence transfer included sending copies of the licence certificate to four justices of the peace, a district inspector of police and the local newspaper, *The Cavan Celt*.

F.W. ran the bar until his death in 1943, when his wife Julia became licensee. Although, Julia was licensee until 1972, her son Gerard, who is the current licensee, carried out most of the work in the bar. Now aged 75, Gerry was the youngest of nine children and says he has worked in the bar since he was a boy.

As a quiet country bar, he says his pub hasn't had a very eventful history. But he has many tales about the nonsense that surrounded the bona fide laws that allowed a person to avail of alcoholic refreshment at almost any hour after travelling a distance of over three miles. When the laws were in operation, drinkers in Shercock would walk to nearby Ballytraynor to enjoy a drink, while drinkers in Ballytraynor walked in the opposite direction to enjoy their pints in Shercock. The laws were ridiculous, but closely monitored. "The guards would watch a man who claimed to be a bona fide traveller to make sure he did not go into another pub once he left the pub where he was drinking," says Gerry. "The law allowed you to drink in only one pub when you were a traveller, you couldn't go into another in the same town. The law was also very strict about the distance you travelled: there was a schoolteacher who used to come in town for a drink, but he wouldn't be allowed go into the first pub he came to. He would have to drink at the top of the town to go the full three miles."

These days, most of the pub's day-to-day management is in the hands of Gerry's son Frank, but Gerry remains licensee and regularly tends the pumps. "I enjoy the work," he says. "If I didn't do it, I'd miss the *craic*. This is a country pub where most of the customers are farmers. It's not a teenagers' bar or one of those theme bars you get up in Dublin."

Dublin Pubs of Historic Architectural Merit

Northside

Nealon's	Capel Street, Dublin 1
Mulligan's	Stoneybatter, Dublin 7
Alfie Byrne's	Chancery Place, Dublin 7
Conway's	Parnell Street, Dublin 1
Ryan's	Parkgate Street, Dublin 8
Kavanagh's	Aughrim Street, Dublin 7
Hanlon's	Hanlon's Corner, NCR, Dublin 7
Gaffney's	Fairview, Dublin 3
The Hut	Phibsboro, Dublin 9
Hedigan's	Prospect Road, Glasnevin, Dublin 9
Kavanagh's	Prospect Square, Glasnevin, Dublin 9

Southside

Mulligan's	Poolbeg Street, Dublin 2
Regan's	Tara Street, Dublin 2
The Palace Bar	Fleet Street, Dublin 2
Bowe's	Fleet Street, Dublin 2
The Brazen Head	Bridge Street, Dublin 8
O'Neill's	Suffolk Street, Dublin 2
The Stag's Head	Dame Court, Dublin 2

The International Bar	Wicklow Street, Dublin 2
The Long Hall	South Great George's Street, Dublin 2
The Lord Edward	Christ Church Place, Dublin 8
Kehoe's	South Anne Street, Dublin 2
McDaid's	Harry Street, Dublin 2
Neary's	Chatham Street, Dublin 2
The Swan	Aungier Street, Dublin 2
Cassidy's	Camden Street, Dublin 2
Bambrick's	South Richmond Street, Dublin 2
The Portobello	Richmond Street, Dublin 2
Toner's	Baggot Street Lower, Dublin 4
Doheny and Nesbitt	Baggot Street Lower, Dublin 4
Searson's	Baggot Street Upper, Dublin 4
Slattery's	Rathmines Road Lower, Dublin 6
Sandyford House	Sandyford
Sorento House	Dalkey

(Compiled by Frank Fell of the Licensed Vintners Association and Michael Hedigan, vintner)

A Note on Money

Before decimalisation in 1971, prices were often marked with the initials L.s.d, an abbreviation for "librae, solidi, denarii", which is the Latin for pounds, shillings and pence. There were 20 shillings in the pound and 12 pence in the shilling (ie 1L = 240d).

In the conversion from "old pence" to new pence in 1971, a shilling (12d) was made the equivalent of 5p, with the result that the new 1p coin was worth between 2¼d and 2½d. Coins in circulation immediately before decimalisation were: the crown (worth five shillings); the half-crown (worth two and six); the florin (two shillings); the shilling; the thrupenny bit (3d); the penny; the ha'penny (½d); and the farthing (¼d).

A commemorative ten-shilling coin was minted in 1966, but a ten-shilling banknote that was used in general circulation. While the Royal Mint in England continued to issue sovereign coins until 1917 and half-sovereign coins until 1915, there were six banks in Ireland issuing one pound and ten-shilling banknotes.

Throughout the 19th and early 20th century, banknotes were far more common in Ireland than in England, despite the fact that English sterling and Irish sterling were amalgamated in 1826. A proclamation in 1701 had officially fixed the value of an English shilling at 13d Irish (ie £100 English = £108 6s 7d Irish), but trading circumstances before the 1820s had caused a great deal of fluctuation between the two currencies.

During the 17th and 18th centuries, there was also a wider range of coins in circulation, including: the five guinea coin (£5 5s); the two guineas (£2 2s); the half-guinea (10s 6d); the third of a guinea (7s); quarter guinea (5s 3d); the double-florin (4s); the groat (4d); the tuppence (2d); the half-farthing (1/8d); and the quarter-farthing (1/16d).

Following decimalisation, a guinea became equivalent to £1.05 Irish punts, which surprisingly allows for a very easy euro conversion. The value of three guineas is almost four euro exactly, with €400 = 300 guineas and a ha'penny).

APPENDIX C

Liquid Measures in 19th Century Ireland

1 Wine Gallon	= 231 cubic inches wine
1 Beer Gallon	= 282 cubic inches ale or beer
1 Imperial Gallon	= 277.274 cubic inches
1 Pint	= 4 gills
	= 4 naggins
1 Quart	= 2 pints
1 Pottle	= 4 pints
1 Gallon	= 8 pints
1 Firkin	= 9 gallons of beer
1 Anker	= 10 gallons of wine
1 Kilderkin	= 18 gallons of beer
1 Rundlet	= 18 gallons of wine
1 Barrel or "Tierce"	= 42 wine gallons or 44 beer gallons
1 Hogshead	= 63 wine gallons or 66 beer gallons
1 Butt	= 2 hogshead wine or 3 barrels beer
1 Tun	= 4 hogshead wine or 252 wine gallons

Bibliography

Agreement subletting the farming of licenses for wine and spirits from Theobold, Earl of Carlingford, Sir Chichester Wrey and Sir Thomas Clifford, with copy of the letters patent granting the farm, 30 July 1665, National Library manuscript.

Allen, Gregory (1999), *The Garda Síochána: Policing Independent Ireland 1922–82*, Gill & Macmillan.

Bullingbrooke, E.D. (1787), *The Duty and Authority of Justices of the Peace and Parish Officers for Ireland*, George Grierson.

Bulson, Roy (1969), *Irish Pubs of Character*, Bruce Spicer.

Carney, James (1985), *Medieval Irish Lyrics*, Dolmen Press.

Cassidy, Constance (1996), *The Licensing Acts 1833–1955*, Round Hall Sweet & Maxwell.

Cassidy, Constance (1996), *The Licensing Handbook*, Round Hall Sweet & Maxwell.

Connolly, S.J. (ed.) (1998), *The Oxford Companion to Irish History*, Oxford University Press.

Cronin, Denis, Jim Gilligan and Karina Holton (ed.) (2001), *Irish Fairs and Markets*, Studies in Local History, Four Courts Press.

Dineen, Patrick (1927), *Foclóir Gaedhilge agus Béarla*, Irish Text Society.

Duffy, Seán (ed.) (1997), *Atlas of Irish History*, Gill & MacMillan.

Kearns, Kevin C. (1996), *Dublin Pub Life and Lore: An Oral History*, Gill & Macmillan.

Kelly, Fergus (1988), *A Guide to Early Irish Law*, Dublin Institute for Advanced Studies.

Kelly, Fergus (2000), *Early Irish Farming*, School of Celtic Studies, Dublin Institute for Advanced Studies.

MacLysaght, Edward (1979), *Irish Life in the 17th Century*, Irish Academic Press.

Magee, Malachy (1998), *Irish Whiskey: A 1000-Year Tradition*, O'Brien.

Malone, Aubrey (2001), *Historic Pubs of Dublin*, New Island Books.

McCusker, John J. (2001), *Comparing the Purchasing Power of Money in Great Britain from 1600 to Any Other Year*, Economic History Services.

McGuffin, John (1978), *In Praise of Poteen*, Appletree.

McGuire, Edward B. (1973), *Irish Whiskey: A History of Distilling, the Spirit Trade and Excise Controls in Ireland*, Gill and Macmillan.

Merry, Tom (ed.) (1949), *Where to Drink: Well-Known Irish Bars and Lounges*, Tom Merry Publishing.

Ó Dónaill, Niall (1992), *Foclóir Gaeilge-Béarla*, An Gúm.

O'Connor, Kevin (1999), *Ironing the Land: the Coming of the Railways to Ireland*, Gill & Macmillan.

Ó Drisceoil, Diarmuid and Donal Ó Drisceoil (1997), *The Murphy's Story: The History of Lady's Well Brewery, Cork*, Murphy Brewery Ireland Ltd.

O'Gorman, Andrew (1983), *A–Z of the Bar Trade*, Bartenders' Association of Ireland.

O'Gorman, Andrew (1994), *A Handbook for the Licensed Trade*, A.O'Gorman.

O'Gorman, Andrew (2000), *Irish Whiskey Old and New*, Irish Guild of Sommeliers.

Phipps, William (1825), *The Vintners Guide*, The Fair Trading Vintners Society and Asylum of the City of Dublin.

Pritchard, David (1997), *The Irish Pub*, Real Ireland.

Protz, Roger (1997), *Classic Stout and Porter*, Prion.

Ryan, John Clement (1992), *Irish Whiskey*, Irish Heritage Series, Eason & Son Ltd.

Sargent, William Albert (1890), *The Liquor Licensing Laws of Ireland from 1660–1890*, William McGee.

Scott, Yvonne (1999), *Survey of Licensed Premises in Ireland 1999*, Drinks Industry Group of Ireland.

Vintners' Federation of Ireland (1936–2002), *The Licensed Vintner and Grocer*, inc. *The Licensed Trader* and *Licensed Vintner and Licensed Grocer*, various issues.

Woods, James (1981), *The Liquor Licensing Laws of Ireland*, James V. Woods.

Index